THE MORAL UNIVERSE OF SHAKESPEARE'S PROBLEM PLAYS

THE MORAL UNIVERSE OF SHAKESPEARE'S PROBLEM PLAYS

VIVIAN THOMAS

BARNES & NOBLE BOOKS
Totowa, New Jersey

© 1987 Vivian Thomas

First published in the USA 1987 by
BARNES & NOBLE BOOKS
81 ADAMS DRIVE
TOTOWA, NEW JERSEY, 07512

Library of Congress Cataloging-in-Publication Data

Thomas, Vivian.
   The moral universe of Shakespeare's problem plays.

   Bibliography: p.
   Includes index.
   1. Shakespeare, William, 1564-1616 — Tragicomedies.
2. Shakespeare, William, 1564-1616 — Ethics.
3. Shakespeare, William, 1564-1616. Troilus and
Cressida. 4. Shakespeare, William, 1564-1616. All's
well that ends well. 5. Shakespeare, William, 1564-1616.
Measure for measure. 6. Troilus (Greek mythology) in
literature. I. Title.
PR2981.5.T46   1987   822.3'3   86-28839
ISBN 0-389-20708-X

Contents

To my mother and the memory of my father

Acknowledgements

My desire to write this book arose out of long, intense and often passionate discussions with my extramural students. The questions and debates to which these classes gave rise did much to stimulate my approach to the problem plays in general and *Troilus and Cressida* in particular. My second debt of gratitude is to four remarkable teachers: Bill Gregory, John Howells, Luigi Pasinetti and Tom Rees. Finally, I should like to thank Rachel Hodgkinson who typed part of the initial manuscript, and my wife, who completed the task and contributed greatly to clarifying expression and removing errors. The mistakes and blemishes that remain are my own.

A Note on the Text

All references are to the New Arden editions of Shakespeare's plays: *Troilus and Cressida* edited by Kenneth Palmer, *All's Well that Ends Well* edited by G. K. Hunter, and *Measure for Measure* edited by J. W. Lever. References to Chaucer's *Troilus and Criseyde* are from Nevill Coghill's Penguin edition. All other quotations and references to Shakespeare's source materials are drawn from Geoffrey Bullough's invaluable *Narrative and Dramatic Sources of Shakespeare*, volumes II and VI. The bibliography has not been extended to include articles in order to keep it within reasonable bounds. A number of the most significant articles on the plays are to be found in the Macmillan Casebook series on *Troilus and Cressida* and *Measure for Measure*. Wells (ed.), *Shakespeare: Select Bibliographical Guides* and Ure, *Shakespeare: The Problem Plays* contain extensive bibliographies on the problem plays; Jonathan Dollimore's *Radical Tragedy* has a wide-ranging bibliography of relevant background literature.

1
Concepts and Perspectives:
Why Problem Plays?

The purpose of this chapter is to convey a clear sense of the emergence and evolution of the term 'problem play' and the nature of the arguments surrounding the grouping of various plays under this heading. Having summarised the views of the most significant contributors to this debate an attempt will be made to isolate the key features of the genuine problem plays and to specify characteristics and themes which they share. By sifting through the ideas and approaches which have been most influential in shaping critical perceptions of these plays as a group, it will become clear why the categorisation and terminology attaching to them have proved both controversial and durable. Through careful analysis of the difficulties arising from the most seminal studies it should be possible to formulate a satisfactory definition of the term 'problem play' and to state precisely why, if the term is to be of value, the designation is applicable to only three of Shakespeare's plays.

Historically, the linking of these plays is both intriguing and illuminating. Dowden began the process in his book *Shakspere: His Mind and Art* (1875), referring to them in the Preface to the third edition as 'serious, dark and ironical' comedies. He perceives a sharp cleavage between these plays and the romantic comedies:

> *Twelfth Night* resumes all the admirable humorous characteristics of the group of comedies which it completes. Then the change comes; *All's Well that Ends Well* is grave and earnest; *Measure for Measure* is dark and bitter. In the first edition of this work I did not venture to attempt an interpretation of *Troilus and Cressida*. I now believe this strange and difficult play was a last attempt to continue comedy made

when Shakespeare had ceased to be able to smile genially, and when he must be either ironical, or else take a deep, passionate and tragical view of life.[1]

It is apparent that Dowden recognises a change of tone and mood from the romantic comedies: *All's Well* is 'grave and earnest'; *Measure for Measure* 'dark and bitter'; and *Troilus and Cressida*, which he assumes is chronologically the last of the three, is 'ironical'. If these plays can be called comedies, for Dowden they constitute a special kind of comedy. Moreover, within the grouping, *Troilus and Cressida* is the strangest and least amenable to being encompassed by any definition of comedy. Nevertheless, despite misgivings, Dowden believes *Troilus and Cressida* to be a comedy of sorts — a 'comedy of disillusion' — though he admits to being perplexed by Shakespeare's 'intention' and the 'spirit' in which he wrote the play.[2] Dowden avers that 'a mood of contemptuous depreciation of life may have come over Shakespeare, and spoilt him, at that time, for a writer of comedy'. Only the presence of Isabella submerges this mood in *Measure for Measure*, Dowden feels, but he insists on a close affinity between *Troilus and Cressida* and *Timon of Athens*: 'we must notice a striking resemblance in its spirit and structure to *Timon of Athens*'.[3]

No modern scholar would attempt the task which Dowden set himself: 'to connect the study of Shakespeare's works with an inquiry after the personality of the writer, and to observe, as far as is possible, in its several stages the growth of his intellect and character from youth to full maturity'.[4] What, for Dowden, represents a change of mental state would, for modern scholars, constitute a movement in interest or style — an attempt to discern patterns and relationships within the drama — rather than in the mind of the dramatist. It is all the more interesting, therefore, that like Dowden, modern scholars have been struck by the strangeness of these plays; by their unwillingness to be placed or located with other conventionally accepted groups of plays; by certain affinities which they share with each other — and with other plays, namely *Hamlet* and *Timon of Athens*.

Dowden, the first critic to group these plays together, was inclined to refer to them as comedies. F. S. Boas, however, who brought *Hamlet* into the grouping, believed that they merited a distinct classification. Writing in 1896, he chose to adopt a term which had been applied to the plays of Ibsen and Shaw: 'problem plays'. It was neither an identity of approach or centre of interest between Shakespeare and those modern playwrights which attracted him to this phrase, but rather a sense of aptness: they shared certain affinities but above all were difficult to classify, so why not problem plays? The term has survived, though with frequent misgivings on the part of scholars.

What, then, were the reasons adduced by Boas for linking these plays? He argues:

> All these dramas introduce us into highly artificial societies, whose civilisation is ripe unto rottenness. Amidst such media abnormal conditions of brain and of emotion are generated, and intricate cases of conscience demand a solution by unprecedented methods. Thus throughout these plays we move along dim untrodden paths, and at the close our feeling is neither of simple joy nor pain; we are excited, fascinated, perplexed, for the issues raised preclude a completely satis-factory outcome, even when, as in *All's Well* and *Measure for Measure*, the complications are outwardly adjusted in the fifth act. In *Troilus and Cressida* and *Hamlet* no such partial settle-ment of difficulties takes place, and we are left to interpret their enigmas as best we may. Dramas so singular in theme and temper cannot be strictly called comedies or tragedies. We may therefore borrow a convenient phrase from the theatre of today and class them together as Shakespeare's problem-plays.[5]

There is something imprecise, but nevertheless true, about Boas's suggestion that these societies are 'ripe unto rottenness'. Indeed, the decadence of Troy was at the centre of the Royal Shakespeare Company's 1985 – 6 production, being portrayed by a set redolent of a decaying mansion still affording crystal brandy glasses and decanters. Vienna is so overripe that Angelo is called upon to provide a purgation, while in the Court of France there is a clear sense that the qualities associated with the older generation are not to be found in the young. Again, his observation that 'abnormal conditions of brain and emotion are generated', thereby pro-ducing 'cases of conscience' which 'demand a solution by unprece-dented methods', is so vague as to be of questionable value. But Boas is surely right when he says that 'at the close our feeling is neither of simple joy nor pain'. These plays are puzzles which — even if we exclude *Hamlet* — cannot adequately be described as comedies.

3

Boas, then, distinguishes these plays from the rest of the Shakes-pearian canon in terms of the texture of the societies which they contain; the problematical nature of the questions which they pose; and the impossibility of achieving a totally satisfactory resolution. The audience is left perplexed — still pondering the problems even when reconciliation and harmony is nominally afforded them (as in *All's Well* and *Measure for Measure*). What Boas fails to do is to convince the reader that *Hamlet* really falls into the group. His main point is that the atmosphere of obscurity which envelops these plays 'closes most thickly round *Hamlet*'.[6] Not only is the play manifestly a tragedy, but it is a particular kind of tragedy — the most popular kind of tragedy to occupy the stages of Elizabethan and Jacobean England — a revenge tragedy. *Hamlet* has its share of problems but they are effectively contained within the mode of tragedy. The genuine problem plays evade any such adequate clas-sification. *Hamlet* would have been recognised as forming part of the tradition so clearly established in the mind of the Elizabethan playgoer by Kyd's seminal play *The Spanish Tragedy*. In contrast to the immensely popular revenge tragedies, George Bernard Shaw makes the illuminating observation that 'in such unpopular plays as *All's Well*, *Measure for Measure* and *Troilus and Cressida*, we find him ready and willing to start at the twentieth century if only the seventeenth century would let him'.[7]

W. W. Lawrence, writing in 1930, gives careful consideration to the comments of his predecessors, removes *Hamlet* from the group and attempts greater precision in delineating their funda-mental features:

> The essential characteristic of a problem play . . . is that a perplexing and distressing complication in human life is presented in a spirit of high seriousness. This special treat-ment distinguishes such a play from other kinds of drama, in that the theme is handled so as to arouse not merely interest or excitement, or pity or amusement, but to probe the compli-cated interrelations of character and action, in a situation admitting of different ethical interpretations.[8]

Here the problems in the plays are seen as perplexing, and open to varying ethical interpretations. Moreover, the problems may be abstract but they are embodied in and acted out through tensions encountered by the characters who find themselves trapped in specific situations. One point omitted by Lawrence is that, in order for the audience fully to engage the intellectual or moral problems, Shakespeare affords them a considerable degree of detachment. This is most obviously the case in the most complex of the three plays, *Troilus and Cressida.*

Lawrence returns to Dowden's emphasis on problem 'comedies' and justifies his position in a way which is both logical and practical:

> The term 'problem play', then, is particularly useful to apply to those productions which clearly do not fall into the category of tragedy, and yet are too serious and analytic to fit the commonly accepted conception of comedy. Indeed, when the problem play becomes tragedy, it is, I think, best considered under that rubric; at all events, there is no difficulty in so classifying it.[9]

But Lawrence does not rest his case there: he insists that 'the "problem" mood must not only be prominent in the action; it must dominate it'.[10] Thus the serious or dark strains in the romantic comedies do not make them problem plays. 'Still less', says Lawrence, 'do the tragic elements in a tragicomedy make of it a problem play.' In contrasting the essentially 'theatrical' qualities of the tragicomedy with the 'analytical' nature of the problem play Lawrence quotes Professor Ristine's view of tragicomedy: 'It presents no transcript from life; it neglects portrayal of character and psychological analysis for plot and theatricality; it substitutes dramatic falsity for dramatic truth; it emphasises novelty, sensation, surprise, startling effect.' Thus, for Lawrence, 'the controlling spirit in a problem play must obviously be realism'.[11] This, however, does not preclude the presence of non-realistic elements in the drama. Lawrence, like Dowden before him, sees these plays as constituting a 'radical departure' in Shakespeare's art; they present the 'serious and realistic treatment of a distressing complication in human life, but without a tragic outcome'.[12]

After providing perceptive comments about the nature of the problem plays, Lawrence states unequivocally that 'They are of course greatly inferior to the better known dramas written by Shakespeare in the opening years of the new century.'[13] This view is now highly questionable and it is significant that the popularity of these plays has continued to increase since Lawrence expressed his negative view with such confidence. Not only is the modern world catching up with Shakespeare, but it is now arguable that

Troilus and Cressida is Shakespeare's most remarkable work and perhaps his greatest achievement. The Achilles' heel of Lawrence's analysis is his claim that the conflicting ethical interpretations affect only a modern audience. Shakespeare's audience, Lawrence claims, would have possessed a familiarity with the conventions and assumptions embodied in the plays and therefore would not have experienced the conflicting judgements to which a modern audience is subject. Thus Lawrence unintentionally devalues the ethical dilemmas to which these plays give rise: all is explained by simply acquiring the perspective of Shakespeare's (assumed) audience.

E. M. W. Tillyard's study, *Shakespeare's Problem Plays*, published in 1950, pays generous tribute to the work of Lawrence, but substitutes 'plays' for comedies in his title, and reinstates *Hamlet* to the group. Tillyard is not enamoured of the term yet sees it as the most useful available. However, he makes a distinction between *Hamlet* and *Troilus and Cressida* on the one hand and *All's Well* and *Measure for Measure* on the other. Indeed, the distinction is such that Tillyard's forewarning that he uses the term problem plays 'vaguely and equivocally' is no exaggeration. He begins with an analogy to express the essential division within the group:

> There are at least two kinds of problem child: first the genuinely abnormal child, whom no efforts will ever bring back to normality; and second the child who is interesting and complex rather than abnormal: apt indeed to be a problem for parents and teachers but destined to fulfilment in the larger scope of adult life. Now *All's Well* and *Measure for Measure* are like the first problem child: there is something radically schizophrenic about them. *Hamlet* and *Troilus and Cressida* are like the second problem child, full of interest and complexity but divided within themselves only in the eyes of those who have misjudged them. To put the difference in another way, *Hamlet* and *Troilus and Cressida* are problem plays because they deal with and display interesting problems; *All's Well* and *Measure for Measure* because they *are* problems.[14]

Despite providing a definition of the problem plays which separates them into two distinct groups, Tillyard does partially rescue the situation by asserting that they share a sombreness of mood arising out of their interest in speculative thought and a psychological exploration that results in an intense sense of realism. Like other writers on the subject before him, Tillyard makes some perceptive points about the nature of the plays but fails to establish a meaningful framework for analysing them as a group.

Almost a decade later, A. P. Rossiter took up the question of the problem plays in lectures which were later published under the title, *Angel with Horns* (1961). He begins by commenting that these plays were written during the period of Shakespeare's greatest versatility: twelve varied plays written between 1597–8 and 1604. Rossiter suggests, therefore, that they do not form a triumvirate, but share a pattern of interests and methods which spill over into other plays. Nevertheless, he does propose a particular strength in the bonds which hold together three of the plays (he excludes *Hamlet*) — even though he thinks of them as 'tragi-comedies', perceiving the essence of this mode as 'an art of inversion, deflation and paradox', which has as its subject 'tragi-comic man'. Thus 'genuine tragi-comedy is marked by telling generalisations about the subject, *man*, of a seriousness which is unexpected in comedy and may seem incongruous with it'.[15]

Despite the change of name (though he also refers to them as problem plays) certain aspects of these plays are once more delineated: 'inversion, deflation and paradox' and concern with the nature of man. Rossiter goes on to specify four major concerns which are embodied in each of these plays. First they 'share a common evaluation of conventionally accepted "nobilities" . . . All are deflated'. Secondly, 'ideal' figures are placed in the pattern in such a way that cynicism is checked. Thirdly, 'these plays involve us in discoveries, always of a bad reality beneath the fair appearances of things: revelations, painful in the extreme — and we are *made to feel the pain* — of the distressing, disintegrating possibilities of human meanness'. And fourthly, they are all 'profoundly concerned with seeming and being: and this can cover both sex and human worth'. Rossiter does add a further element which he sees as forming one of the overall qualities of the problem plays: 'shiftingness' by which he means that 'All the firm points of view . . . are felt to be fallible.' Ultimately, Rossiter suggests:

these plays throw opposed or contrary views into the mind: only to leave the resulting equations without any settled or soothing solutions. They are all about 'Xs' that do not work out. *Troilus and Cressida* gives us a 'tragedy-of-love' pattern that is not tragic (nor love?); *All's Well* a 'happy ending' that makes us neither happy nor comfortable; *Measure for Measure* a 'final solution' that simply does not answer the questions raised.[16]

Once more a penetrating critic is left confronted by a sense of perplexity. Interestingly, although he perceives a need to range more widely in the pursuit of themes and interests which are embodied in these plays, it is precisely the problem plays which leave him with a peculiar sense of perplexity or open-endedness. They seem to provide puzzles that refuse to yield solutions. Unlike Tillyard, Rossiter makes no distinction between the nature of the problems associated with *Troilus and Cressida* on the one hand and *All's Well* and *Measure for Measure* on the other. Moreover, he recognises that they belong to a genre which inevitably excludes *Hamlet*.

Peter Ure, writing in 1961, reverted to a quartet of plays by excluding *Hamlet* from the group but including *Timon of Athens*. He declined to provide a tight definition, embracing Tillyard's disclaimer that he intended to use the term 'vaguely and equivocally'. Nevertheless, Ure commences his discussion of these plays by identifying their shared characteristics:

> the probing of character under the test of situations which raise conflicting ethical interpretations; the replacement of the strain of occasional melancholy which is found even in Shakespeare's most festive comedies by an urgently satirical and disfiguring temper; a willingness even in comedy to draw near to pain and death; a curious interweaving of romantic and even fantastic tales with realistic characterisation, which itself sometimes moves towards allegory and symbol; an art who's occasional apparent contempt and carelessness about what W. B. Yeats called the 'wheels and pulleys' of drama, the machinery for achieving consistency and smooth running, mediate the reach and pressure of a mind profoundly aware that energy and meaning in the theatre may spring from the attempt to embody in its forms the very resistance which life offers to being translated into expressive modes of art . . . [Finally] their language is often extremely hard to construe. It is tough and subtle, compounded of unexpected words, daring and resonant images, and strangely subterranean and occluded rhythms. For all readers this is the first and most vital 'problem'.[17]

This summary is of considerable value though some of the points require qualification. For instance, the reference to the inter-mingling of fantastic tales with realistic characters applies much more accurately to Shakespeare's romances and applies not at all to *Troilus and Cressida*. And Ure is no more convincing in his attempt to establish a close connection between *Timon of Athens* and the other three plays than Boas or Tillyard are in relating them to *Hamlet*. However, Ure's comment on language is particularly pertinent.

In setting out his case for recognition of the true or genuine problem plays, Ernest Schanzer, writing in 1963, rejects the idea that a meaningful distinction can be made on the basis of genre. He questions the validity of previous contributors as follows: Boas is denounced for claiming that *All's Well* and *Measure for Measure* are problem plays on grounds of their moral problems and yet are, after close analysis, found to be devoid of moral 'perplexity'. The problem which Boas discerns in *Hamlet*, Schanzer maintains, is of an entirely different kind (the psychological inscrutability of the hero), while *Troilus and Cressida* presents the problem of inter-preting the meaning of a complex play and discerning the connec-tion between the war plot and love story. Thus, though Boas finds the chief primary connecting link in 'the atmosphere of obscurity that surrounds them', Schanzer denies the validity of attaching this label to plays which exhibit different kinds of problems. Likewise, although admiring the greater precision of Lawrence in approaching this question, he points out that having claimed their essential affinity is one arising from the 'different ethical interpre-tations' to which the plays give rise, Lawrence goes on to argue that there would have been no such diversity of response in an Elizabethan audience. Hence Schanzer says of Lawrence, 'His concept of the Problem Play and his view of the proper interpreta-tion of the three plays he discusses under the label are irreconcilable, because they point in opposite directions.'[18]

Schanzer's conclusion on previous writing on the problem plays is that critics have employed definitions that are either too vague or equivocal (such as Boas and Tillyard respectively) or have produced interpretations of the plays which are at variance with their precise definitions (Lawrence, for example). Thus he sets out to provide a definition which is unambiguous and genuinely applies to three plays: *Julius Caesar, Antony and Cleopatra* and *Measure for Measure*. His definition of the problem play, therefore, has nothing to do with genre (he sees *Measure for Measure* as a comedy).

Rather the problem play is:

> A play in which we find a concern with a moral problem
> which is central to it, presented in such a manner that we are
> unsure of our moral bearings, so that uncertain and divided
> responses to it in the minds of the audience are possible or
> even probable.[19]

Schanzer argues that neither *All's Well* nor *Troilus and Cressida* exhibit a moral problem (for the latter play he suggests that the central issue is a metaphysical one: what is value?); and likewise he invokes A. C. Bradley in dismissing the suggestion that Hamlet's delay is 'prompted by moral scruples'.[20] Thus Schanzer not only discards the previous definitions of the term but creates an entirely new grouping which has nothing to do with earlier perceptions.

Whatever arguments can be adduced in favour of the establishment of this new triumvirate, the grouping has not secured a place in critical writing if for no other reason than that there are fascinating interrelationships which are shared by the three Roman plays, not least being their common source material, which results in their being treated as a group. Moreover, the Roman plays have powerful connections with the English history plays, especially the consideration of morality and ambition in the political sphere. Schanzer's comments on individual plays are valuable, but for the present discussion his book is most notable for constituting a direct challenge to the peculiar association of *Troilus and Cressida*, *All's Well* and *Measure for Measure*. Schanzer is unique in wishing to discard all previous definitions and groupings for the plays while preserving the term problem play and attaching it to an unusual triumvirate.

The most recent extended contribution to this question is Northrop Frye's *The Myth of Deliverance: Reflections on Shakespeare's Problem Comedies* (1983). Frye's book is devoted to a consideration of Shakespearian comedy, but he is interested in establishing a connection between *All's Well* and *Measure for Measure* and the Romances (see esp. pp. 8 and 32–3). Frye dismisses such issues as the 'realistic' nature of the problem plays and their concern with 'serious' social issues as a 'pseudo problem'. His view is that 'while *Troilus and Cressida* is admittedly an experimental play in a special category, the other two are simply romantic comedies where the chief magical device used is the bed trick instead of enchanted forests or identical twins'.[21] For Frye, then, the question of genre is a matter of structure. In his summary he sets out the characteristic structure and purpose of Shakespearian comedy and portrays *All's Well* and *Measure for Measure* as romantic comedies with *Troilus and Cressida* set apart as representing something unique in the Shakespearian canon. It is worth quoting Frye's summary paragraph almost in full as it sums up his argument with singular clarity and comprehensiveness:

> Two of Shakespeare's problem plays, then, are fairly typical comedies in which redemptive forces are set to work that bring about the characteristic festive conclusion, the birth of a new society, that gives to the audience the feeling that 'everything's going to be all right after all.' Such plays illustrate what we have been calling the myth of deliverance, a sense of energies released by forgiveness and reconciliation, where Eros triumphs over Nomos or law, by evading what is frustrating or absurd in law and fulfilling what is essential for social survival. But comedy is a mixture of the festive and the ironic, of a drive toward a renewed society along with a strong emphasis on the arbitrary whims and absurdities that block its emergence. There is a much larger infusion of irony in *Measure for Measure* and *All's Well* than in, say *As You Like It* or *Twelfth Night*, and of course there are many comedies, especially in modern times, where the ironic emphasis is too strong for the drive toward deliverance, and where the play ends in frustration and blocked movement. In Shakespeare's canon the play that comes nearest to this is *Troilus and Cressida*, a play that, whatever else it may do, does not illustrate the myth of deliverance in comedy.[22]

What Frye states is quite acceptable but for one crucial point: many critics and vast numbers of theatregoers choke on the very consummation which they readily accept in Shakespeare's romantic comedies. They don't believe in the happy endings of *All's Well* and *Measure for Measure*. They feel that there is something wrong and are driven back to a reconsideration of all that has gone before. As a consequence the perspective of these plays seems radically different from that of the romantic comedies. Frye perceives that these plays raise questions about the relation between drama and life, of illusion to reality, an affinity they share with the romances — plays which explore this matter with singular insistence. Nevertheless, he does not take sufficient account of the fact that the forced nature of the endings of these plays calls into question the validity of the solution. We have the structure of romantic comedy but not the world of romantic comedy — and the questions dismissed by Frye as pseudo problems once more need to be posed.

Significantly Frye rejects the view that *Troilus and Cressida* is a problem 'comedy'. For Frye 'It is a kind of history play, for the Trojan war was the normal beginning of secular history in Shakespeare's day.' However, 'The play also seems to be a tragedy, what with the death of Hector, the destruction of Troilus' trust by Cressida, and the bitter final scene, with Troy approaching its final catastrophe.'[23] It is telling to find such a distinguished critic expressing his ambivalence so candidly. Evidently *Troilus and Cressida* does not conform to any of the traditional categories. The Epistle to the Quarto edition of the play calls it a comedy while the title page refers to it as a history. The editors of the First Folio appear to share Frye's uncertainty, placing the play between the tragedies and the histories, though the circumstances leading to that decision are obscure. (The title of the play does not appear in the catalogue, which suggests that the editors found difficulty in obtaining a satisfactory text or that there was some problem over copyright.) Directors and reviewers have sometimes indicated a preference for strengthening the tragic dimension of the play by denying the last word to Pandarus, thereby closing the play with the Trojans retiring to Troy oppressed by the knowledge of their inevitable defeat. Interestingly Frye does draw attention to one common feature of the three plays: namely, the presence of railers. Even so, he makes a perceptive distinction between Thersites and his counterparts in the other plays: 'while the slanders of Lucio and Parolles are the wildest fantasy, the railing of Thersites is close to the facts'.[24] Here, then, is another intriguing example of a parallel between the plays but one which characteristically reveals *Troilus and Cressida* in slightly different focus.

One critic who has been unequivocal in his classification of *Troilus and Cressida* is Oscar James Campbell. He has described the play as 'comicall satyre' — a term invented by Ben Jonson and applied to three of his own plays: *Everyman Out of His Humour* (1599), *Cynthia's Revels* (1600 – 1) and *Poetaster* (1601). Two other plays placed firmly in this category by Campbell are Marston's *Jack Drum's Entertainment* (1600) and *What You Will* (1601). Campbell points out that 'a "satire" or "satyr", in the critical terminology of the Renaissance, implied a distinctive artistic

method and a well-defined literary type devoted to the denunciation, exposure, or derision of some kind of folly and abuse'.[25]
Thus Campbell sees *Troilus and Cressida* as providing an example of
Shakespeare following dramatic fashion as the play was written
'during the years when the vogue of comical satire was at its
height'.[26]

Although Campbell is able to cite a number of parallels between
Troilus and Cressida and the satirical comedies which he analyses in
depth, the feeling of the modern reader is of the extent of the
differences between Shakespeare's play and those with which it is
compared — differences which are not simply attributable to the
resources of the dramatists. One example will suffice to illustrate
how wide of the mark Campbell is in relating *Troilus and Cressida* to
these comical satires:

> Ulysses and Hector are commentators — representatives of
> the author. Like Macilente, Felice, and Quadratus, they are
> philosophers of a sort. The pair expound the political theories
> which their creator had illustrated in some of the chronicle
> histories, and the ethical system which he was to embody in
> many of his tragedies. Thersites and Pandarus are buffoons
> — original variations of the type which Carlo Buffone repre-
> sented. They are just as contemptuous as the *raisonneurs* of the
> follies and sins which the play exposes, but are so abandoned
> in their methods of reprehension that they break all the rules
> of artistic decorum. However, they awaken the boisterous
> laughter which all Elizabethan audiences demanded from
> some part of every comic drama. They serve as equivalents of
> the louts and clowns of other kinds of comedies.[27]

The inadequacy of this view becomes evident on only slight
acquaintance with Shakespeare's play. Ulysses and Hector are not
the representatives of the author: they are treated with ironic
detachment. Likewise the interpretation of Pandarus and
Thersites by Campbell comes nowhere near capturing the complexity of the relationship of these characters to the overall
dramatic design. Campbell becomes aware of the unsatisfactory
nature of his analysis in the last page of his book where he refers to
Shakespeare's 'temperamental unfitness for the composition of an
effective comical satire'. What Shakespeare has done, implies
Campbell, is to transcend the dramatic mode which he was
attempting to utilise: 'The sustained intensity of his mind, joined

to his tendency toward philosophical lyricism, lent the play a depth of tone which makes his satire ring with universal meanings.'[28] In other words, Shakespeare aimed at producing a comical satire, missed the mark and produced something else! What influence the plays discussed by Campbell exerted on Shakespeare is open to question, but his implied conclusion is correct: what Shakespeare actually produced cannot be adequately described as comical satire.

What emerges strongly from this summary of some of the most significant and influential commentaries on the problem plays is a sense of the uncertainties and contradictions which characterise the discussion. *All's Well* and *Measure for Measure* are seen as possessing close affinities and almost fall into the category of romantic or festive comedy (a status which they achieve for Northrop Frye). Yet there is a distinct feeling that despite the ostensible harmony that is achieved at the end of these plays there is a tension which precludes a whole-hearted belief in the joyful resolution. Critics, and audiences, find their minds driven back to the questions provoked by the preceding action. The sense of release characteristic of Shakespeare's romantic comedies is not there. The predominant feeling is not one of emotional surrender but one of mental agitation and questioning.

There is general agreement that *Troilus and Cressida* lacks even the structure of romantic comedy despite being suffused with comic elements. For Frye the play stands alone, and in a sense he is right; there is nothing quite like *Troilus and Cressida* anywhere in Shakespeare or indeed in English drama. Nevertheless, a number of strong connecting links have been discerned between *Troilus and Cressida*, *All's Well* and *Measure for Measure* and it is worth specifying their precise nature in an attempt to evaluate the argument for grouping together these three plays as opposed to other possible combinations.

The first significant unifying feature of these plays is that we are left pondering the questions raised by the action rather than contemplating the sense of loss characteristic of tragedy or of feeling the release or joy inherent in Shakespeare's romantic comedies. Whatever affinities these plays may share with *Hamlet* or *Timon of Athens* the feelings engendered by those plays are different and belong distinctly to the world of tragedy. Thus we are caught up with the problems which form the stuff of these plays and feel at a loss to categorise them. They are truly problem plays. The matter of genre is not merely one of wanting to pigeonhole plays out of an excessive sense of order. Rather, the nature of the contemplation provoked by these plays is such that we ponder both the social realities encompassed by them and the dramatic form in which they are embodied. Incongruity is perhaps the word that most effectively conveys the feeling of the audience: it does not really believe in the happy end and is more engaged by the concerns of character, relationships and institutions, both inside and outside the drama. As for *Troilus and Cressida*, bewilderment appears to have been historically the most characteristic response, and in recent times there has been a temptation to tilt the play towards tragedy in order to diminish the ambivalence of the audience which this play usually engenders.

Second, each of the three plays possesses a crucial debate scene which focuses sharply on the central themes. Moreover, the scene occurs in almost an identical position in each play. In *Troilus and Cressida* (II.ii.) the issue is one of value, worth and honour; in *All's Well* (II.iii.) the critical question relates to human valuation in terms of intrinsic and extrinsic considerations; the debate in *Measure for Measure* (II.ii.) centres on law and justice.

Third, all the plays interrogate the relationship between human behaviour and institutions. Each play is concerned with authority, hierarchy, decision-making and the consequence of these decisions for the society as a whole and for particular individuals. Who are the decision-makers (in the Trojan war)? What are the foundations for these decisions? What are the consequences? What is the nature of obligation and privilege (in the French court)? How far can the law go in controlling human behaviour (in Vienna)? What is the nature of the obligation placed on a ruler? These are merely a few of the most central questions relating to human behaviour and social institutions in the plays.

Fourth, these plays are particularly concerned with contrasts between appearance and reality. Continually an attractive exterior gives way to an unattractive interior. The great hero Achilles resorts to murder when he is incapable of defeating his enemy by fair means; Bertram has fine breeding and upbringing but behaves despicably. Parolles has an extravagant manner which covers a coward's heart. Angelo is a most precise and unrelenting judge but descends to the lowest depths of depravity. Occasionally this aspect is emblematic: the soldier in sumptuous armour killed by Hector turns out to be diseased.

Fifth, all the plays provoke a considerable degree of detachment. This feature is most marked in *Troilus and Cressida*, where

Pandarus and Thersites are key figures in ensuring that the audience is not afforded the luxury of identifying too closely with any of the characters. But this feature is also present in the other two plays: despite the passionate intensity created through the collision of characters, the action is placed in such a way that the issues remain clear and constantly on the surface. The use of irony, paradox and deflation are essential elements in maintaining the detachment of the audience. There are exemplary characters but they form part of the structure that underlines the questioning of characters like Isabella and Bertram. Moreover, scurrilous individuals like Thersites, Parolles and Lucio have an attractive side and represent features of life that make for human vitality: Thersites precludes sentimentality by constantly reminding the audience of stark realities; Parolles' dishonesty is charmingly innocuous compared with Bertram's vicious lying; Lucio's scandalous tongue and disreputable behaviour must be checked, but his refusal to be put down represents a defence against the authoritarianism of Angelo — it is he, after all, who presses Isabella to persist with and reinforce her plea on Claudio's behalf.

Sixth, Thersites, Parolles and Lucio share another characteristic which links the plays: they are not clowns or fools but denigrators. Thersites exposes the boils on the body politic with his savage insights; Lucio delights in scandalous lies and abuses his associates — particularly the woman who has borne his child; Parolles lacks the sharpness and bite of Thersites and Lucio but seeks to deceive through presenting a false appearance to the world. Interestingly, they all play a major role in the action but remain outsiders. Thersites is tolerated with amusement or contempt by his associates but his status remains the same throughout the course of the play and his presence makes the audience continually aware of the bleakest interpretation of the action. Like Thersites, both Parolles and Lucio have tongues which run away with them but ultimately it lands them in trouble which changes their status. But if Lucio is a liar and a scoundrel he presents a healthy counterweight to Angelo's interpretation of justice in sexual matters and he uses his energy to drive Isabella to greater exertions in an attempt to save Claudio. Moreover, while his interruptions in the last scene are irritating he represents a type which cannot be bludgeoned into subservience — a valuable antidote in any society threatened with totalitarianism. Parolles is the most innocuous of the three: he neither exposes nor commits a significant crime, unless his willingness to surrender secrets to the enemy is taken seriously. However, he does attempt to perpetrate fraud by pretending to be what he is not and it is he who experiences the greatest change of circumstances by the end of the play: he is given a new and humbler role. Parolles' vices do not go deep, they are effectively beyond his own control and he is easily exposed for what he is. Contemplation of his character and actions inevitably produces a more severe questioning and judgement upon Bertram's character and actions. Thus it is evident that there are significant differences between these characters in terms of behaviour and dramatic function, but as Northrop Frye recognises, each of them provides 'a focus for slander and railing'.[29]

Seventh, a major theme in these plays is honour. The plays all invite a probing of this concept and insist on separating its various strands. Bertram inherits honour, but surprisingly the King, among others, expresses the hope that Bertram will prove worthy of his inheritance: honour derived from ancestry has to be re-affirmed by the behaviour of the recipient. Moreover, honour can be attained in different ways, but different kinds of honour are not necessarily interchangeable. The Countess insists that Bertram cannot recover the honour lost in his treatment of Helena by means of his exploits on the battlefield. Angelo has behaved in a totally dishonourable way in his treatment of Mariana, but seems oblivious of the fact when we first encounter him. His conscious abandonment of honour is rapid after his initial meeting with Isabella. Hector asserts the primacy of honour over life but simplifies the equation by failing to recognise the dependence of others on his life. Moreover, for his chief antagonist honour can be put on and off like a suit of armour depending on the circumstances. Throughout these plays honour is a central concept and theme which, however significant in other Shakespeare plays, is so intimately linked to the major themes that it binds them together.

Eighth, these plays are all peculiarly concerned with sex. At the centre of the Trojan war are two faithless women who are fought over, enjoyed and denigrated. (Of the four outstanding cases of jealousy in Shakespeare three of the women are incapable of infidelity. Only in *Troilus and Cressida* do we find a mad outburst of jealousy which is justified.) Diomedes provides an annihilating evaluation of Helen while Troilus has to endure the agony of watching Cressida's betrayal. But women are both sex objects and symbols. Troilus is prepared to risk his arm to regain a tarnished love token, while the very existence of Troy is gambled through the retention of Helen. Angelo will treat a novice like a whore for sexual gratification and yet will execute a man for consummating his unofficial marriage with the woman he loves and by whom he is loved. Meanwhile sex as a commodity and a means of livelihood displays a vitality and ubiquity which is beyond the reach of the most restrictive legal system. Bertram is prepared to seduce and dishonour a woman without a blush or a moment's remorse and then denounce her in public as a prostitute. Yet he is loved by a woman remarkable for her virtue, perception and energy. Love and lechery feature powerfully in all three plays and provoke serious questions about sexual attraction, sexual desire and repression and the extent to which institutions ought to impinge on these fundamental human drives.

Ninth, disillusionment is close to the centre of these plays and is intimately connected with love and lechery. By the end of the play Troilus is disillusioned with both love and war — as indeed are most of the major characters long before the end. The Countess and the King are bitterly disillusioned by the failure of Bertram to measure up to his father, while several of the young men are disillusioned by the incongruity between Bertram's performance on and off the battlefield. Angelo is disillusioned about his moral rectitude: he is shocked and distressed when he discovers his vulnerability. In the latter two plays disillusionment may be dispelled by the rapid adjustment which takes place at the conclusion of the action — even so the audience may feel disillusioned that characters as worthy as Helena and Mariana can be so deeply attached to such dubious characters as Bertram and Angelo. In *Troilus* the sense of disillusionment is pervasive: the Greeks scent victory but they have long since relinquished their ideals. The audience is deprived of any illusions about the ability of human beings to conduct their most vital affairs in a rational manner.

Tenth, the other side of the disillusionment which the three plays exhibit, is a passionate desire to believe in total integrity: a wholeness and beauty in life which cannot be tarnished. Hector is emphatic in placing honour before life itself, and believes that the code to which he adheres is universal. His dying words express disbelief that this code can be discarded by Achilles. Helen thinks of Bertram as god-like ('my idolatrous fancy/Must sanctify his relics' (I.i.95–6)) but has to adjust to a reality that is very different. However, she moves from image to reality without any apparent sense of disillusionment except for one poignant moment (when Bertram refuses to kiss her farewell). It is as if her integrity will be enough for both of them. The confidence of several other characters in the play, however, suffers more severely and the King is evidently disillusioned with life before he is healed by Helena — a disillusionment which is made abundantly clear by his references to the hopes, beliefs and expectations he had held when younger and surrounded by such men as Bertram's father. Isabella yearns for the nunnery, and an austere regime, presumably to live in a world that is pure. Her encounter with Angelo forces upon her a recognition that the world outside the nunnery is far worse than she imagined. But what is the consequence for her after this initial disillusionment? She shows herself capable of an astonishing capacity for forgiveness and perhaps has developed the ability to live in an impure world. She seems as impervious to the destructive consequences of disillusionment as Helena. Arguably idealism triumphs over disillusionment in two of these plays, but that interpretation may be limited to the characters in the drama. The audience may experience a severe sense of disillusionment in all three plays while recognising the force of the aspiration for wholeness or purity in a flawed universe.

Another explicit concern of these plays is with the matter of identity and kinship. Virtually every character in *Troilus and Cressida* is identified in terms of kinship and several implications are suggested. Even the illegitimate Margarelon and Thersites emphasise the kinship network, and the one man who relinquishes his place in this pattern, Calchas, virtually loses his identity. Although the pattern is not as ubiquitous or persistent in the other two plays it still plays a remarkable role. *All's Well* opens with comments on two dead fathers and these live on vividly in the minds of others. Helena is the adoptive child of the Countess who would gladly receive her as a daughter-in-law. Lafew promises that the King will be a second father to Bertram, and later agrees that his own daughter be allowed to marry the prodigal son. Diana is accompanied by her mother and is advised by her. In *Measure for Measure*, Isabella and Julietta play at being cousins; Isabella has temporarily to leave her chosen vocation to fight for the life of her brother; Mariana initially loses Angelo because her brother is lost at sea; Lucio denies his paternity in order to avoid marriage to a whore. Angelo demands Claudio's head but he can be satisfied with a substitute because death creates a kinship through disguising identity; Claudio's fear of death with all its implications leads Isabella to doubt the fidelity of her mother. Mistress Overdone has run through more husbands than stockings. Thus once more a pattern that is discernible in several plays is greatly accentuated in the problem plays.

A number of critics appear to feel that there is something peculiar about the societies portrayed in these plays. It was Boas who suggested that they are 'highly artificial societies' and that an 'atmosphere of obscurity surrounds them'. What decidedly seems the case is that in each instance we enter a society which is introspective and manifests a sense of having a major problem. The Greeks and Trojans have punched themselves to a standstill and no longer seem to possess the capacity to change direction: they lack the energy and imagination to transform their situation. The disasters of the past have not illuminated their difficulties in any way but press down upon them like a dead weight. Vienna seethes with a licentiousness that is a matter of concern to the Duke but which is hardly a serious social threat in comparison with the unfeeling harshness of one of the outstanding deputies in the state. However, the feeling remains that if Angelo has been transformed there is little likelihood of transforming Vienna. *All's Well* also conveys a feeling of social strain: it is an ageing society: one in which a gap has opened up between the generations and there are too few talented young people mature enough to take the place of those who have died or are about to relinquish their positions. In varying degrees the leaders in these societies recognise that they are confronted by a social problem. In the case of *Troilus and Cressida* the failure of both societies is manifest, but in *All's Well* and *Measure for Measure* the audience is left with a dim awareness that these societies have not resolved their problems. Nowhere else in Shakespeare is the feeling articulated in this way. *The Tempest* leaves the audience doubting the ability of any state to remain invulnerable to the manoeuvres of the politically ambitious, but that remains, as it were, one of the ongoing contests or tensions intrinsic to the political process. In the problem plays something less tangible and therefore more intractable is alluded to. Paradoxically, *Troilus and Cressida* is less problematical in this sense: the failure of the society is apparent and this directs attention to the parallels between the world of the Trojan War and the world inhabited by the audience. This is one of the reasons why *Troilus and Cressida* now appears so fresh and so meaningful to a modern audience. We share the problems of the Trojans and Greeks — the possession of an advanced civilisation under severe threat, slipping inexorably beyond rational control — and are fascinated by it; we don't quite understand the full extent and nature of the problems of Vienna and the French court because they are only partially articulated. They remain obscure.

The final unifying characteristic is the toughness of the language. Although the language of each play is very distinctive (only *Troilus and Cressida* is rich in imagery) these plays contain many speeches which are not merely ambiguous but have a construction which is positively awkward: the verse occasionally exhibits a strain and tension which reflects the stress of conflicting emotions within the characters who voice them. The significance of this phenomenon will be considered in the chapters on the individual plays and will be evaluated in the concluding chapter.

The foregoing summary has provided an indication of the way in which the concept of the problem play has been perceived by some distinguished critics during the course of the past century. Definitions have varied, the plays encompassed by the term have changed and perceptions of the essential elements which go to make up the plays have differed. Nevertheless, there have been common points of reference and these have been delineated and developed during the preceding discussion. Moreover, additional parallels and comparisons have been made in order to suggest the relevance of the term problem plays when attached to *Troilus and Cressida, All's Well* and *Measure for Measure*. The most significant of these connections will be underlined in the concluding chapter.

What is essential, however, before proceeding to detailed discussion, is to have a clear definition of the term problem play which will provide a useful framework for the ensuing analysis. The term problem play is here used to encompass three plays which defy absorption into the traditional categories of romantic comedies, histories, tragedies and romances, but share striking affinities in terms of themes, atmosphere, tone and style. In particular, they explore fundamental problems relating to personal and social values within a framework which makes the audience acutely aware of the problems without providing amelioration through the provision of adequate answers or a dramatic mode which facilitates a satisfactory release of emotions.

Notes

1. Edward Dowden, *Shakspere: A Critical Study of his Mind and Art*, 3rd edn (Routledge and Kegan Paul, London, 1875), p. vi.
2. Ibid., p. vii.
3. Ibid., p. viii.

4. Ibid., p. xiii.
5. F. S. Boas, *Shakspere and his Predecessors* (John Murray, London, 1896), p. 345.
6. Ibid., p. 384.
7. G. Bernard Shaw, *Plays Pleasant and Unpleasant*, Revised edn (2 vols., Constable, London, 1906), vol. 1, p. xxi.
8. W. W. Lawrence, *Shakespeare's Problem Comedies*, 3rd edn (Penguin, Harmondsworth, 1969), p. 21.
9. Ibid., p. 22.
10. Ibid., p. 22.
11. Ibid., p. 23.
12. Ibid., p. 25.
13. Ibid., p. 26.
14. E. M. W. Tillyard, *Shakespeare's Problem Plays*, 3rd edn (Penguin, Harmondsworth, 1970), p. 10.
15. A. P. Rossiter, *Angel with Horns*, 4th edn (Longman, London, 1970), p. 117.
16. Ibid., pp. 126–8.
17. Peter Ure, *Shakespeare: The Problem Plays*, 3rd edn (Longman, London, 1970), pp. 3–4.
18. Ernest Shanzer, *The Problem Plays of Shakespeare: A Study of 'Julius Caesar', 'Measure for Measure', 'Antony and Cleopatra'* (Routledge and Kegan Paul, London, 1963), pp. 1–3.
19. Ibid., p. 6.
20. Ibid., pp. 8–9.
21. Northrop Frye, *The Myth of Deliverance: Reflections on Shakespeare's Problem Comedies* (Harvester Press, Brighton, 1983), p. 3.
22. Ibid., p. 61.
23. Ibid., p. 62.
24. Ibid., p. 65.
25. Oscar James Campbell, *Comicall Satyre and Shakespeare's 'Troilus and Cressida'*, 4th edn (Huntington Library Publications, California, 1970), p. viii.
26. Ibid., p. 185.
27. Ibid., p. 232.
28. Ibid., p. 234.
29. Northrop Frye, *The Myth of Deliverance*, p. 65.

2

Shakespeare's Use of His Source Material

i. *Troilus and Cressida*

As *Troilus and Cressida* is the most complex of the three plays, so too is the source material that Shakespeare draws on more rich and varied than the stories which provide the narrative material for *All's Well* and *Measure for Measure*. The title of the play and Shakespeare's material for the love story are taken from Chaucer's poem *Troilus and Criseyde*, along with Henryson's sequel, *The Testament of Cresseid*, which up to 1721 was printed as Chaucer's (though Shakespeare probably detected the different authorship). For the war story Shakespeare's main sources were almost certainly William Caxton's *Recuyell of the Historyes of Troye* (*c.* 1474), John Lydgate's *Troy-Book* (1513) and George Chapman's translation of Books I–II and VII–XI of Homer: *Seaven Bookes of the Iliades*. (The first instalment was published in 1598.)

Shakespeare may also have read one or more of the numerous translations of the *Iliad* which were available in English, French and Latin. In addition he probably drew on Virgil's *Aeneid* and Golding's translation of Ovid's *Metamorphoses* (1567). Ulysses' famous speech on order may have been influenced by Elyot's *The Governour* (1531), Hooker's treatise *Of the Lawes of Ecclesiasticall Politie* (1593) and the Homilie on obedience. Another possible source cited by Bullough, Muir and Palmer is Robert Green's *Euphues his Censure to Philautus* (1587).

The two major works which lie behind Shakespeare's medieval sources are the *Ephemeris Belli Troiani* of Dictys the Cretan, belonging to the fourth century AD and purporting to be based on an

23

eyewitness account, and the pro-Trojan version by Dares Phrygius, *De Excidio Troiae Historiae*, which dates from the sixth century.

Dares' work was rendered into Latin hexameters by Joseph of Exeter in the twelfth century. Although Dares describes Troilus, Diomed and Briseis, the love story emanates from Benoit de Sainte-Maure's *Roman de Troie*, dating from the second half of the twelfth century, which effectively takes up the story with the departure of Briseida from Troy. Benoit's French verse was translated into Latin prose by Guido delle Colonne, and it was his *Historia Troiana* (1287) which became the most widely used version of the love story. However, Chaucer's immediate source, Boccaccio's *Il Filostrato*, drew more heavily on Benoit because of his more compelling treatment of the love triangle.

Although the embryo of the love story is to be found in Benoit it was Boccaccio who was responsible for the creation of a genuinely moving poem which focuses directly on the lovers from the beginning of Troilo's wooing of Criseida to her betrayal of Troilo for Diomed. Not only is the poem infused with passionate feeling but Boccaccio, who changes the name of Troilus' sweetheart from Briseida to Criseida, introduces the key character of Pandarus, thereby providing the potential for a great deal of the comic irony found in Chaucer and Shakespeare. A good indication of the scope of Chaucer's transformation is given by F. N. Robinson, who points out:

> The *Filostrato* was the immediate and principal source of Chaucer's *Troilus* . . . a simple story of passion and sorrow has been expanded into what has often been called a psychological novel. In thus elaborating the *Filostrato* Chaucer improved the plot, and made the setting more vivid and more appropriate to its period. He gave the dialogue, which was good in the Italian original, his characteristic naturalness and humour, and sometimes a subtlety that is hardly matched in the best conversational passages in the *Canterbury Tales*. He enriched the whole narrative with moral and philosophical reflection. And above all, he transformed the characterisation.

> Not only is the plot altered and elaborated, apparently with repeated use of the *Filocolo*, the *Roman de Troie*, and the *Eneas*; and the characterization improved, perhaps under the influence of Ovid; but songs are derived from Petrarch, and, probably, Machaut; a series of portraits are taken from Joseph

of Exeter; and the whole poem is packed with popular proverbs and allusions to literature, both ancient and medieval.[1]

To this extensive list of sources and influences should be added ideas drawn from Boethius and Dante. Chaucer, in the *Hous of Fame*, lists the chief authorities on the Troy story as Homer, Dares, Dictys, Boccaccio, Guido delle Colonne and Geoffrey of Monmouth whose *Historia Regium Brittaniae (c.* 1139) narrated the story of Aeneas' flight from Troy and settlement in Italy, and the expulsion of his great grandson Brute who reached Albion to become the founder of London. It was this latter account which linked Britain to Troy thereby creating a sentimental attachment to the Trojans which intensified the tragic force of the destruction of that great city and its civilisation.

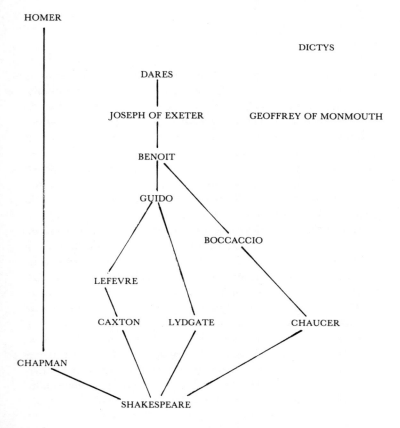

Both medieval versions of the war story used by Shakespeare derive ultimately from the same source. William Caxton's *The Recuyell of the Historyes of Troye*, which was the first printed book in English, was translated in 1471 and published *c*. 1474. Caxton's work was a translation of Raoul Lefevre's fifteenth-century French prose translation of Guido delle Colonne's *Historia Troiana*. John Lydgate's *Troy-Book* which was begun in 1412 and published in 1513 and again in 1555 was translated directly from Guido. Nevertheless, there were a number of differences between the versions of Lydgate and Caxton which offered suggestions for Shakespeare in his reshaping of the narrative.

A diagrammatic representation of the main lines of transmission of the Trojan war story in Shakespeare will provide a useful summary before examining the ways in which the dramatist shaped the diverse material that was directly available to him (see p. 25).

Chapman's Homer

The most striking change undertaken by Shakespeare relates to the withdrawal of Achilles from the battle. In Homer, Agamemnon is pressed into returning Chryseis to her father in order that the priest will revoke his plea to the gods to punish the Greeks with a visitation of the plague. Agamemnon only reluctantly agrees to relinquish his prisoner, displaying an arrogance which characterised his initial response to the priest. Moreover, as compensation he insists on taking Achilles' lovely captive, Bryseis, despite an attempt by Nestor to dissuade him. Thus the severity of the public quarrel between Agamemnon and Achilles and the subsequent humiliation inflicted on the latter causes an irrevocable breach between the men that leads to the withdrawal from the war of Achilles and his Myrmidons. Shakespeare suppresses this entire incident, and, for some time, he withholds Achilles' reason for not fighting (his love of Polyxena). Consequently the Grecian warrior appears petulant in contrast with Homer's hero who displays an understandable resentment against an overbearing and unjust commander. During the course of the play the concepts of value, worth and measurement are powerfully developed by Shakespeare whereas they are significant but minor and scattered in Homer. For instance Achilles, who complains of the disparity between his achievement and rewards, says:

yet by the valure got
Of my free labours thy rude lust will wrest in to thy lot:
In distribution of all townes, wun from our Trojan foes
Still more then mine to thy heapt store th'uneven
    proportion rose,
But in proportion of the fight the heaviest part did rise,
To my discharge, for which I find much praise and little
    prise.
But Ile endure this ods no more, t'is better to retire,
And to my countrie take my fleet, not feeding thy desire
Both with the wracke of my renowne and of my wealth
    beside,
Exhausted by the barbarous thirst of thy degenerat pride.[2]

Shakespeare appears to draw heavily on Book II of Homer, which contains a vivid description of Thersites, and Ulysses' speech on the necessity of order through hierarchy. This is delivered to dissuade the army from leaving Troy:

The anger of a king is death; his honor springs from *Jove*.
His person is in spight of hate protected in his love.
But if he saw the vulgar sorte, or if in crie hee tooke
A souldier with exclaimes for flight: him with his mace hee
    stroke,
And usde these speeches of reproofe: wretch keepe thy
    place and heare
Others besides thy Generall that place above thee beare:
Thou art unfit to rule and base without a name in war
Or state of counsaile: nor must Greekes be so irregular
To live as every man may take the scepter from the king:
The rule of many is absurd, one Lord must leade the ring
Of far resounding government: one king whome *Saturnes*
    sonne,
Hath given a scepter and sound lawes, to beare dominion.[3]

Although brief, this contains the embryo of the speech in Shakespeare. The difference in context, however, is significant. In Homer, Ulysses is seeking to quell a disorganised dissolution of the army and has to round off his speech by recalling Calchas' prophecy that the Greeks will triumph over Troy after ten years. Shakespeare's Ulysses offers an explanation for the Greeks' failure to subdue Troy. He not only states the case for order and discipline

through hierarchy but points out that the fundamental principle
has already been breached — through the example of Achilles.

Turning to Thersites, Homer describes him as:

> A man of tongue, whose ravenlike voice a tuneles jarring kept,
> Who in his ranke minde coppy had of unregarded wordes,
> That rashly and beyond al rule usde to oppugne the Lords,
> But what soever came from him was laught at mightilie:
> The filthiest Greeke that came to *Troy*: he had a goggle eye:
> Starcke-lame he was of eyther foote: his shoulders were
>   contract
> Into his brest and crookt withall: his head was sharpe
>   compact,
> And here and there it had a hayre. To mighty *Thetides*
> And wise *Ulisses* he retaind much anger and disease:
> For still he chid them eagerlie: and then against the state
> Of *Agamemnon* he would rayle: the Greekes in vehement hate
> And high disdaine conceipted him: yet he with violent throate
> Would needes upbraide the General, and thus himselfe
>   forgot.[4]

Thersites, disfigured and despised, provides a perceptive critique
of Agamemnon's behaviour, denouncing his greed, lust and his
dishonourable treatment of Achilles which sets a bad example to the
entire army:

> *Atrides*, why complainst thou now? what dost thou covet more?
> Thy thriftie tents are full of coine, and thou hast women store,
> Faire and well favorde, which we Greekes at every towne
>   we take
> Resigne to thee . . .
>   who my selfe, or any other Greeke,
> Should bring thee captive? or a wench, fild with her sweets of
>   youth,
> Which thou maist love and private keepe for thy insaciate
>   tooth?
> But it becomes not kings to tempt by wicked president
> Their subjects to dishonestie: O mindes most impotent,
> Not Achives but Achian gyrles, come fall aborde and home:
> Let him concoct his pray alone, alone Troy overcome,
> To make him know if our free eares his proud commandes
>   would heare

In any thing: or not disdaine his longer yoke to beare,
Who hath with contumely wrongd, a better man then hee,
Achilles, from whose armes, in spight that all the world
   might see,
He tooke a prise won with his sword, but now it plaine
   appeares,
Achilles hath no splene in him, but most remislie beares
A femall stomacke: else be sure, the robberie of his meede,
O *Agamemnon*, would have prov'd thy last injurious deede.[5]

Thus Homer's Thersites sees Agamemnon himself as precipitating
the breakdown in order. Thersites insists that power of command
rests upon moral behaviour and cannot simply be enforced.
Shakespeare, by accentuating Thersites' scurrility, not only paves
the way for more devastating denunciations of individuals and the
war but also creates greater complexity through ambiguity. How
are we to take Thersites' views?

Homer's Thersites is promptly beaten by Ulysses for his inter-
vention but the reader is left more with an awareness of his perception than his subsequent humiliation. Indeed, his speech rings
true: we perceive the unpleasant reality of a wilful and incompetent leader that totally undermines Ulysses' case for unquestion-
ing acceptance of the rule of hierarchy. In contrast, Shakespeare's
character never exhibits this kind of directness: he is not capable of
producing a sustained oration; he fires insults and evaluations like
arrows; he perceives the stupidity and shabbiness that pervades the
battlefield and council chambers but is limited to impotent railing.
Nevertheless, despite the abuse that scholars have hurled at
Thersites, Shakespeare makes him a critic who sees through the
pretensions of the heroes and understands the true nature of the
war: 'All the argument is a whore and a cuckold' (II.iii.74–5).
Perhaps Thersites' denunciation of Agamemnon, coming fast on
the heels of Homer's description of him, gave Shakespeare the
germ of a character who is deformed, irascible and perceptive. A
man who sees only one side of life but sees it clearly.

Again, Hector's challenge to the Greeks comes from Homer,
but in *The Iliad* it is a much more serious affair. On receiving the
challenge all the Greek warriors are silent. However, after
Menelaus makes a futile gesture, Nestor evokes a response from
nine of the best warriors who put themselves forward for a lottery.
The lottery is genuine though the winner, Ajax Tellamon, is
clearly the Greeks' choice. Shakespeare, in contrast, has a rigged

lottery which forms part of a scheme to promote Ajax to the position of foremost warrior in the camp in order to precipitate an emulative response from Achilles. But the differences do not end there. Shakespeare makes the duel a gentle affair between blood relatives with Hector possessing such superiority that he can display courtesy and magnanimity. Moreover, the duel forms only part of a major scene which shows the leading characters in new circumstances: enemies are temporary friends and harmony prevails with the exception of Achilles' appalling breach of decorum. In Homer the duel is a serious matter — with no suggestion of consanguinity — in which Hector fares the worse. Nevertheless, even here Ajax insists that Hector must be the first to call a halt to the fight signifying the general view that Hector is the superior warrior. Hector does so in a way which displays his courtesy and humanity — features that are central to Shakespeare's portrait.

The duel in Homer precedes the Trojan debate on whether to give up Helen, whereas Shakespeare has Hector announce his challenge at the culmination of the debate scene. But like the comparison between Ulysses' speeches on order in Homer and Shakespeare respectively, the Trojan debate is slight and undramatic in Homer. Significantly, it is Antenor who states the case in Homer for surrendering Helen; whereas that character, praised for his wisdom in Shakespeare, never speaks a word (in Caxton he 'spacke moche').[6] Paris offers restitution of the wealth he brought from Argos but refuses to part with Helen, a view which is sanctioned by Priam. Shakespeare makes the debate scene one of the high points of the play: Hector defeats Troilus and Paris in argument, presents an overwhelming case for returning Helen, then makes an about turn with a decision to keep her. Shakespeare, therefore, gives full scope to the arguments and to the major participants, before establishing a course of action which is illogical and indefensible — on grounds other than the quest for honour and fame. Priam is a passive chairman content merely to set forth the Greek conditions and to chastise Paris for self-indulgence: 'You have the honey still, but these the gall' (II.ii.145).

Two other features of the debate scene need to be examined. Shakespeare opens the scene with the Greeks' proposal for peace which includes a catalogue of the costs of the war — costs which apply to both sides. The enormity of the past losses specified, Hector implies, and Cassandra makes explicit, what the ultimate cost may be — the total destruction of Troy. It is against this background that the subsequent debate takes place, thereby exposing the unthinking rashness of Troilus and the self-indulgence of Paris. Moreover, the audience gains an uncomfortable awareness of the disparity between the narrowness of the decision-making body, the King and leading princes of Troy, and the breadth of suffering that has already occurred and will continue in the future. Although the debate in Homer is perfunctory, the messengers who make the offer to the Greeks reveal a sense of widespread disillusionment with the war and Helen — 'From whose joy all our woe proceeds' — and contempt for Paris as the cause of the trouble: 'would he have died before'. These hints of dissatisfaction ('all the Peeres of Troy' urge Paris to relinquish Helen) are greatly developed by Shakespeare: virtually everyone expresses disgust at the misery and death emanating from the pursuit of a worthless woman. Interestingly, the Trojan messengers in Homer refer to Helen not by name but as 'Menelaus' wife'.[7] Shakespeare in the Prologue refers to her as 'Menelaus' queen'. In both cases her status is beyond question: she belongs to Menelaus. Homer's Greeks reject the offer of wealth and determine not to accept Helen as a bribe even if she were offered. They perceive the Trojan offer as an indication of weakness and Diomed insists that to depart without victory would constitute inconstancy.

It is at this point in Homer that Nestor proposes a new compact between Achilles and Agamemnon. The latter repents his ill-treatment of Achilles and promises the return of Bryseis 'untoucht' along with rich gifts. When the ambassadors encounter Achilles he is engaged in playing the harp and singing:

> And loving sacred musicke wel made it his exercise:
> To it he sung the glorious deedes of great Heroes dead,[8]

This is in sharp contrast to Shakespeare's Achilles whose artistic pursuits do not extend beyond an appreciation of Patroclus' and Thersites' parodies of the Greek leadership.

The appeal of the ambassadors is initially to Achilles' pity for the plight of the Greeks, but they pursue a number of arguments: duty; the attainment of fame through magnanimity; the extent of the compensation he is awarded by Agamemnon; glory through triumph over Hector. But Achilles dismisses the appeal by Ulysses, contrasting his efforts on the Greek part with the rewards he has received:

> No overplus I ever found, when with my mindes most strife
> To do them good, to dangerous fight I have exposde my life,[9]

Achilles rounds off his complaint by saying that in stealing Bryseis, Agamemnon committed the very same crime that brought the Greeks to Troy. This argument completely undermines the justification for the war, and indeed Achilles threatens to sail for home on the following day. The ambassadors leave empty-handed but far from accepting the validity of the argument advanced by Achilles, Ajax denounces him for an excess of pride:

> . . . great *Thetis* sonne hath storde
> Prowde wrath within him as a wealth, and will not be
>   implorde:[10]

Likewise Diomed scorns Achilles for his pride:

> Would God *Atrides* thy request were yet to undertake;
> And all thy gifts unoffered; he's prowde enough beside:
> But this ambassage thou hast sent will make him burst with
>   pride.[11]

Shakespeare may well have been influenced by this incident in Homer in creating two brilliant scenes: in II.iii. Ajax denounces Achilles for pride while being brimful himself thereby attracting the laughter and contempt of the Greek leadership. Ulysses' attempted seduction of Achilles (III.iii.) is much more subtle than the equivalent event on Homer. Ulysses employs his superior intellect in an endeavour to stir up Achilles' emulation. Before doing so, however, he has the entire Greek leadership snub Achilles to jolt him out of his sense of comfortable superiority. In the process of attempting to stimulate Achilles' desire for unquestioned superiority, Ulysses explores such issues as fame, mortality, Time and human nature. Ulysses' ploy fails to drag Achilles back into the fighting but it opens up a consideration of values and concepts which are central to the play.

Thus in Chapman's *Seaven Bookes of the Iliades* there are a number of key incidents which may have influenced Shakespeare: Ulysses' speech on order; the description of Thersites and his accurate denunciation of Agamemnon; Hector's challenge and duel with Ajax; the Trojan debate over the continuation of the war and the disillusionment of the messengers; the appeal to Achilles to rejoin the fight. However, in all these cases Shakespeare diverges significantly from the Homeric episodes in such a way that he is evidently working to a very different design. Moreover, in the matter of the cause of Achilles' withdrawal from the war Shakespeare jettisons the vital quarrel between the Greeks' general and their most powerful warrior. Consequently Shakespeare's Achilles appears more petulant and churlish than his Homeric counterpart.

In addition to the relevance of these incidents for Shakespeare's play, Chapman's version supplies the dramatist with suggestions for imagery and concepts. The matter of quantification in Shakespeare's play may have originated in the significant references in this source, two of which have already been cited. Hector's lengthy challenge to the Greeks contains a telling reference to fame and time:

> That when our ages in the earth shall hyde their periode,
> Survivors sayling the blacke sea may thus his name renew;
> . . .
> Thus shall posteritie report, and my fame never dy.[12]

Food imagery is also used by Hector in the challenge when he insists that the war

> Will never cease till *Mars* by you his ravenous stomacke fills
> With ruinde *Troy*, or we commaund your mightie Seaborne
> fleete.[13]

There is one striking echo of Chapman in Shakespeare: Agamemnon says that had he ten counsellors like Nestor 'Then *Priams* hightopt towers should stoope',[14] which is close to:

> Yon towers, whose wanton tops do buss the clouds,
> Must kiss their own feet.
> > (IV.v. 219–20)

A little less close is Nestor's wish that

> now my youthful spring
> Did floorish in my willing vaines . . .[15]

Which is close in association with his insistence in Shakespeare that he is prepared to encounter Hector, whose youth is 'in flood', with his 'three drops of blood' (I.iii. 299–300).

Throughout Homer there are constant references to ancestry

which again may have been one of the impulses behind Shakespeare's deployment of blood relationships as a structural feature of his play. Although the verbal and conceptual connections between the poem and the play are intriguing it would be mistaken to see these examples as anything more than slight pressures on forces that were coming to life in Shakespeare's imagination.

The death of Hector, which is described in Book XXII of Homer, was not translated by Chapman until 1611 and could not, therefore, have been utilised by Shakespeare. But there can be little doubt that he had recourse to Homer's account in some form. The outstanding features of this critical moment in the story are: the magnificent descriptions of Achilles; the pleas of Priam and Hecuba to Hector not to fight with the 'homicide'; Hector's flight around the walls until he is deceived into standing to fight by Pallas Athene; and his plea to Achilles both before the fight and after he is mortally wounded that the corpse of the loser be treated with respect; Achilles' contemptuous response and savage treatment of the body which is bound to his chariot by the heels and dragged around the battlefield. Achilles' language and actions reveal a degree of inhumanity which is shocking and contrasts sharply with Hector's behaviour on this and other occasions. The great Myrmidon looks like a magnificent warrior but behaves like a blackguard. Interestingly, the Myrmidons are ready to strike at Hector, if necessary, so that even in Homer the mighty Achilles has support at hand should things go badly for him. It is not surprising that Shakespeare searched deeper for the soul of the Grecian hero and found a cowardly gang leader rather than a magnificent warrior.

Golding's translation of Ovid's *Metamorphoses* (1567) is a probable source, and Books XII and XIII are of special interest because they describe the death of Achilles and the dispute between Ajax and Ulysses for his armour. Ajax contrasts his own feats in battle with Ulysses' cowardice and underhand methods before calling into question Ulysses' ancestry and asserting his own descent from Jove, claiming Achilles as 'cousin german'.[16] The attack is devastating, but Ulysses responds by naming his ancestors and claiming descent from deities on both sides (*Jupiter and Mercuree*). He then asserts the superiority of his role as leader and decision-maker as well as fighter. When Ulysses is awarded the armour Ajax kills himself.[17] This Ajax is far more articulate than Shakespeare's and is scornful of leadership, whereas in the play Ajax is easily flattered by the leadership and is hostile only to Achilles. However, there is a telling remark made by Shakespeare's Ulysses when he complains that Achilles despises 'policy':

> Count wisdom as no member of the war,
> Forestall prescience, and esteem no act
> But that of hand.

(I.iii. 198 – 200)

Shakespeare may well have recollected Ovid's description of Ajax's contempt for policy as opposed to physical prowess when describing the attitude of the disenchanted Achilles.

Lydgate

John Lydgate's *The Hystorye Sege and Dystruccyon of Troye* (1513) provides a description of major characters and key incidents which would have been of great value to Shakespeare in his reshaping of the war story. Ulysses is described as noble and full of wiles,

> In counseylynge discrete and full prudent,
> And in his tyme the most eloquent,[18]

and this conforms with Shakespeare's portrait. In contrast to Shakespeare's Ajax, Ajax Telamon is described as 'discrete and vertuous', a gifted musician, a 'noble kynght' who was 'Devoyde of pompe hatynge all vaynglorye'.[19] The only thing Shakespeare's Ajax has in common with this character is military prowess. Neither is Ajax Oyleus much like Shakespeare's, apart from his enormous physique and brute strength: his speech is 'rude and reckeles' and he is a 'cowarde'.[20] Diomede is presented as powerfully built, formidable, but mean and testy,

> For lytell worthe of disposicyon,
> And lecherous of complexyon,[21]

Here Shakespeare steers a mid-course making Diomed proud, self-confident and lecherous but also perceptive.

Lydgate restricts his comments on Cryseyde, acknowledging the greater powers of his master, Chaucer. However, he refers to her striking beauty and contrasts her virtues with her one weakness.

> Full symple and meke and full of sobernesse,
> . . .
> Goodly of speche, fulfylled of pyte,
> . . .
> And, as sayth Guydo, in love varyable;
> Of tendre herte and unstedfastnesse
> He hir accuseth, and newfongylnesse . . .[22]

Her variableness in love is contrasted with Troilus' staunchness:

> Therto in love trewe as any stele,
> . . .
> Without chaunge and of one herte entere.
> He was alway faythfull, juste and stable,
> Perseveraunt and of wyll immutable
> Upon what thynge he ones set his herte,

Moreover, as a knight he is unsurpassed:

> Except Ector there ne was such another.[23]

Whereas in Shakespeare's play Hector's fatal mistake is to allow Achilles to go free when he has the opportunity of killing him, for Lydgate the crucial blunder occurs when Hector declines to burn the Grecian ships at the behest of his cousin, Ajax Telamon. This is followed by a second error when the Trojan council grant the Greeks a three-months' truce even though Hector points out that their appeal is based on a shortage of food. Here, then, is material strongly suggestive of Trojan folly or naïvety.

It is during the truce that Calchas pleads with Agamemnon to exchange Antenor for Cressida. The Trojans agree to the exchange less willingly than the Greeks, but Lydgate points out that once the decision was made by the Parliament it could not be repealed. Shakespeare's Troilus seems to recognise the finality of such a decision when he asks 'Is it so concluded?' (IV.ii. 68) The truce also provides an opportunity for Hector to visit the Greeks for which 'in herte caught an appetyte'.[24] Shakespeare has Achilles say:

> I have a woman's longing,
> An appetite that I am sick withal,
> To see great Hector in his weeds of peace,

> (III.iii. 236–8)

And this is in keeping with Lydgate's description of how Achilles longed to see Hector, the man behind the armour.

When the great adversaries meet in Achilles' tent the latter promises to kill Hector. First for the wounds he has suffered at Hector's hands, but much more importantly as revenge for the killing of Patroclus whom Achilles loved dearly. The tenderness of this love is missing in Shakespeare, but Achilles' feeling for his friend is such that he immediately forgets his vow to Hecuba and goes roaring on to the battlefield to find Hector, the slayer of Patroclus. Shakespeare, then, transposes the incident: in the play the killing of Patroclus acts as the catalyst which drives Achilles into action on the fateful day. In Lydgate, Hector responds calmly to Achilles' threat but challenges him to single combat. Unlike the duel in Shakespeare, where Hector brags that the challenge will rouse the factious Greeks, in Lydgate the challenge is designed to prevent further deaths: if Achilles wins Priam will submit his city and power to the Greeks; if Hector wins the Greeks will sail away leaving the Trojans in peace. Achilles accepts the challenge with alacrity but the allies of the champions refuse to risk everything on the outcome of the duel. Interestingly, during the interview Hector is calm whereas Achilles is ill-tempered. This contrast in personalities is carried into the play — though with considerable adjustment. Achilles plays the braggart to such an extent that he provokes an uncharacteristically violent outburst from Hector, for which he apologises to the assembled Greeks and Trojans:

> You wisest Grecians, pardon me this brag:
> His insolence draws folly from my lips;
>
> (IV.v. 256 – 7)

Having described the desperate passion of Troilus and Cryseyde on learning of their forced separation, Lydgate points out that Guido sees merely a false woman capable of affecting an elaborate show of love and grief. In putting Guido's case he expresses himself as follows:

> And though so be that with a woeful eye
> They can outwarde wepe pyteously,
> The tother eye can laffe covertly,[25]

Which is very close to Cressida's confession of divided loyalties once she has succumbed to the advances of Diomed:

Troilus, farewell! One eye yet looks on thee,
But with my heart the other eye doth see.

(V.ii. 106–7)

Neither Lydgate nor Shakespeare, however, accept Guido's interpretation of Cressida as an example of the falsity of women.
Rather, they perceive a woman convinced of the depth of her affection while she is with Troilus, but unable to sustain the feeling
when she is apart from him. Hence the poignancy of the self-
denunciation in the lines just cited. Lydgate asserts that if women
are by nature inconstant, as Guido maintains, men should suffer
patiently,

For if women be double naturelly
Why shulde men ley on them the blame?[26]

A point of departure between Lydgate and Shakespeare is that
the latter depicts Cressida's swift surrender to Diomed in a sordid
manner and under the observation of Troilus, Ulysses and
Thersites, whereas the former has Diomed win her in a courtly
fashion sending her Troilus' captured horse (an incident used by
Shakespeare but possessing in the play a quality of incongruity —
a chivalric gesture in a world that has outlived chivalry) and
winning her only after a long period of suffering. This contrast is
instructive: in Shakespeare's play Cressida keeps Troilus at bay in
order to intensify his ardour and enjoy her power over him, but
she can't keep Diomed waiting five minutes: he is a man who
insists on instant payment; a lecher who knows what he wants and
will settle for nothing less. Lydgate's Diomed can be kept waiting
and pining by Cressida as he belongs to the tradition of chivalry.
This unity of tone in Lydgate contrasts with Shakespeare's juxtaposition of chivalry with coarseness, providing an ironic commentary on the gap between ostensible values and patterns of
behaviour and the actual values and impulses that motivate
human beings.

Shakespeare stays fairly close to Lydgate's description of the
weeping and desperate pleas made to Hector not to fight on the
fateful day. However, Shakespeare does not place Helen or
Polyxena alongside Andromache, Cassandra and Hecuba.
Neither is Hector restrained from taking the field as he is in
Lydgate's account, where he does not fight until his brother
Margareton is killed. A further difference between the two

accounts is that Shakespeare has Cassandra present Hector's death to him in such a way that he experiences the future event in the present, producing an effect which is much more potent than anything in Lydgate.

Again Shakespeare follows Lydgate only part of the way in dealing with Hector's death. Lydgate provides an elaborate description of the magnificent armour that entices Hector to kill a Greek king before riding off with his corpse to strip it. In order to secure the armour Hector forgoes the protection of his shield and is spotted by Achilles who

> all that ylke day
> For hym alone in awayte so lay,
> If in myschefe of hate and of envye
> In the felde he myght hym ought espye.[27]

He then charges at Hector, who is unaware of his approach, and pierces him through the heart with a spear. Achilles is then wounded by a Trojan and is carried from the field. The day closes with Hector's body being carried to Troy with reverence. Shakespeare adopts the armour incident but intensifies the duplicity and viciousness of Achilles by having him surround the unarmed Hector with his Myrmidons who then kill him before giving the credit to Achilles. Moreover, only a short while before this event Hector has had an advantage over Achilles in a fair fight and has let him go. Thus whereas Lydgate sees the folly of Hector arising from covetousness,

> That sodaynely was brought to his endynge
> Oonly for spoylynge of this ryche kynge.[28]

Shakespeare has him commit the additional fault of adopting a code of conduct in warfare that is unrealistically generous — as Troilus has pointed out — which he discovers for himself when he makes his plea to Achilles:

> I am unarm'd: forego this vantage, Greek.
>
> (V.viii. 9)

Finally, Shakespeare departs from Lydgate in that Achilles is uninjured and so is left revelling in the prospect of the destruction of Troy and insulting Hector's body by dragging it around the battlefield at the tail of his horse. Shakespeare denies Hector the tragic dignity afforded him by Lydgate and reveals the full hopelessness of the Trojan situation through the ranting of Troilus.

Achilles' withdrawal from the fighting through his love of Polyxena occurs after the death of Hector in Lydgate. His reason for returning to the battle is the desperate situation of the Greeks who are on the brink of defeat, due largely to the tremendous deeds of Troilus. Achilles instructs his Myrmidons (many of whom have been maimed, as in Shakespeare) to prepare a trap for Troilus. When they have surrounded him, killed his horse and hacked off his armour, Achilles attacks him from behind, chops off his head and drags his body around the field at the tail of his horse. Lydgate expounds at length on the greatness of Troilus and the cowardice and malice of Achilles, finally chastising Homer for so praising a cowardly brute.

Clearly Shakespeare takes material from the deaths of both Trojan heroes and conflates them when describing the death of Hector. His approach to history is not to denounce Homer, even by implication, but to provoke a wariness in the audience about 'history'. We are constantly left asking, what really happened? As in so many ways, the modern world is only just catching up with Shakespeare in adopting a sceptical approach to official history.

Caxton

In his introduction to *The Recuyell of the Historyes of Troye* Caxton states that the French version of the story which he is translating is based on many Latin versions. Unlike Lydgate, Caxton recounts the destruction of Troy by Hercules and its refounding by Priam who had five legitimate sons and three daughters (and 30 illegitimate sons). Of the Trojans left alive and taken into captivity by the Greeks was Priam's sister Exiona who became the mother of Ajax. It was in revenge for the refusal of the Greeks to repatriate Exiona that Paris captured Helen.

Caxton describes the magnificence of Troy whose towers seem to reach 'unto the hevene',[29] — in Shakespeare they 'buss the clouds' (IV.v. 219) — and its place as a centre of trade and commerce. He also enumerates the names of the six gates of the city — as Shakespeare does in the Prologue. Unlike Lydgate, who provides a brief account of the Trojan discussion about whether they should seek an end to the war, Caxton provides a vivid and extensive presentation of the debate about whether they should send a force to visit vengeance on the Greeks and secure the release of Hesione. Clearly Shakespeare, whose debate is over the *continuation* of the war, draws heavily on Caxton. Caxton has Priam make an appeal for revenge to Hector into whose hands he places authority. Hector argues with modest dignity that before embarking on such a project they should all contemplate the possible consequences. He maintains that it is folly to jeopardise the lives of everyone in Troy merely to enable their aunt to live out her last few years in her homeland. Hector is immediately opposed by Paris who is eager to undertake a mission to inflict damage on the Greeks and capture a noble lady who can be exchanged for Hesione. He supports his argument by reference to his vision of the goddesses and their promises. Deiphobus supports Paris with the argument that contemplation of the outcome of an action is a formula for permanent inaction (a view expressed by Troilus in the play). However, Helenus weighs in by referring to his powers of prophesy and warns that if Paris undertakes the proposed enterprise they will all be destroyed. His warning silences the disputants, until Troilus bursts forth by denouncing Helenus as a coward (as he does in the play) and rejecting prophesies and revelations as a guide to action. His passionate speech wins the day despite further prophetic warnings from one Pantheus. When she hears of the decision to send Paris into Greece, Cassandra prophesies the entire destruction of Troy and pleads with Priam on her knees 'drowned in terys'.[30] As in Shakespeare's play she is disregarded.

One crucial difference between this debate scene and that in the play — apart from the fact that the one debate precedes the war and the other takes place after seven years of desperate fighting — is that Shakespeare's Hector suddenly reverses his position, determining to continue the war after arguing persuasively for the return of Helen. In Caxton Hector simply lends his silent assent to the mood of the meeting; Shakespeare makes him more culpable. Moreover, in the play the Greeks are making a generous offer, relinquishing all right to reparations, merely requiring the return of Helen. The Trojans, therefore, have the benefit of years of experience and of suffering and death and must be aware of the realistic possibility that Troy will be destroyed. By transposing the debate, therefore, Shakespeare shows the Trojan decision-makers in a far poorer light. They can use their past experience to reconsider their situation but persist in following the road to destruction.

Not only that, but the announcement of Hector's challenge at the end of the scene, with its avowed purpose of rousing the Greeks, reveals an astonishing naïvety. Instead of capitalising on Greek dissention they are intent on uniting their enemies.

Referring back to Dares, Caxton provides brief but telling portraits of the chief characters. In contrast to Shakespeare's Ajax, the Ajax Telamon of Caxton is described as being 'with oute pompe'. Ulysses, the fairest of an impressive array of Greek heroes, and also the most gifted orator, is 'deceyvable and subtyll . . . a right grete lyar'. Diomedes' fighting prowess is allied to unattractive traits: he is brutal to his servant, 'luxuryous' and, 'false in his promesses' — a characteristic cited by Thersites in the play (V.i. 90–4). Two little peculiarities that Caxton attributes to Hector are a stammer and a lisp. But above all else he is extolled for his supremacy among the Trojans as a warrior and a man: 'Ther yssued never oute of Troye so stronge a man ne so worthy. Ne ther yssued never oute of his mouthe a vyllaynous worde . . . Ther was never knyght better belovyed of his peple than he was.' Shakespeare preserves these human qualities of Hector making him the most attractive character in the play. Troilus is described as a fighter second only to Hector. Perhaps most interesting from the standpoint of Shakespeare's translation of these characters is Antenor, described by Caxton as 'a ryght wyse man', an opinion echoed in the play, who 'spacke moche' — which is in sharp contrast to Shakespeare's character who does not speak a single word. The implication of Antenor being allocated the quality of wisdom and silence is that good sense would be ignored in circumstances where the key decision-makers are determined to perpetuate the war. Of the lovely women described by Caxton, Polyxena outshines them all.[31]

Before the war takes place the Greeks send Diomedes and Ulysses as ambassadors to persuade the Trojans to return Helen and compensate them for the damage inflicted by Paris. Agamemnon advocates this peace mission on the grounds that no one can foretell the outcome of an enterprise, but also that by giving the Trojans the opportunity of restoring Helen the Greeks will have justice on their side and so be blameless for the destruction of Troy. In presenting his case Agamemnon points out that the present situation would not have arisen had the Greeks not responded so arrogantly to the Trojan request for the return of Hesione. Evidently neither side can claim to be free of blame. In both cases pride overrides reason.

During the meeting in Troy Diomedes and Aeneas become locked in an argument which is close in tenor to their quarrel in the play (IV.i).

For Caxton the crucial moment in the war comes when Hector encounters Ajax Telamon in battle and discovers that he is his 'cosyn germaine'[32] being the son of Hesione. After embracing Ajax and inviting him to take his place on the Trojan side (which is refused) Hector offers to do Ajax any service he requires. The latter requests that Hector withdraw his men from battle — which he does even though they are burning the Grecian ships and have victory within their grasp. Hence Caxton concludes,

> This was the cause wherefore the Trojans lost to have the victorye, to the whiche they myght never after atteyne ne come, for fortune was to them contrarye. And therefore Virgile sayeth, Non est misericordia in bello, that is to saye, There is no mercy in bataill.[33]

Here, then, the Trojan defeat is not preordained, the gods don't decide, as in Homer, and even fortune cannot prevent the Trojans securing victory at that moment. The ultimate cause of the Trojan defeat is poor judgement or misplaced generosity. Shakespeare does not incorporate this scene in the play, but he has Troilus chastise Hector for extravagant generosity, and it is that excess of generosity which causes Hector's death when he relinquishes his power over Achilles — and thereby brings about the fall of Troy.

Something which might well have caught Shakespeare's eye is Caxton's reference to Hector striking King Thoas such a blow that he cut off half his nose. Lydgate commented on Hector mutilating Greeks and these two references may have come together in Shakespeare's mind to inspire his description of the Myrmidons after they have encountered Hector:

> Together with his mangled Myrmidons
> That noseless, handless, hack'd and chipp'd, come to him,
> Crying on Hector.
>
> (V.v. 33–35)

It is this King Thoas who is later exchanged for Antenor, along with Breseyda who, Caxton comments, is named by Chaucer 'Creseyda'.[34] His only other remark on this exchange relates to the loathing the Trojans felt for Breseyda's father, Calchas.

The exchange takes place during the three-months' truce granted to the Greeks, and it is during this time that Hector visits Achilles in his tent at the latter's request. Caxton's description of the scene, with Achilles vowing vengeance for the death of Patroclus — 'hym that I moste lovyd of the world'[35] — and accepting Hector's challenge to determine the outcome of the war through their single combat, is very close to Lydgate's, though there is less emphasis on the contrast between Achilles' coarse bragging and Hector's calm courtesy. Caxton diverges slightly from Lydgate, however, in that Priam is willing to risk everything on Hector's prowess, whereas the rest of the Greeks and Trojans decline the challenge. This challenge is very different from the one that occurs in Shakespeare, in that Hector is seeking a quick end to the conflict and is confident that he can effect victory for the Trojans. Moreover, it is made calmly in response to Achilles' threats. The challenge in Shakespeare possesses no clear advantage for the Trojans. On the contrary, Hector seems aware that it might have a beneficial effect on the Greeks.

According to Caxton's account Cressida parts from Troilus in great sorrow, 'Ther was never seen so moche sorowe made betwene two lovers at their departyng',[36] but is received graciously by the Greeks from whom she receives presents. In addition she is the immediate recipient of Diomed's pledge of love which she does not refuse. So comfortable is she in her new surroundings that she soon forgets Troy and Troilus. Thus Caxton neither denounces her like Guido, nor defends her like Lydgate, but rather expresses sadness: 'O how sone is the purpos of a woman chaungid and torned, certes more sonner than a man can saie or thinke.'[37] Shakespeare retains this presentation of a woman who leaves her lover in great sorrow and distress but soon finds that she is devoid of genuine depth of feeling or constancy. His Troilus adopts Guido's censure: an argument which is countered by Ulysses — 'What hath she done, prince, that can soil our mothers?' (V.ii. 133)

A major point of difference between Caxton's account and the play is that he describes how Cressida keeps Diomed in hope without giving herself to him: 'And she answered hym right wysely, gyvyng hym hope wyth oute certaynte of ony poynte, by the whyche Dyomedes was enflamed of alle poyntes in her love.'[38] This is precisely the strategy which Cressida successfully employs with Troilus, but Shakespeare's Diomedes disdains nice courtship: he will not tolerate dalliance and insists on immediate gratification.

Again Caxton is close to Lydgate in narrating the story of Andromache's dream and the desperate attempt to prevent Hector from fighting on the fateful day. However, Caxton adds a touch not in Lydgate which Shakespeare takes up: 'Hector was angry and sayd to his wyf many wordes reprochable'.[39] In the play Hector says 'You train me to offend you; get you in.' (V.iii. 4)

In both Caxton and Lydgate Hector takes the field only after Margarelon is killed, and when he does so he wreaks havoc among the Greeks, wounding Achilles in the thigh. The latter creeps up on Hector and catches him undefended when he is stripping the rich armour from a victim. Caxton, however, does not pause to moralise over Hector's action as Lydgate does. In both accounts Achilles is wounded by King Menon and is carried back to the camp while the Trojans march dolefully towards Troy. Shakespeare, then, chooses a much bleaker conclusion than is supplied by his main sources and intensifies the irony inherent in the situation. His Achilles is more cowardly and ruthless, his Hector more magnanimous (Achilles does not escape but is allowed to flee) and his action in taking the armour more surprising because it is not a commonplace in the play as such actions are in Homer, Lydgate and Caxton (in all three Hector is involved in an undignified scramble for the armour of Patroclus).

Another significant transposition of material by Shakespeare is Achilles' love for Polyxena which commences in Caxton on the anniversary of Hector's death, whereas in the play it is the cause of Achilles' withdrawal from the fighting. In Caxton's account Achilles addresses an assembly in an attempt to bring the war to an end (in order to win Polyxena in marriage) before withdrawing his own men from the fighting. Interestingly he makes a statement which is used in a variety of ways by a number of characters in the play: 'Helayne is nothing of so grete prys that ther behoveth to dye for her so many noble men'. He adds that they can leave with honour because they have killed Hector and many other nobles and they retain 'Exione, to whome Helayne may not compare in nobleness'.[40] Helen is not a pearl beyond compare (Menelaus might find equally attractive women); they have already paid too much and exacted too much for her.

When Ulysses leads a delegation to entice Achilles back into the fight he makes an appeal to the latter's need to preserve his renown. But quite unlike the exchange in Shakespeare, Caxton's Achilles responds with perception and dignity citing the worthy people who have already wasted their lives in a bad cause, including Hector, whom he confesses was a stronger man than himself. Finally, he concludes his argument by saying, 'For I have no more entencion to putte me more in danger, and love better to lese my renomee than my lyf, for in the ende ther is no prowesse but hit be forgoten.'[41] Shakespeare's Ulysses plays on the argument that reputation has constantly to be renewed through action, whereas Caxton's Achilles puts forward the logical implication of this by maintaining that as all fame is transient it is not worth dying for. Not only do Ulysses and Nestor fail to persuade Achilles, but they go away and put the case for peace countering Menelaus' claim that Troy was virtually defeated, since Hector is dead, with the view that the Trojans have in Troilus a warrior who is almost the equal of Hector. It is at this point that Calchas makes a crucial interjection by insisting that the gods have determined on the destruction of Troy. Achilles permits his Myrmidons to join the battle after further persuasion by Agamemnon and Nestor, and it is as a consequence of the beatings they receive at the hands of Troilus that he breaks his word to Hecuba and rejoins the war — only to be wounded by Troilus in their first confrontation.

Once Achilles recognises that Troilus is his superior in arms he arranges for his Myrmidons to encircle Troilus and cut him off from support. After they have killed Troilus' horse and beaten his armour from him Achilles moves in and cuts off his head. He then ties Troilus' body to the tail of his horse and drags him through the camp. Caxton concludes his description of the scene with a moral evaluation: 'O what vylonnye was hit to drawe so the sone of so noble a kynge that was so worthy and so hardy! Certes yf ony noblesse had ben in Achilles he would not have done this vylonye'.[42] And this is precisely the point from which Shakespeare begins. He finds the finer qualities attributed to the character in Caxton and Lydgate incompatible with his brutality. Shakespeare picks up all the suggestions of stupidity and dishonesty attaching to leaders and heroes in his sources and brings them to the foreground: he demythologises the Trojan war: there is courtesy, dignity and magnanimity to be found in Hector, but there is also a refusal to face up to the bleak realities of the situation. Having exposed the danger and futility of the conflict, Hector then justifies it by reference to honour; when he has his arch enemy at his mercy he lets him go — only to die minutes later, the victim of murder. He can hardly believe that he is going to be murdered, and is even less aware that his body will be defiled in an ignoble display of triumph.

What Shakespeare achieves through careful selection and transposition is an astonishing clarity of exposition. The inconsistencies and apologies of the sources have been discarded and a starker and more realistic, though not necessarily true, version of the war emerges. Moreover, the subject does not remain as a calamitous event in history, but operates as a paradigm for misrule and human folly. The fall of Troy is a recurrent event in history; entire cultures rise and fall, not as a matter of necessity, but as a consequence of the subjection of human reason to pride or ideology.

The ideology of Homer is heroism and possesses a kinship with the ideology of chivalry, but they are not identical. Shakespeare embodies the ethos of chivalry in the play and the cult of the hero, but exposes a tension between ostensible values and the bleaker realities of human conduct which operates beneath the surface. The great thinker and orator of the sources is in the play an arch manipulator. The greatest Grecian warrior is a coward and a fraud: but the Greeks win. The Trojans, for all their achievements, are decadent. Troilus knows the passion of the heart but is a headstrong fool who never learns. He can become disillusioned but not enlightened. Hector is an intelligent man with admirable human qualities to support his martial prowess, but he refuses to see life as it is. Ultimately he is a noble fool, responsible for his own death and the destruction of Troy.

Chaucer

Shakespeare's love story and three major characters are taken from Chaucer. Moreover, the tone of the poem is close to Shakespeare's, possessing irony, playful ambiguity and pathos. As E. Talbot Donaldson rightly claims,

> Shakespeare understood Chaucer's poem for what it is, a marvellous celebration of romantic love containing a sad recognition of its fragility, a work full of ironic contradictions and yet ringing true in a way that far more realistic literature fails to do.[43]

Taking Pandarus first, Shakespeare's debt to Chaucer is obviously enormous. Although Pandaro is Boccaccio's invention, as Nevill Coghill points out,

The most beguiling, and, at first sight, the most apparent change is in Chaucer's handling of the character of Pandarus. In place of Boccaccio's fashionable young man, cousin of Criseyde, and in no sense a striking personality, he offers us her worldly-wise and witty uncle, of unstated age, . . . He is full of stratagems, proverbs, jokes and fibs, a character memorable in the ways in which a Shakespeare or a Dickens character is memorable. He is the first great study in idiosyncrasy and personality in modern English literature.[44]

Chaucer's Pandarus, then, is very close to Shakespeare's. Chaucer not only provided Shakespeare with a story and ready-made characters but rendered him characters who had become established as archetypes: Criseyde as the inconstant lover, Pandarus as the quintessential go-between and Troilus as the constant lover (a position reinforced, if not established, by Henryson's poem). They already have a place in history, and a great deal of the ironic pleasure derived from Shakespeare's play is their swearing about the future to an audience which already knows their destiny — a future at variance with the vows they make.

Another point of tangency between the poem and the play is the extent to which they provide their audience with a sense of detachment. Detachment does not cancel feeling but provides for cool analysis of the situation and feelings of the characters, heightening both insight and understanding and deepening sympathy. Much of the detachment is effected through the role of Pandarus who seldom leaves the lovers together in the poem or the play. The young lovers are not allowed the luxury of being alone: tenderness and delicacy are always diminished by the commentary of Pandarus. When they finally come together in the play (III.ii) Pandarus provides running commentary and joins in the embraces. He derives as much pleasure from his part in the transaction as either of the lovers. In the poem he shares a bedroom with the lovers on their first night and provides the directions for Troilus to make the necessary progress from his knees and worship, to the bed and fulfilment (even helping him undress). In the morning Pandarus is on Criseyde's bed, teasing her about her encounters — even lifting the corner of the sheets to kiss her (III. 225). Shakespeare's Pandarus is equally playful on the morning after but does not share the lovers' bedchamber nor does he tease Cressida in her bed.

A significant difference between the poem and the play arises from the greater concentration of the latter. In the poem Pandarus twice steers Troilus and Criseyde into a bedroom — on the first occasion she is brought to comfort the young man who is ostensibly on the brink of death — whereas in the play they come together only on the fateful night that they consummate their love. Chaucer's pair have a period of three years between Troilus seeing and falling in love with Criseyde and her departure from Troy, though it is not clear how long they have together as active lovers. Shakespeare's lovers have only one night before Cressida is whisked off to the Grecians.

It is evident from the opening scene of the play that Troilus has been in love with Cressida for some (indeterminate) time and is impatient with Pandarus' slow progress. Indeed, it is in response to Troilus' complaint that Pandarus begins to exhibit his delightful absurdity, and his pleasure in playing the role of go-between (though he protests vigorously about the thankless nature of his efforts), expounding the analogy between courtship and baking. Chaucer's Pandarus is seen at work from the moment he exacts from Troilus the cause of his unhappiness. When he is successful in getting Criseyde to accept Troilus as her 'servant' he goes down on his knees to Cupid, celebrating the accord and quickly slipping into a practical gear by promising to take care of arrangements for the future (III. 27 – 8).

Chaucer's Pandarus has a momentary attack of conscience when he confesses that the role he has been playing on Troilus' behalf is virtually that of a bawd (III. 36 – 40). However, he acquits himself of the charge and is supported by Troilus (III. 57) on the grounds that there is a distinction between a man who acts out of love of his friend and one who works for financial reward. The dubious nature of this distinction is ironically pointed up by Troilus who offers to secure either of his sisters, Polyxena or Cassandra, or even Helen should Pandarus want one of them (III. 59). This offer, which provokes amusement rather than censure in the reader, virtually transforms the women themselves into coins. Thus Pandarus in evincing a moment of conscience, or in trying to clear himself of an indictment which he realises can easily be made by anyone conversant with the situation, draws the reader's attention to the true nature of his role.

Indeed, Chaucer's narrator informs us at the very moment when Pandarus is about to creep into Criseyde's bedchamber, to prepare her for Troilus' entrance, that he is one 'who knew the ancient dance/At every step, and point therein,' (III. 100). In other words, he is the complete professional. Later, when Troilus is sick with grief at the loss of Criseyde, Pandarus protests that he is overdoing things as he has at least had his satisfaction (IV. 57). In other words, it is sexual gratification which appears to be the supreme goal for Pandarus. This cynical man has no understanding of Troilus' deeper current of emotion. His cynicism is underlined when he advises Troilus to look around as he is able to find a dozen women fairer than Criseyde (IV. 58).

In a sense, Shakespeare's Pandarus is less self-aware: he is even more shallow and amusing than Chaucer's while being less cynical. Chaucer's Pandarus fades out from the poem, whereas Shakespeare's remains a vital presence. He is disregarded by the Trojan nobility who call to take Cressida to the Greeks and is denounced as a procurer by Troilus when the latter receives Cressida's dishonest letter. Although he is humiliated and experiences rapid physical decline through (venereal) disease, Pandarus provides an epilogue and rounds off the play with a song. He is shallow and pathetic, unaware of his own voyeuristic nature. He has done everything for the best of both parties, whereas Chaucer's Pandarus has consciously exploited his niece for the benefit of his friend.

Although Chaucer's Pandarus is willing to exploit his niece she seems to have the measure of him and uses him as effectively as he believes he is using her. Cressida's superiority over her uncle is even greater than Criseyde's: she quickly sets a trap for him and catches him off balance in their first encounter (I.ii.). Her soliloquy makes it plain that her admiration for Troilus exceeds anything that Pandarus can claim for him. Shakespeare's heroine has all the subtlety of Chaucer's but she is more witty, and takes a more obvious delight in teasing Pandarus.

Despite their close kinship, Shakespearian critics have been inclined to see Cressida in a less favourable light than Criseyde. Even such an intelligent and perceptive critic as Kenneth Muir makes a stark contrast between the two characters:

> Chaucer treats his heroine with gentleness and sympathy; she is a young widow, charming, pliable, and timid. Chaucer evades any direct explanation of her unfaithfulness and excuses her as much as he can. We are led to understand that she turns to Diomed, not out of sexual desire, but because she is lonely and isolated in the Greek camp and because she is always tempted to take the line of least resistance.

Shakespeare's Cressida has not been married and she is a
coquette by temperament, sharpening the appitite of both
men by her tactics.[45]

This hostility has been denounced by Donaldson who has mounted
a sturdy defence of Shakespeare's heroine. His starting point is as
follows:

> I can think of no literary characters who have been subjected
> to criticism less cool-headed than Criseyde and Cressida; and
> when they are treated together they tend to become the two
> halves of a companion picture, in which the good qualities of
> the one are exactly balanced by the bad qualities of the other.
> Criseyde is written up at Cressida's expense, and Cressida is
> written down to Criseyde's advantage.[46]

First, there is the question of Cressida's lively wit which is sufficiently ambiguous to permit interpretations which contain a good
deal of sexual suggestion. Donaldson claims that critics have been
prejudiced by knowledge of her ultimate betrayal of Troilus and
that 'she figures no more prominently in Eric Partridge's study of
Shakespearian obscenity than many of her more innocent
sisters'.[47] This is a valid point but Donaldson leans rather heavily
in favour of a near innocent Cressida in attempting to correct the
imbalance which he is attacking. For instance, when Troilus smiles
at Cressida's request, on hearing knocking at the door, 'My lord,
come you again into my chamber', she protests 'You smile and
mock at me, as if I meant naughtily.' (IV.ii. 37–8) She may have
made an innocent remark and Troilus smiles at the unintended
double entendre. Evidently they both enjoy the joke but Donaldson
protests that by making a bawdy interpretation of an innocent
remark Troilus is 'treating her as if she were a whore'.[48] But if this
is going too far one way, Donaldson is probably correct in criti-
cising Arnold Stein's suggestion that Cressida has 'a trick . . . of
slyly provoking immodest jokes at which then she can be embarrassed'.[49]

This enigmatic quality of Cressida goes right to the heart of the
play, but before exploring it in depth it is necessary to make some
detailed contrasts between Cressida and Criseyde. First, Criseyde
is a widow, whereas Cressida is a maid, probably a virgin.
Secondly, Criseyde succumbs to the attention and attractions of
Diomede after ten days (the last day by which she promised to

return to Troilus) but does not surrender physically for some (unstated) time. In contrast, Cressida commits herself to Diomed only one night after she has consummated her love with Troilus. Thirdly, Criseyde and Troilus have enjoyed a considerable though unknown period of love-making whereas Troilus and Cressida have only one night together. Fourthly, Troilus observes Cressida's betrayal, whereas Chaucer's Troilus anxiously awaits Criseyde's promised return for ten days, walking the walls expectantly — while Pandarus looks on knowingly. When Criseyde writes to Troilus she reveals considerable guile, dissembling first, and later, in response to his letter, casting doubt on the nature of his love and his fidelity. Troilus knows for certain that he has been betrayed only when he sees his brooch on a coat captured from Diomede (although Cassandra has previously warned him of the betrayal by means of interpreting a dream). In both cases the hero suffers agony: in the poem the anguish is long-drawn out; in the play the betrayal is observed brutally at first hand. The experiences, though very different, appear equally painful. Cressida, like her counterpart in the poem, writes a duplicitous letter, but in the play it has no power to deceive.

Despite the significant differences between the two situations the women are remarkably alike. Both appear subtle and intelligent and probably mean to be loyal when they pledge themselves to their sweetheart. Both are reluctant to leave Troy and both discover very quickly, with misgivings, that they are not capable of love. Here there is at least as much cause for sympathy for human frailty as there is for antagonism toward a woman who has betrayed her lover.

One major problem in both versions of the story relates to the surrender of the woman by Troilus. In each case she is being exchanged for Antenor (though in Chaucer's story the Trojans have to relinquish a king in addition to Criseyde). Troilus appears more culpable in Chaucer's version because he is present in Parliament when the question is debated (with many protesting against the exchange, including Hector). He says nothing on the grounds that Criseyde might be annoyed by his interference! Clearly he was in a position where he *might* have been able to prevent the exchange. Shakespeare avoids this peculiarity by having the decision made without the knowledge of Troilus. He is presented with the *fait accompli*. His response to the news of the exchange is: 'Is it so concluded?' (IV.ii. 68) Presumably there is absolutely nothing he can do. He is shocked and thwarted. Nevertheless,

students of the play are generally dissatisfied by his meek acceptance of the agreement especially in the light of his forceful defence
of the retention of Helen during the debate scene (II.ii.). Cressida,
in contrast, protests that she will not go until Troilus himself tells
her that there is no choice. In Chaucer's tale, Troilus, having sat
silent during the debate, contemplates absconding with Criseyde
but she insists that such a course will damage both of them: Troilus
will be denounced for leaving his country in its hour of need and
she for seducing him from his obligations. Rather than attempt to
defeat the arrangement by fleeing, she insists that she will deceive
her father and secure her return to Troy (expressing considerable
confidence in her wiles). Thus much of the sympathy for Crisyde
and Cressida emanates from the initial 'betrayal' by Troilus. They
are counters in a transaction — and are not consulted.

Something closely related to this matter is the issue of secrecy.
Much is made of this in both versions. Secrecy was one of the conventions in 'courtly love'. Because

> an illicit or even adulterous relationship was so often
> envisaged, the need for secrecy was paramount; but apart
> from the more practical aspect of this need for secrecy, in that
> it was a protection against the risk of a husband's discovery, it
> was also a protection against gossip — 'wicked tongues'. To
> be talked about was shameful; no one must ever suspect that
> your mistress is your mistress;[50]

This, then, can explain the desire for secrecy as Shakespeare's play
embodies many medieval elements. (Though Paris clearly perceives what is going on and in all probability everyone else will
soon.) Even when students recognise the significance of the convention they are still not completely satisfied. Why, they ask, does
Troilus never mention marriage? It may be that Shakespeare has
been happy to allow the awareness of the courtly love convention
of secrecy to operate in the back of the mind of the audience.
Shakespeare's alteration of Chaucer's story is significant and he
undoubtedly diminishes ill-feeling towards Troilus, but there
remains a residue of dissatisfaction with the hero.

As for Criseyde, she tears her hair and exclaims against fate
before falling into a faint. (The narrator puts a sly gloss on things
by suggesting that the violence of her reaction on hearing the news
is accentuated when she sees Troilus (IV. 118).) Troilus swears
that he would have killed himself had she not revived and Criseyde

adds that in such a case she would have done likewise. However, she cuts short the disquisition on suicide by suggesting that they go to bed immediately (IV. 178). The entire scene, with Pandarus crying his eyes out, is infused with comic irony. Moreover, once Criseyde is over the shock she is formulating her scheme for a swift return to Troy leaving no doubts about the contempt which she feels for her father (IV. 196–202). She even suggests that peace will probably be agreed in the near future. Hence she leaves Troy almost bubbling with confidence and chastising Troilus for his lack of trust. Shakespeare's Cressida is not nearly so self-assured at this point but is even more vigorous in reproving Troilus for his anxieties about her fidelity. Nevertheless, she prepares to leave Troy only after Troilus has insisted that there is no remedy (IV.iv. 29–30).

The critical moment in the interpretation of Shakespeare's Cressida is that which takes place when she enters the Greek camp. Chaucer's Criseyde is led straight to her father's tent by Diomede, but Shakespeare invents a scene which has fuelled the debate over the interpretation of Cressida. She is kissed in turn by the Greek leadership, initially in silence, but finding her feet in time to discomfort Menelaus and possibly humiliating Ulysses. The nub of the question is whether the Greeks audaciously treat Cressida as a prize of war, to which she eventually reacts with considerable vigour, or whether she has such an inviting eye that they merely respond to what they detect in her — looseness. At the centre of the problem is what precisely happens in the interchange between Cressida and Ulysses. When he asks 'May I, sweet lady, beg a kiss of you?' (IV.v. 47) is it his prelude to the kiss or a deliberate manoeuvre intended to secure the offer and reject it? When Cressida replies, does she say 'Beg then' or 'Beg two'? The latter could be delivered invitingly, whereas the former suggests a put down. In the 1985 Stratford production Juliet Stevenson accompanied her retort 'Beg then' with a snap of the fingers followed by a firm indication that Ulysses should fall to his knees. If this is what Shakespeare intended, Ulysses' long speech on Cressida is not a matter of objective appraisal but the spiteful riposte of a man who has suffered public humiliation. Donaldson is one of those who leans firmly to the latter interpretation, commenting picturesquely, 'It seems clear that a pretty young woman should not defeat a middle-aged self-proclaimed thinker in a small battle of wits, or deny him a kiss that others have received. Sour are the grapes of his wrath.'[51] More will be said about the incident later.

It is sufficient for the moment to indicate Shakespeare's invention of the scene and the problems of interpretation which it presents.

If the two versions diverge at the point where the heroine enters the Greek camp, they converge in their estimation of the character of Diomede. Chaucer's narrator indicates that he was a man 'who knew his way about' (V.16); he adds that Diomede was cunning and a boaster. Shakespeare presents him in his clash with Aeneas as a self-confident, even arrogant man who has a very clear perception of the world. His magnificent denunciation of Helen leaves no doubt that this is a character who has no illusions. In addition, both Ulysses and Thersites disparage him. The former comments:

'Tis he, I ken the manner of his gait:
He rises on the toe; that spirit of his
In aspiration lifts him from the earth.

(IV.v. 14 – 16)

The precise meaning of this statement may be open to question, but it appears to imply arrogance and self-assertion on the part of Diomed. Thersites' estimation of Diomed presents no problem of interpretation. He refers to Diomed as 'That dissembling abominable varlet' and a 'Greekish whoremasterly villain' (V.iv. 2 – 7).

Although Diomed possess similar characteristics in Chaucer and Shakespeare, the character behaves very differently in the two versions. In both cases there is an immediate move to win Cressida, but Chaucer's Diomede adopts a more cautious approach. In presenting himself as a servant to Creseyde he claims that he has had no other love before. Having made his initial move he waits ten days before going to Calkas' tent — 'as fresh as a branch in May' (V.121). He successfully insinuates himself with Criseyde gaining from her a promise that no other Greek will win her love if she does not choose him. Moreover, she gives him her glove. This being the latest day she has promised to return to Troilus the gesture is significant. She decides to stay with the Greeks. The following day Criseyde presents Diomede with a brooch given to her by Troilus — to which the narrator draws attention, asking why she should give this particular token — a horse of Troilus' and a 'pennon of her sleeve' (V.149). Although he gains her heart on the eleventh day after she has left Troy (and she exhibits some remorse that she will lose the immortality of being the pattern of fidelity and instead be reviled for faithlessness (V.152)), Diomede does not gain possession of her body for some time. The narrator, however, is unable to indicate the precise length of the wait (V.156).

The difference between the courtship style of Chaucer's Diomed and Shakespeare's leads Kenneth Muir to discern a sharp distinction in character:

> Shakespeare's Diomed is also a coarsened version of Chaucer's. Whereas in Chaucer's poem he is a noble warrior who wins Criseyde by his long and eloquent wooing, in Shakespeare's play he hardly bothers to woo Cressida. He never pretends to love her and obviously depises her. This degrading of Diomed's character is a corollary to the alteration in Cressida's.[52]

The weakness of Muir's interpretation is that it presents far too generous a portrait of Chaucer's Diomede. Shakespeare's Diomed woos Cressida with forceful insistence. He is a man of the world who has no time for teasing or promises. He wants Cressida's body and he insists on immediate possession. His courtship is the antithesis of Troilus's tremulous worship. She, in turn, is unable to play the waiting game with him: she has to make an immediate declaration or lose him. Cressida wavers momentarily but succumbs with astonishing speed to Diomed's harsh directness. Does she accept Diomed as an alternative to being fair game for the rest of the camp, or is she a woman, who once awakened to the full force of her sexuality needs a man? Students differ widely in their response to the scene. For some Cressida is a victim: a mere woman in a man's world who has to learn survival. For others she is a frightened young woman, weak and vulnerable who surrenders to the admittedly brutal persuasions of Diomed. Then again, she is seen as a slut or a whore.

One of the most fascinating features of the relationship between Chaucer's poem and Shakespeare's play is the passionate debates that have arisen over the character of Criseyde and of Cressida. Chaucerian and Shakespearian critics both discern a duality in the character presented. It is worth paying some attention to the discussions of Criseyde before attempting to discover the ways in which Shakespeare modified or transformed the heroine he found in Chaucer.

J. S. P. Tatlock is unequivocal in placing Chaucer's Criseyde above and beyond Boccaccio's. For him the latter is 'an attractive, sensual Neopolitan aristocrat, capable of any trivial impulsiveness, little more than a lay-figure to carry her part, therefore without any great conflicts, personality, or interest'. In contrast Chaucer's Criseyde is 'far more charming and dignified and less easy to win than Criseida'. Moreover, 'It is the greatest mistake in the world', Tatlock insists, 'to think her the kind of woman who has to have a lover.' He then presents the quintessence of Criseyde as follows:

> The picture of the growth of her love is perfect, with a wonderful balance of feeling and good sense; a cool head and a warm heart are not inconsistent, and make a poised character. Yet unquestionably she is apt for love, takes to the thought and to Troilus at once, and has plenty of spontaneous coquetry. It is the antithesis here which makes her one of the most appealing and deeply touching women in all poetry. The only trait which in the least prepares us for her undoing is her softness. She is no more fearful or even timid than any woman of her general type would be — in all the circumstances; softness is the word, and together with tenderness is her most endearing trait. There is no strand of steel in her make-up; and no 'courtly love' affectation . . .[53]

But having been won so whole-heartedly to this Criseyde, Tatlock then turns to her betrayal which he sees as totally at odds with the above portrait:

> on the tenth day we are told quite baldly the origins of her decision to remain, — the peril of the town, her need of friends, what Diomed had said, and his high station; reasons laughably inadequate compared with the interior warmth of the earlier picture. None of this is mere coquettish pastime, for which she is in no mood, but there is also no love, nor even desire, — it is mere calculation.[54]

Thus despite the antitheses which Tatlock discerns in the presentation of Criseyde's character he does not see any of the qualities as accounting for the changed behaviour of the heroine in the Greek camp. His explanation of this duality is twofold:

> in early literature human character is apt to be conceived and presented as static and not changing; to be given two Criseydes (as we pretty much are) is unusual, and a whole

series of steps would be amazing. It is surprising that moderns should expect this, or a complete preparation. But the chief reason is still more medieval. History and story had not yet made their declaration of mutual independence, and this traditional story to all practical intents was history. The first and only thing everyone knew of Criseyde is that she was faithless;[55]

The inadequacy of this argument is partly recognised by Tatlock, when he claims that the purpose of Chaucer 'was not to explain how an attractive woman became faithless . . . but how infinitely appealing a woman notoriously to become faithless could be'.[56] Even if Tatlock is correct in locating Chaucer's centre of interest, this fails to overcome the problem of how such a gifted poet as Chaucer portrays a character who appears intrinsically incapable of unfaithfulness and then proves unfaithful. Given the necessity of Criseyde's faithlessness, surely it is within the poet's capacity to draw the portrait in such a way that the reader believes that the act of betrayal is carried out by the same character who is Troilus' warm-hearted lover.

What, in fact, seems odd, and this is germane to the discussion of Shakespeare's Cressida, is that critics find it so hard to accept that an attractive and sincere woman can be capable of faithlessness — even with an unattractive individual and in a shabby way. A reading of the poem which pays careful attention to the irony and subtle shifts of tone, conveys the impression of a woman who is sincere, attractive and vital but not incapable of breaking faith. Chaucer provides these fine qualities and produces a feeling of pathos when Criseyde falls, but does not create a sense of disbelief for the modern reader. It is through our awareness that life is like this that the pain is felt. The idea of two Criseydes only arises if it is felt that Chaucer has created a character like Hermione, Imogen or Desdemona who then proves faithless.

But, having argued this case, it is, nevertheless, true that a sense of incongruity between Troilus' sweetheart and Diomede's is widely perceived by students of Chaucer. It is worth, therefore, paying some attention to Arthur Mizener's view of this question in order to comprehend how deep and pervasive is the sense of duality associated with Chaucer's heroine.

Our conviction that in real life or in a psychological novel the Criseyde of the Fifth book must have been different from the

Criseyde of the early books to act as she did is no doubt true. And that Chaucer should have intended to imply no causal interaction between what Criseyde does and what she is therefore runs counter to all our habits of thought on this subject. Yet Chaucer's poem, looked at without prejudice, offers, I believe, no evidence that he intended Criseyde's unfaithfulness to appear either the cause of a change, or the consequence of an established vice, in the character he presents to us. In fact, there are grounds for an initial presumption to the contrary, for it is only if there is a contrast between what she is and what she does that Criseyde's fate is tragic. A Criseyde whose fall is the product either of an inherent vice or of a change for the worse in her character is at best an object of pathos.[57]

Once more, there is a clear suggestion that the poem produces two Criseydes. The problem is resolved by an appeal to a convention which is at variance with a modern psychological approach. If this answer is satisfactory it is surprising that students of Chaucer have spent so much time on the matter. What seems to be the case is that many critics have so idealised Criseyde in Troy, that they find her incompatible with Criseyde in the Grecian camp. A good example of a refusal to recognise the range of tone and suggestion in the poem is provided by Mizener's astonishing comment on the 'morning after' scene when Pandarus peeps under the sheets to tease Criseyde. He expresses the view that this constitutes a 'beautiful presentation of two witty but tactful people'.[58] Shakespeare's Pandarus and Cressida are positively coy in relation to Chaucer's parallel scene.

Yet, the sense of incongruity that has been experienced by students of Chaucer cannot be ascribed simply to an excess of seriousness on their part, a failure to detect the comic and ironic tones in the poem. Rather, it is attributable to the sense of shock at the suddenness of the betrayal and the unattractive nature of the character to whom Criseyde succumbs. Shakespeare evidently felt this because he accentuated both elements: one night after sleeping with Troilus — hopelessly lost in love — Cressida is in bed with Diomed; moreover, he is cruder than Chaucer's lover — he tells Cressida to deliver her body to him or go elsewhere. It would appear that Shakespeare felt the shock of the poem and wished to preserve it. After all, everyone knew that the heroine was going to be unfaithful: both the poet and the dramatist felt that the way to provoke a thoughtful response to the situation was to surprise their audience.

The complexity of the situation created by Shakespeare will require further comment later, but it is worth noting here that although the time span for the betrayal is longer in the poem than in the play, the sensation experienced by readers is one of speed and of inadequate motivation. Criseyde succumbs too easily and too quickly, especially in the light of the way in which she responds to Troilus' courtship. The question which then arises in the reader's mind is why, if Criseyde is not simply a light woman, does she give way? There is after all, then, a mystery. Criseyde is enigmatic. Mizener feels acutely the lack of motivation provided by Chaucer for Criseyde's betrayal, and suggests an answer:

> Nor does Chaucer, in any serious psychological sense, motivate Criseyde's physical betrayal of Troilus. She betrays Troilus because the action requires it, because she had to if the tragic possibilities of the main action, 'the double sorowe of Troilus', were to be worked out completely, and not because of anything in her character which made that betrayal inevitable. Chaucer says she is guilty, but he never shows us a woman whose state of mind is such as to make the reader believe her capable of betraying Troilus . . .
>
> The character of Criseyde is primarily an instrument for, and a unit in, a tragic action; it is therefore statically conceived and is related to the action by congruence rather than by cause and effect. For both Troilus and Criseyde are victims of an act determined, not by Criseyde's character, but by the dramatic necessities of the action.[59]

This view unintentionally challenges the artistic integrity of the poem — unless we accept the suggestion that this method was a perfectly acceptable medieval convention. James Lyndon Shanley, however, expresses the view that

> At no time do we feel that Criseyde is unworthy of love . . . we cannot feel that Troilus was well rid of her. We can only accept the fact that, gentle and lovely as she was, Criseyde could not stand fast in 'trouthe'.[60]

Here is a recognition that the Criseyde of Troy is capable of being unfaithful. Even so, it would appear that the character in

Chaucer's poem and in Shakespeare's play remains an enigma, inviting interpretation but unwilling to yield a simple solution.

Chaucer's version depicts the full anguish of Troilus in his recognition of betrayal (though he does not renounce Criseyde) and has him wishing to meet Diomede on the battlefield. His wish is granted but he fails to kill his rival (V.252). The narrator states that Troilus is killed by Achilles' spear (V.258–9) despite the fact that he was the finest warrior after Hector. Unlike the other medieval sources there is no indication whether Troilus is killed in a fair fight or not. The war, even at the moment of his death, features merely as a vague background to the love story. And this, of course, is the biggest change of all between Chaucer and Shakespeare. The dramatist intertwines the love story and the war story so that they provide reciprocal comment. The very nature of the drama ensures that Shakespeare concentrates and compacts the material which he takes from Chaucer, gives full vent to the comedy and pathos, and deepens and enriches the irony. Having said all that, Shakespeare must have glowed with pleasure as he read Chaucer's poem, appreciating the enormous dramatic potential of the piece and marvelling at the subtle movements which effect such changes in tone and feeling.

ii. *All's Well that Ends Well*

Shakespeare's source for this play was a story in Boccaccio's *Decameron*. The story, which was well known, was available in a popular French version translated by Antoine le Macon (1545), but Shakespeare would certainly have been familiar with the English translation by William Painter where it appears as novel 38 in *The Palace of Pleasure* (1566–7 and 1575). The section of the *Decameron* to which this story belongs (Day III) is concerned with the mutability of fortune, focusing particularly on people 'who by dint of their own efforts have achieved an object they greatly desired, or recovered a thing previously lost'.[61]

The story is notable for its simplicity and clarity of design. It begins by explaining that the Count of Rossiglione had maintained a physician in his household because of his poor health. After his father's death the young count, Beltramo, goes to the court as a ward of the King. He is soon followed by Giletta, the daughter of the physician. Giletta's pretext for following Beltramo is her ability to cure the sick King. Although he has refused further treatment, because of the suffering caused by the continued failure of his physicians, the King soon acquiesces to Giletta's offer of help believing that she has been sent by God. Nevertheless, he invites Giletta to name her own penalty for failure and she requests death by burning if she fails to effect the cure within eight days.

In response to this acceptance of a penalty the King offers Giletta a reward in the form of a husband. She promptly responds by asking to be allowed to make her own choice, making the proviso that he shall not be of royal blood, and gains the King's immediate assent. Once she names Beltramo as her choice, however, the King is loath to grant him to her, but even more unwilling to break his word. When Beltramo is informed he is scornful of Giletta on the grounds of her lowly birth, but immediately accepts the King's authority — even though he insists that he will never be content with the marriage. Instead of returning to his estate in accordance with the King's command, Beltramo directs his wife to Rossiglione, without consummating the marriage, and goes off to fight for the Florentines in their war with the Senois.

Returning to Rossiglione, Giletta shows great diligence in putting the estate in good order and wins the loyalty and affection of her subjects. She then sends a message to Beltramo offering to leave the estate if he so wishes in order that he can return home. In response Beltramo 'chorlishly'[62] replies that she can do what she likes for he will not live with Giletta until she wears his ring on her finger and bears a son by him. On receipt of the letter Giletta causes deep distress to her servants by informing them that she is to devote the rest of her time to pilgrimages, never to return home. She makes her way to Florence and by 'Fortune' lodges next door to the poor young woman who is being pursued by Beltramo. Giletta comes to an agreement with the girl's mother whereby an arrangement will be made to accommodate Beltramo's desires but that Giletta will substitute for the girl in bed. The gentlewoman, who is scrupulous in spite of her poverty, agrees to the proposal and secures the ring from Beltramo ('although it was with the countes ill will').[63]

On several occasions Giletta shares a bed with Beltramo, and soon becomes pregnant. Believing that the young woman has left Florence and that Giletta's departure from home is permanent, Beltramo accedes to requests from his subjects to undertake the management of his estate. The gentlewoman is reluctant to nominate a reward for her assistance to Giletta but blushingly asks for one hundred pounds. Giletta responds by bestowing on her money and jewels worth almost ten times the amount requested.

Giletta returns home only after she has given birth to twin sons, who strongly resemble their father. She arrives in the midst of a banquet being given by Beltramo on the Feast of All Saints. Giletta wearing her pilgrim's clothes presents herself, along with her sons and the ring, to her husband, reminding him of his promise. Beltramo accepts his wife immediately and they live happily ever after.

Leaving aside for the moment the additional characters introduced by Shakespeare, there are some significant differences in the treatment of the story. Most strikingly, Beltramo is quick to acknowledge the King's authority in disposing of him in marriage to Giletta; Bertram has to be threatened with the King's displeasure before he yields. Evidently he accepts the privileges of court without recognising his obligations as a subject. While on the one hand Bertram emphasises the importance of blood and status, on the other, he seems oblivious of the implications of such considerations in terms of his subjection to the King. Moreover, Shakespeare's King is remarkable in that he insists on the essential equality of human beings:

> Strange is it that our bloods,
> Of colour, weight, and heat, pour'd all together,
> Would quite confound distinction, yet stands off
> In differences so mighty.
>
> (II.iii. 118–21)

Whereas the King in Boccaccio's story, after some initial hesitation, commends the marriage on the grounds that Giletta is wise, fair and loves Beltramo — considerations which transcend social status — Shakespeare's King insists that he will make Helena equal with Bertram through the wealth which he intends to bestow on her. The question of social origins, he insists, is irrelevant:

> From lowest place when virtuous things proceed,
> The place is dignified by th'doer's deed.
> Where great additions swell's and virtue none,
> It is a dropsied honour. Good alone
> Is good, without a name; vileness is so:
> The property by what it is should go,
> Not by the title.
> Honours thrive

When rather from our acts we them derive
Than our foregoers.

(II.iii. 125–37)

Thus the clash between the King and Bertram is a dramatic high point in the play, focusing sharply on the question of value and worth, whereas in the source the conflict is much milder with the King philosophically suggesting that things may well turn out for the best despite some disparity in social standing. Moreover, in the story the interview between the three parties appears to be in private, whereas in the play this is a public occasion so that the latter is much more embarrassing. So much is this the case that Helena offers to forget her reward rather than endure further humiliation.

The immediate consequences of the betrothal are also very different. In the story Beltramo is expected to leave the court and return home with his wife, whereas in the play Bertram steals away leaving a letter to acquaint the King with his actions, thereby storing up future difficulties for himself. The feeling in the story is that Beltramo is not likely to experience adverse repercussions from leaving his wife in charge of things in Rossiglione and going his own way. Bertram, however, is placing himself in direct conflict with the King as soon as he leaves for the Italian wars. Beltramo, it seems, goes to fight because it is a convenient way of keeping clear of his wife. Bertram, on the other hand, is immensely eager to go to the wars in order to prove his manhood and acquire honour.

Once in Italy Beltramo quickly establishes his military reputation and is clearly a young man in possession of sparkling martial qualities. He also catches the eye of the ladies. Beltramo is described as 'a curteous knight, and wel beloved in the City'[64] but nothing more is said of his achievements. What is striking about Shakespeare's young hero is the disparity between his qualities as a soldier and his actions as a man. He is indifferent to the news of the death of Helena and is set on a determined course of seducing a young woman and leaving her to cope with the consequences — the possibility of which he recognises and about which he makes a joke. Beltramo is also intent on seduction but the sordid nature of his behaviour is much less vivid in the story and there are comments of disapproval by his peers as there are in the play. Part of the difference in effect is brought about by the presentation of the young woman, Diana, in the play, who undertakes the manoeuvres herself, whereas in the story she is merely spoken of and the business is conducted solely by her mother. Consequently Bertram emerges as more callous than his counterpart in Boccaccio's story.

Even within the framework of the story which he inherits from Boccaccio, Shakespeare heightens our response to the behaviour of the young hero and creates a major issue out of the question of the role of breeding in the determination of human worth. Indeed, this critical issue of the assessment and estimation of individuals becomes the fulcrum on which the play is balanced. Intimately related to this matter is the conclusion: in the story Beltramo is astonished when his wife appears with his two sons but he responds quickly and positively to the situation. There is nothing equivocal about his words and actions. In contrast, Shakespeare creates a scene in which Bertram is exposed as totally unprincipled. His denunciation of Diana as a prostitute and his willingness to resort to any ploy to save his own reputation is utterly despicable. When Helena finally appears to rescue him, therefore, it is by no means clear whether he is once more making a desperate attempt to save himself from humiliation. As his wife kneels before him, Beltramo is in command; Bertram has run out of options. In place of Boccaccio's simple happy ending, we are invited to make up our own minds about this highly ambiguous conclusion.

In addition to effecting subtle but significant changes in the story before him, Shakespeare expands the whole by introducing four major characters and a sub-plot. Most significant is the Countess about whom we are told nothing in the narrative. Shakespeare's character impresses us immediately as a woman of great feeling and perception. She loves Helena, treats her as a daughter and delights in the prospect of having her as a daughter-in-law. Thus Bertram's mother holds an entirely different view from that espoused by her son of the role of breeding in evaluating human worth. Moreover, she is explicit in insisting that he will not be able to retrieve the honour he loses in his treatment of Helena by the acquisition of honour on the battlefield. Different kinds of honour are not interchangeable. One of the striking features of the play is the astonishing depths to which Bertram falls, and the way in which he does it, given his remarkable parentage. (The King's comments on Bertram's father leave no doubt that he was an admirable man noted for his ability to establish a comfortable relationship with anyone, regardless of social position.)

Not only is the Countess's character of great significance but her very presence ensures that Bertram is more firmly anchored in his community. Beltramo can wander abroad free from any concern other than whether the estate is run efficiently, whereas Bertram experiences the powerful pull of emotional bonds. There is never any doubt that he will have to return to his own country and his own home, and will, therefore, have to re-establish himself. One of the ironies of the play is that when Helena is believed dead, Bertram is the recipient of generous forgiveness, by his mother and the King, and is soon set fair to marry a young woman of high social standing. Just when it seems as if all his misdeeds are safely behind him, the world comes crashing down through questions about Helena's ring which he is wearing (without realising it is hers) and the emergence of Diana to require marriage and public acknowledgement of the wrong which he has done her.

Next in significance of the characters invented by Shakespeare is Parolles who is at the centre of the sub-plot. This colourful charlatan adds immensely to the joy of the play and provides an extra dimension to Boccaccio's tale. Parolles is a counterfeit coin attempting to pass as current gold. He wishes to enjoy the status and prestige of a successful soldier and man of the world while possessing the heart of a coward and a weak brain. He covers his deficiencies with an extravagant tongue and flamboyant clothes which deceive only the untutored eye and mind. However, when his littleness is exposed he accepts the evaluation of his worth and is grateful for securing a humble position. There is no doubt that Parolles becomes honest. Does Bertram? Bertram fails to see through Parolles until his true nature is exhibited. Being the last to discover Parolles, Bertram is also the most cruel in his condemnation and the least forgiving. Thus Parolles in a number of ways acts as a mirror in which we see Bertram.

The third of Shakespeare's invented characters, Lafew, also forms part of the older generation. He is quick to find the true worth of Parolles but accepts the penitent with alacrity, providing him with a place in his household. Lafew has perception, understanding and magnanimity, qualities closely associated with the older generation. As he helps reintegrate Parolles so too is he prepared to marry his daughter to Bertram as part of the process of rehabilitating the fallen hero. Early in the action it is he who establishes such quick rapport with Helena and prepares the ground for her first encounter with the King. Lafew is a vital intermediary between the King and his subjects: unpretentious, intelligent, loyal, industrious and dependable. His worth is beyond question.

Lavatch, clown-cum-servant, provides another vital element in Shakespeare's scheme. In a social sense he is as redundant as Lafew is necessary. We learn that the old Count took pleasure in him but nobody else appears to appreciate his humorous wisdom. Even the Countess seems to see his worth purely in terms of his connection with her dead husband. Significantly he and Bertram never speak. Lavatch would be quick to recognise the young man's lack of sympathy with him, though he jokes with Helena. He is part of an older generation and has lost touch with the present. Lavatch recognises Parolles for what he is, but feels at ease with Helena. Her range of sympathies and perceptions clearly extend wider than those of any other character in the play.

Ironically, if Lavatch is a man who has outlived his usefulness, it is the King, during his sickness, who most poignantly expresses a feeling of redundancy: 'I fill a place, I know't' (I.ii. 69). Yet if there is a feeling that France is not yet ready to do without the King or Lafew, Lavatch is an anachronism. Nevertheless, down-to-earth humour has its place. Does Shakespeare introduce this character to suggest that a society which has no place for a Lavatch is over-refined and over-sophisticated?

It is clear that Boccaccio's story had considerable appeal for Shakespeare, but what it provided was an initial drawing for what was to become an oil painting. He invents new characters, creates a sub-plot, changes the balance of the narrative, and from Beltramo's disdainful reference to Giletta's humble origins Shakespeare develops a powerful theme relating to human worth. Whereas in Boccaccio fortune and endeavour act to reinforce each other (albeit in a perfunctory manner), in Shakespeare's play Helena has to operate against the destiny that has placed her in a position which seems irredeemably beneath that of Bertram. In place of a satisfactory and straightforward story of a good woman who wins a happy future through intelligent endeavour, Shakespeare gives us a complex and ambiguous drama which contains only the possibility of a happy ending.

iii. *Measure for Measure*

The story of the corrupt magistrate, who abuses the trust and loyalty of a virtuous young woman and executes her husband or brother, has a long history which has been traced in great detail by Lascelles, who refers to it as 'the story of the monstrous ransom'.[65]

Even St Augustine provides a version with the aim of showing how dangerous it is to draw moral judgements without careful consideration of the facts of a situation and the motives involved in the particular case.

Bullough provides valuable documentation of Shakespeare's most likely sources, the most significant of which are Giraldi Cinthio's novella *Hecatommithi* (1565) — of which there was no English translation before the eighteenth century so that Shakespeare would have had to resort to the original or a French translation by Gabriel Chappuy (1584); Cinthio's dramatisation of the tale, *Epitia* (1583); George Whetstone's play *Promos and Cassandra* (1578); Whetstone's novella, published in *Heptameron of Civill Discourses* (1582), and reprinted in 1593 under the title *Aurelia*; and the possible source of Whetstone's play, *Philanira*, a Latin tragedy by Claude Rouillet, printed as one of four plays in his *Varia Poemata* (1556), and later published in a French translation (1563 and 1577).

A number of the analogues reproduced by Bullough are interesting in revealing the value put on this tale as a means of elaborating the principle of just rule. While all of these accounts create a sense of outrage in the reader, they focus on the principle of good government rather than on serious considerations of human psychology. Given the differences which exist between the variants of the story upon which Shakespeare draws, it is illuminating to observe those elements which he elects to incorporate in his play and those which he chooses to discard.

In the analogues provided by Bullough the victims are husband and wife whereas in Whetstone and Cinthio they are brother and sister. Bullough's view of the connection between the play and the source material is as follows:

> The relation of *Measure for Measure* to earlier versions of the Isabella-story is not easy to assess, but Shakespeare seems to have been stimulated largely by Whetstone's play and also by Cinthio's novella. Several recent scholars have argued that he also knew *Epitia* and I agree with them. *Epitia*, much more than *Promos*, is a play about the nature of justice and authority, and the contrast between Shakespeare's Escalus and Angelo resembles closely the opposition between the Podesta and the Secretary, who discuss justice and mercy and the duties of judges in terms not unlike those in *Measure for Measure* . . . In *Epitia* a happy ending was made possible by

the substitution of a hardened criminal for Vico, and Shakespeare's Barnadine may be the result . . . In both *Epitia* and *Measure for Measure* a woman pleads with the heroine for the villain's life; in Cinthio it is Angela, in Shakespeare Mariana.[66]

Cinthio's novella has, like *Measure for Measure*, Austria for its setting. The Emperor Maximian offers his dear friend Juriste the governorship of Innsbruck, warning him of the danger implicit in accepting the responsibility. Juriste being 'more pleased with the office to which the Emperor called him than sound in knowledge of his own nature'[67] willingly takes up the post and acquits himself with credit until he encounters Epitia, an eighteen-year-old virgin who appeals to him on behalf of her brother. Vico is condemned to die for committing rape. Epitia argues that as Vico can right the wrong he has done by marrying the girl, who is willing to have him, Juriste ought to exercise mercy.

Juriste is so 'smitten with lustful desire'[68] for Epitia that he defers execution and affords her a second interview. He insists at their meeting that there can be no legal justification for the exercise of clemency, but, nevertheless, offers to mitigate the penalty if he be allowed to enjoy her. Epitia is given a further day to reflect, with the incentive that she may become Juriste's wife thereby removing the stain of dishonour about which she expresses herself so strongly. Vico pleads with his sister to accept the arrangement begging her to remember their ties of blood and the horror of execution. He also affirms the integrity of Juriste's promise of marriage. Epitia is deeply moved by love of her brother and returns to Juriste to fulfil her side of the bargain. However, even before they retire to bed Juriste gives orders for Vico's immediate execution.

Epitia is horrified when, the following morning, she receives the corpse of her brother from the goaler with the words 'This is your brother whom my lord Governor sends you freed from prison'.[69] The young woman draws on the resources she has acquired through her training in philosophy to quell the violence of her anguish and appeals to Maximian. When confronted by the Emperor, Juriste loses his self-possession but attempts to divert Epitia from her suit by proffering his love. Maximian, however, castigates him and insists that they marry to remove the blemish on Epitia's honour. Juriste accepts with alacrity; Epitia reluctantly. Once the marriage ceremony is over Maximian shocks

Juriste by passing the death sentence on him. Epitia now feels compassion for the man and questions the extent to which she has been motivated more by desire for revenge than by the principle of justice. She proceeds to make an eloquent and successful plea on Juriste's behalf. Maximian relents but threatens his former friend with severe retribution if he fails to bestow on Epitia the love which she deserves. The caution proves unnecessary as Juriste becomes a loving husband.

This story, then, has a number of key elements that carry over into Shakespeare's play: an attractive and eloquent young woman who appeals to a magistrate on behalf of her brother; a justice who is so overwhelmed by sexual desire for the woman that he departs radically from his normal standard of behaviour and proposes a dishonourable bargain; a prison scene in which a frightened young man pleads with his sister to accept the arrangement; the exposure and condemnation of the deputy by the supreme authority in the state; a reconciliation and happy conclusion.

However, there are some significant differences. In the story the magistrate is able to offer the bait of marriage to the young woman who is not, like Isaballa, a novice. Moreover, when challenged, Juriste quickly surrenders, whereas Angelo behaves brazenly. Both women appeal on behalf of the guilty magistrate in the belief that the brother is dead, but Epitia is feeling compassion for a man who is now her husband and does not need to be persuaded. Isabella responds to Mariana's plea. Finally, Angelo is saved from his evil intent whereas Juriste is left with the burden of his guilt.

This last element is treated differently by Cinthio in his dramatised version of the story. Vico is saved by the Captain to make a last-minute appearance and a genuinely happy ending. The surprise to Epitia is great because she has been completely deceived by the substitute corpse. A fascinating parallel between this version and Shakespeare's is that Angela, who is Juriste's sister, pleads with Epitia to beg for her brother's life. But unlike the compliant Isabella in *Measure for Measure*, Epitia is adamant: until she discovers that her brother lives she is intent on bringing about Juriste's death. Whereas in Cinthio's novella the reluctant wife sues for her husband's freedom, without encouragement, in his play she can bring herself to forgive Juriste only when she finds her brother has been saved.

Another significant change effected by Cinthio in his play is that Juriste becomes more cynical by claiming that he kept his word to Epitia in sending her brother to her:

I promised his release, but not alive;
And so I have fulfilled all that I promised;
But never did I plight my troth to her
To take her as my wife.[70]

Thus Juriste seeks escape from one of his promises by means of a verbal quibble, while he is prepared to lie outright over the promise of marriage. When Juriste's sister is brought forward to support Epitia he insists that the law does not allow a sister to testify against her brother.

This cynicism is akin to Angelo's when he denounces Isabella as a liar. However, the circumstances and the psychology of the two men are very different. Juriste contemplates freeing Vico, in flagrant breach of the law, but is afraid to do so because of the warning of the Podesta, who insists that the full force of the law must be implemented. Angelo, in contrast, is dealing with a man who has merely committed the crime of anticipating the marriage vows rather than being convicted of rape, and has as an associate Escalus, who strongly favours mercy. But the details relating to circumstances are insignificant when contrasted with the matter of psychology, for in neither of Cinthio's versions is there much psychological probing of Juriste. What psychological exploration takes place relates to Epitia. Shakespeare finds a role in his sources for Angelo but not a character. Angelo is entirely his own creation.

George Whetstone's two-part play, *Promos and Cassandra*, is closer to Shakespeare than either of Cinthio's versions of the story At the outset we find that the law against fornication had been allowed to lapse until re-activated by Promos. Moreover, the first man to fall foul of the law, Andrugio, like Shakespeare's Claudio, is guilty merely of anticipating the marriage bonds in contrast to Cinthio's miscreant who commits rape. Immediately, then, the convicted young man is being presented in a much more sympathetic light by Whetstone and Shakespeare.

A major difference between Cinthio and Whetstone is that the latter introduces an additional social stratum: there is an active and vibrant world of minor officials and common people, including prostitutes. Both Whetstone and Shakespeare have the news of the young man's arrest first reported and discussed by the common people. However, there is a significant difference between Whetstone and Shakespeare in their exploration of the lives of the lower orders. In *Promos and Cassandra*, Promos has a deputy Phallax who is totally corrupt and who operates with the sanction of his superior. In turn Phallax has two informers, aptly named Gripax and Rapax, who devise ways of exploiting people. What this low-life action reveals, therefore, is the way in which corruption in the state works its way through to the lowest level, resulting not only in injustice but in extortion and the exploitation of the weakest members of society. Thus the sub-plot reinforces the moral of the main action. The survivors among the lower orders are prostitutes like Lamia who becomes the mistress of Phallax. Interestingly, when Phallax is finally exposed and removed from office he merely prepares to move on to another city where he knows he will be able to prosper by means of his well-practised guile.

Shakespeare turns all this around. We don't see a poor populace ground down by corrupt officials, but rather an underworld of rampant sexuality and prostitution which appears impervious to the most biting laws. The problem is not one of protecting the poor from corrupt officials — Shakespeare's officers are incompetent and comic rather than corrupt — but rather one of finding a means of achieving some kind of moral order in the face of rampant sexuality. In *Pericles* the pimp Boult excuses his actions to Marina by references to the lack of alternative employment. In *Measure for Measure* the vices associated with sex appear to be so potent that they are not amenable to social solutions.

This more complex treatment of low life which characterises Shakespeare's play is reflected also in the fusion which is effected between the two social worlds. In Whetstone's play the connection is simply one of moral corruption being manifested in both spheres; *Measure for Measure* possesses a physical overlap, with Lucio in particular moving between these social strata. Strikingly, it is Lucio who reports Claudio's plight to Isabella, conveying his request to her to plead with Angelo, whereas in Whetstone's play the young man Andrugio makes his own appeal to his sister in prison.

When she appears before Promos, Cassandra's case is clear and succinct: her brother is very young and has neither raped nor seduced a young virgin, but has transgressed merely through the force of love; and the wrong that has been committed can be quickly rectified. This is in sharp contrast to Isabella's reluctance to plead in mitigration of a sin which she abhors, and her wide-ranging examination of the principles of justice and mercy. The effect on both magistrates is, however, similar. Whetstone's heroine is like Shakespeare's in that her power suddenly to overwhelm the magistrate resides in a beauty devoid of artifice:

> Happie is the man, that injoyes the love of such a wife!
> I do protest, hir modest wordes hath wrought me in a maze.
> Though she be faire, she is not deckt with garish shewes for
> gaze;
> Hir bewtie lures, her lookes cut off fond sutes with chast
> disdain.
> O God, I feele a sodaine change that doth my freedome
> chayne.
> What didst thou say? fie *Promos* fie! of hir avoide the thought,
> And so I will, my other cares wyll cure what love hath
> wrought.[71]

Shakespeare overcomes the difficulties arising from the magistrate falling in love with the young woman whom he could possibly marry, by making her a novice. This removes the possibility of Angelo even thinking of her as a wife and also deepens the magnitude of his lust and his crime. Both magistrates are, however, extremely tough characters. The goaler in Whetstone's play claims that Promos shows compassion to nobody and that the time between sentencing and execution has become extremely brief since he took office. Both Promos and Angelo seem to enjoy inflicting severe punishment and they are alike in the way in which they are suddenly overcome with passionate desire for a young woman.

During their second interview Promos cuts short Cassandra's argument, after she has invoked mercy over rigour in law, by avowing the force of his love and offering to free Andrugio in exchange for enjoying her for one night. Although Cassandra refuses to sell her honour, Promos allows her two days in which to change her mind. A change of heart is quickly effected by Andrugio's passionate plea to his sister, but before he manages to persuade her she presents a posture which is close to that of Isabella's. Like Isabella she begins by warning her brother that:

> All thinges conclude thy death *Andrugio*:
> Prepare thy selfe, to hope it were in vaine.

But in response to questioning she states the nature of the offer made by Promos before claiming that she would rather be tortured or killed than to submit to the proposal:

> If thou dost live I must my honor lose.

Thy raunsome is, to *Promos* fleshly wyll
That I do yelde: then which I rather chose,
With torments sharpe my selfe he first should kyll:
Thus am I bent, thou seest thy death at hand.
O would my life would satisfie his yre,
Cassandra then, would cancell soone thy band.[72]

Both the sentiments and the language of Isabella are close to Cassandra's: rather than surrender to his lust she tells Angelo 'Th'impression of keen whips I'd wear as rubies,' (II.iv. 101); to Claudio she says she is unable to relinquish her virginity but states emphatically there is nothing else that she would not give to save him: 'O, were it but my life' (III.i. 103).

This interview between the brother and sister lacks dramatic potency in Whetstone. Andrugio, like Claudio, is amazed that Promos is insistent on exacting the death penalty for a crime which is less than that which he wishes to commit himself. He insists that Cassandra's fault will not be grievous because it is forced. Further, he discounts her fear of slanderous tongues by arguing that her reputation will be enhanced by such selfishness. And finally, Andrugio insists that Promos' hint of marriage will become a certainty thereby removing any loss of honour. Although Cassandra believes that to give way to Promos is to surrender her honour she exhibits no theological misgivings, nor does she possess the psychological fears that appear to horrify Isabella. Moreover, at no point does she denounce her brother for cowardice: his life is elevated above her own anguish.

After Promos has secured his desire he meditates on the promises which he made and cannot keep: to marry Cassandra, which she insisted on before giving herself to him, and freeing Andrugio. He therefore determines to fulfil one promise by means of a verbal quibble (send Cassandra her brother's body), and the other by denial, trusting to her embarrassment and his power to prevent detection. Fortunately for him, the gaoler is so overcome with pity for Andrugio that he sets him free and substitutes a convenient corpse.

The unscrupulous Phallax reveals that Promos is struck by conscience but even he sees the deed as the blackest possible: 'The Devill himselfe could not have usde a practise more unkind.'[73] Cassandra is ready to kill herself once she has exacted revenge on Promos by taking her case to the King. When the King arrives with his officer, Ulrico, there is great consternation among

Promos' subordinates who have engaged in widespread corruption and petty tyranny. When the common people are invited to bring forth their complaints it soon becomes apparent that abuse of power has been the norm in the city. The King summarises both the situation and the moral of the play:

> I see by proofe that true the proverb is,
> Myght maisters right, wealth is such a canker
> As woundes the conscience of his Maister,
> And devoures the heart of his poore neyghbour.[74]

Confronted by Cassandra, Promos, unlike Angelo, does not attempt to brazen things out: he confesses the truth immediately. Promos' reaction is influenced by the exposure of his underlings and the relatively light punishment meted out to Phallax. Whereas Shakespeare arranges things so that Angelo has the opportunity of confessing while still believing that he is able to evade detection, Promos knows that he is caught. Thus Shakespeare creates additional scope for the moral decline of Angelo.

Once Promos has confessed to his crime the King again underlines the principle of the need for complete impartiality and integrity in the dispensation of justice:

> This over proofe, ne can but make me thinke
> That many waies thou hast my subjectes wrongd
> For how canst thou with Justice use thy swaie
> When thou thy selfe dost make thy will a lawe?[75]

Promos is ordered to marry Cassandra and to suffer execution on the following day. After going through the wedding ceremony Cassandra determines to plead for Promos, not through a sudden accession of love but moved by a sense of duty to her husband. Andrugio, who has been in hiding, discovers the situation, but is disinclined to save Promos because he is conscious that he would be dead if Promos' will had prevailed. However, he is stirred by compassion for the suffering of his sister. Consequently he reveals his identity even though he risks execution by so doing. The King responds by pardoning both offenders and advises Promos that he should make the maximum use of the lessons he has learned:

> Henceforth forethinke of thy forepassed faultes,
> And measure Grace with Justice evermore.

Unto the poore have evermore an eye,
And let not might outcountenaunce their right:
Thy Officers trust not in every tale,
In chiefe when they are meanes in strifes and sutes.
Though thou be just, yet coyne may them corrupt.
. . .
If thou be wyse, thy fall maye make thee ryse.
The lost sheepe founde, for joye the feast was made.[76]

Thus the compassionate gaoler and substitute corpse are key elements in the plays of Whetstone and Cinthio (though not in the latter's novella). This device, which facilitates a happy ending, is adopted by Shakespeare, but not in a straightforward way. Barnadine is a condemned murderer with a convenient head available for removal, but he refuses to give it up to suit the convenience of the disguised Duke and his associates. This is characteristic of the complexity which Shakespeare substitutes for the simplicity to be found in the source material. Ultimately they amount to narratives or dramatisations of the need for judicial integrity. The characters are entirely subordinate to this end and there are no difficult questions of human motivation left in the air.

Thomas Lupton's *Too Good To Be True* (1581) contains a version of the story which has the familiar pattern of a wife giving herself to the judge, in order to secure the release of a husband convicted of murder, and being deceived by him.[77] When she appeals to the Commissioner she reluctantly accepts the decision that she must marry the Judge, whereas he is delighted. Once the ceremony is over, however, the feelings of the main parties are reversed as the death sentence is pronounced on the Judge. The widow feels no compassion for him, nor any sense of wifely duty, and is pleased to see him executed. The reader feels little sympathy for either the husband or the Judge and so the story provides a grim but simple story of justice untouched by any broader issues of human frailty or forgiveness.

The problem of ensuring justice is also the central theme of Barnaby Riche's *The Adventures of Brusanus, Prince of Hungaria* (1592). The King, Leonarchus, leaves the court to wander in disguise among his subjects. He discovers that he is greatly esteemed among the people but recognises that the most virtuous rulers have great difficulty in ensuring that their subordinates are equally scrupulous in the exercise of their duties. Moreover, while men crave for the good order that arises out of the dispensation of punishment for wrongdoing, so too do they hate the oppression emanating from laws that are excessively rigorous. The great art is to achieve a careful balance: 'to use justice with mediocrity, that neither we leane to overmuch severity, nor yet may be ledd by too much lenity'.[78] Here is the dilemma which comes to the foreground in *Measure for Measure*: laws are made for human beings as they *are*, not as some authorities would like them to be. The removal of all vice is not possible , but if attempted results in the transformation of society into a prison.

Riche not only sets forth the problem of establishing the right balance, but has the King explain the need to travel his realm incognito so that he has a full understanding of the social realities outside the court, and a greater awareness of the follies and affectations within it. The Duke in *Measure for Measure* can only find out what Angelo is really like by leaving him in charge in the belief that he is unobserved. Like the Duke, Leonarchus also encounters a rogue, Gloriosus, who is given to lying. However, he derives great pleasure from the astuteness of his son Dorestus in dealing with Gloriosus and the Prince's whole conduct in his absence.

The interest of Riche's tale is that it is particularly concerned with the problem of achieving the right balance between rigour and moderation, in the making and exercise of law. Whereas Shakespeare's main sources suggest that the best way of ensuring justice throughout the realm is by exemplary behaviour at the topmost regions of the hierarchy, Riche implies that constant surveillance of lower officials is essential. What all these sources share is a belief in the necessity of good laws and justices of impeccable integrity who strive to strike the right balance in their treatment of offenders. But the plays or stories all serve their end directly, possessing little interest in psychological exploration of the characters.

Of these possible sources only Barnaby Riche provides a ruler who adopts a disguise so that Shakespeare had very little if anything to suggest his omnipresent Duke. Likewise none of these sources has the bed-trick: the sisters all sacrifice their honour. The addition of the Duke, who controls the action; the deliberate testing of a Deputy who has previously revealed a flaw in his seemingly faultless character; the sister being a novice; and the availability of a discarded sweetheart of the Deputy who facilitates the bed-trick are all innovations of Shakespeare's. Although the lower orders appear in Whetstone's play their nature and function is quite different from their counterparts in *Measure for Measure*.

Notes

1. F. N. Robinson (ed.), *The Complete Works of Geoffrey Chaucer*, 2nd edn (Oxford University Press, London, 1957), pp. 386–8.
2. George Chapman, Translation of *The Seaven Bookes of Homer's Iliades*, Bullough (ed.), *Narrative and Dramatic Sources of Shakespeare* (8 vols., Routledge and Kegan Paul, London, 1966), vol. 6, pp. 115–16.
3. Ibid., p. 120.
4. Ibid., p. 120.
5. Ibid., pp. 120–1.
6. William Caxton: Translation of Raoul Lefevre's *The Recuyell of the Historyes of Troye* in Bullough, *Narrative and Dramatic Sources*, p. 194.
7. Chapman, *The Seaven Bookes of Homer's Iliades* in Bullough, *Narrative and Dramatic Sources*, p. 130.
8. Ibid., p. 133.
9. Ibid., p. 135.
10. Ibid., p. 136.
11. Ibid., p. 137.
12. Ibid., p. 124.
13. Ibid., p. 124.
14. Ibid., p. 123.
15. Ibid., p. 125.
16. Ovid, *Metamorphoses*, Translated by Arthur Golding in Bullough, *Narrative and Dramatic Sources*, p. 153.
17. Ibid., pp. 156–7.
18. John Lydgate, *The Historye Sege and Dystruccyon of Troye* in Bullough, *Narrative and Dramatic Sources*, p. 158.
19. Ibid., p. 158.
20. Ibid., p. 158.
21. Ibid., p. 159.
22. Ibid., p. 159.
23. Ibid., p. 160.
24. Ibid., p. 165.
25. Ibid., p. 171.
26. Ibid., p. 171.
27. Ibid., p. 179.
28. Ibid., p. 178.
29. William Caxton's Translation of Raoul Lefevre's *The Recuyell of the Historyes of Troye* in Bullough, *Narrative and Dramatic Sources*, p. 188.
30. Ibid., p. 192.
31. Ibid., pp. 193–4.
32. Ibid., p. 198.
33. Ibid., pp. 198–9.
34. Ibid., p. 201.
35. Ibid., p. 201.
36. Ibid., p. 202.
37. Ibid., p. 203.
38. Ibid., p. 204.
39. Ibid., p. 205.
40. Ibid., p. 209.

41. Ibid., p. 211.
42. Ibid., p. 214.
43. E. Talbot Donaldson, *The Swan at the Well: Shakespeare Reading Chaucer* (Yale University Press, New Haven and London, 1985), p. 3.
44. Chaucer, *Troilus and Criseyde*, Translated into Modern English by Nevill Coghill, 8th edn (Penguin, Harmondsworth, 1982), p. xvii.
45. Kenneth Muir, *The Sources of Shakespeare's Plays*, 2nd edn (Methuen, London, 1977), p. 142.
46. Donaldson, *The Swan at the Well*, p. 86.
47. Ibid., p. 87.
48. Ibid., p. 94.
49. Arnold Stein, 'The Disjunctive Imagination' in Priscilla Martin (ed.), *Troilus and Cressida* (Casebook Series, Macmillan, London, 1976), p. 187.
50. Chaucer, *Troilus and Criseyde*, Translated by N. Coghill, p. xxiii.
51. Donaldson, *The Swan at the Well*, p. 113.
52. Muir, *Sources of Shakespeare's Plays*, p. 144.
53. J. S. P. Tatlock, 'The People in Chaucer's *Troilus*' in Edward Wagenknecht (ed.), *Chaucer: Modern Essays in Criticism*, 2nd edn (Oxford University Press, New York, 1971), pp. 340–1.
54. Ibid., p. 342.
55. Ibid., p. 343.
56. Ibid., p. 344.
57. Arthur Mizener, 'Character and Action in the Case of Criseyde' in Wagenknecht (ed.), *Chaucer*, pp. 351–2.
58. Ibid., p. 358.
59. Ibid., pp. 361–4.
60. James Lyndon Shanley, 'The *Troilus* and Christian Love' in Wagenknecht (ed.), *Chaucer*, p. 393.
61. Boccaccio, *The Decameron*, translated by G. H. McWilliam (Penguin, Harmondsworth, 1986), p. 231.
62. William Painter, *The Palace of Pleasure* (1575 edn) in Geoffrey Bullough (ed.), *Narrative and Dramatic Sources of Shakespeare* (8 vols., Routledge and Kegan Paul, London, 1968), vol. II, p. 392.
63. Ibid., p. 395.
64. Ibid., p. 393.
65. M. Lascelles, *Shakespeare's 'Measure for Measure'* (Athlone Press, London, 1953), p. 7.
66. Bullough (ed.), *Narrative and Dramatic Sources*, vol. II, p. 406.
67. G. B. Giraldi Cinthio, *Hecatommithi* (1583 edn), Decade 8, Novella 5 (The Story of Epitia) in Bullough (ed.), *Narrative and Dramatic Sources*, vol. II, p. 421.
68. Ibid., p. 422.
69. Ibid., p. 425.
70. G. B. Giraldi Cinthio, *Epitia* (1583) in Bullough, *Narrative and Dramatic Sources*, vol. II, p. 439.
71. George Whetstone, *Promos and Cassandra* (1578) in Bullough (ed.), *Narrative and Dramatic Sources*, vol. II, p. 453.
72. Ibid., p. 461.
73. Ibid., p. 474.

74. Ibid., p. 496.
75. Ibid., p. 499.
76. Ibid., p. 513.
77. Thomas Lupton, *Too Good To Be True* (1581) in Bullough (ed.), *Narrative and Dramatic Sources*, vol. II, pp. 514–24.
78. Barnaby Riche, *The Adventures of Brusanus, Prince of Hungaria* (1592) in Bullough, p. 528.

3

The Fractured Universe: Wholeness and Division in *Troilus and Cressida*

Troilus and Cressida is such a breathtakingly original play that it has been awarded little critical esteem until the last 25 years. Scholars are unsure whether the play was performed in Shakespeare's day. Probably written around 1602, the play was entered in the Stationers' Register on 7 February 1603 and the entry states that it was recently acted by the Lord Chamberlain's men. However, the play did not appear in print until published by Bonion whose entry appears in the Stationers' Register on 28 January 1609. Bonion's original title page indicated that the play had been performed at the Globe, but the page was cancelled during printing. When the play appeared in print it was described in the Epistle as 'a new play, never stal'd with the Stage, never clapper-claw'd with the palmes of the vulgar'. Some scholars have suggested that the play received private performances at the Inns of Court while others have claimed that the play was also acted at the Globe, the Prologue and Epilogue being added or retained only for the Inns of Court performances.[1] Whatever the truth of the matter it is clear that *Troilus and Cressida* was not a popular play or the printer of the Quarto edition would hardly have claimed it had never been performed. Apart from four productions of Dryden's adaptation (1679) in the first half of the eighteenth century, the play was not staged again in England until it was performed in London in 1907. It is probably fair to say that the upward curve in the play's popularity coincided with the Barton-Hall production of 1960-2.

No doubt part of the perplexity occasioned by *Troilus and Cressida* has been due to uncertainty about what kind of play it is supposed to be. It is described as a History by the title page of the 1609 Quarto, but the Epistle to that edition refers to it as a comedy. It was intended for inclusion among the Tragedies of the First Folio of 1623, but was finally placed between the Histories and the Tragedies (the play was omitted from the catalogue so its inclusion was a last-minute affair, possibly because of copyright difficulties). 'Placing' *Troilus and Cressida* has remained a problem. Yet, despite the uncertainty surrounding the play and its meagre stage history, it has at last begun to achieve the status it merits as one of Shakespeare's finest plays, both in the study and on the stage. In this respect the production at Stratford-upon-Avon in 1985 may prove a watershed.

Clearly *Troilus and Cressida* is unique in the Shakespearian canon even though it shares significant affinities with *All's Well* and *Measure for Measure*. Although the play has received a good deal of critical attention in recent years there are still major aspects of the play which have been either ignored or badly neglected. The purpose of this chapter, therefore, is to focus on these key elements which contribute so much to an understanding of the overall design of the play and the intentions of the dramatist. The first part of the chapter will explore the pattern of division which is so central to the play; the second part will examine the process of 'translating the man' or the exploration of the nature of identity; the third part will deal specifically with the imagery of the play; and the concluding section will devote some attention to the RSC's 1985 – 6 production.

The most striking omission in critical appraisals of the play relates to the matter of division, calculation and fragmentation, especially the way in which these characteristics are juxtaposed with a desire for the achievement of unity or wholeness. The process of disintegration throughout the play involves breaking things down into constituent parts and then making comparisons in terms of weight, size, speed, etc., which may frequently be brought together under the rubric of value or worth. But the tension in the play involves a cleavage between the human desire to believe wholly or achieve wholly and the inevitable forcing back into accepting the reality of and necessity for disintegration. This is perhaps analogous to a society possessing universal or holistic views whilst experiencing in daily affairs the reality of the counting house. The tension in Shakespeare's society between religious values on the one hand and commercial values on the other seems to be mirrored by the strains which are apparent in the play.[2] Though the following comments in no way depend on an acceptance of that view, awareness of the possibility may be suggestive in following the ensuing analysis.

The feature of number, division and parts, appears as early as the Prologue: the Grecian princes who set off for war number 'sixty and nine'; Troy is described as 'Priam's six-gated city'; the two armies prepare to confront each other, but despite fundamental division they have a common attitude to the war:

> Now expectation, tickling skittish spirits
> On one and other side, Trojan and Greek,
> Sets all on hazard.
>
> (20-2)

The sense of excitement, though perhaps typical of a prelude to war, is irresponsible and results in everything being gambled on the outcome or 'the chance of war'. Finally, the play itself is not intended to encompass this famous war in its entirety, but

> Leaps o'er the *vaunt* and *firstlings* of those broils,
> *Beginning* in the *middle*, starting thence away
> To what may be digested in a play.
>
> (27-9)

It is significant that these divisions are often closely linked with the food imagery (cooking, eating, regurgitating — 'disgorge' also appears in the Prologue) the pervasiveness of which has been widely recognised.

If the Prologue initiates these features of number, division and separation they are epitomised in the most significant speeches of the play. Before looking at such speeches in detail it is worth selecting some one-line examples which exhibit these features. Nestor is willing to fight Hector whose youth is in 'flood' with his own '*three* drops of blood' (I.iii. 299–300). After Pandarus has praised Troilus to Cressida she reveals that 'more in Troilus *thousand fold* I see' (I.ii. 289) than her uncle is capable of imagining. Cassandra in worrying over the fate of Troy cries 'Lend me *ten thousand* eyes,/And I will fill them with prophetic tears' and suggests that while preparing for the end they pay 'A *moiety* of that *mass* of moan to come' (II.ii. 102–8). Nestor in a magnificent description of Hector's omnipresence claims 'There is a *thousand* Hectors in the field.' (V.v. 19) Diomedes is willing for Aeneas to live 'A *thousand* complete courses of the sun' unless he can claim him as victim, in which case he desires that he die 'with *every joint a wound'* (IV.i. 28 – 30). Hector speaks of the *'many thousand dismes'* lost in the war (II.ii. 19); Troilus talks of Helen as the woman 'whose price has launch'd above a *thousand* ships' (II.ii. 83); and Ulysses claims that 'emulation hath a *thousand* sons' (III.iii. 156).

These constitute the simple examples. For the most part number, bifurcation and separation run right through long speeches making comparisons which range along the spectrum from nothing to infinity and measuring in units of weight, number, segment, time, etc. Troilus is so entranced by Cressida that in trying to conceal his love he fears his heart will 'rive in twain' (I.i. 35) and complains that Pandarus intensifies the agony of his passion by referring to all Cressida's features: 'her eyes, her hair, her cheek, her gait, her voice' (I.i. 54). In the very next scene Alexander describes the mighty Grecian warrior Ajax as 'A lord of Trojan blood, nephew to Hector;' and goes on to describe how this divided man is made up of a multiplicity of attributes, both good and bad: 'There is no man hath a virtue that he hath not a glimpse of, nor any man an attaint but he carries some stain of it.' (I.ii. 13 – 26) Ajax is virtually a symbol of division. Not only is he half Trojan and half Greek but he is the second most powerful warrior on the Greek side and his function, from the standpoint of the leadership, is to be placed alongside Achilles and yoked 'like draught-oxen' to 'plough up the wars' (II.i. 108 – 9). In practice he is emulous of Achilles and having been built up by the Greek leadership and acclaimed as the foremost warrior he becomes as proud and inactive as his rival, thereby symbolising the division in the Greek army which Ulysses analyses in his famous 'degree' speech (I.iii. 75 – 137). Aeneas draws attention to the position of Ajax prior to the duel with Hector. He commences the speech by first insisting on Hector's essential nature in order to counter Achilles' insinuation that Hector is proud and arrogant:

> In the extremity of *great* and *little*,
> Valour and pride *excel* themselves in Hector;
> The *one almost as infinite as all*,
> The *other blank as nothing. Weigh* him well,
> And that which looks like pride is courtesy.
> This Ajax is *half* made of Hector's blood;
> In love whereof, *half* Hector stays at home:
> *Half* heart, *half* hand, *half* Hector comes to seek
> This blended knight, *half* Trojan and *half* Greek.
>
> (IV.v. 78 – 86)

Not only does this speech display characteristics of separation and comparison, it also exhibits the pervasive feature of bodily division and of the conception of the whole as being something which is known to be made up of parts but not always being subject to separation. Ajax is 'blended'. The divided nature of Ajax is pressed even harder in Hector's magnanimous speech which brings the duel to a premature close. Moreover, he insists on the impossibility of dividing Ajax or separating his two components:

> Thou art, great lord, my father's sister's son,
> A cousin-german to great Priam's seed;
> The obligation of our blood forbids
> A gory emulation 'twixt us twain.
> Were thy commixtion Greek and Trojan so
> That thou could'st say *'This hand is Grecian all,*
> And *this is Trojan: the sinews of this leg*
> *All Greek,* and *this, all Troy: my mother's blood*
> Runs on the *dexter* cheek, and this *sinister*
> Bounds in *my father's'* — by Jove multipotent,
> Thou shouldst not bear from me a Greekish *member*
> Wherein my sword had not impressure made
> Of our rank feud; but the just gods gainsay
> That any *drop* thou borrow'dst from thy mother,
> My sacred aunt, should by my mortal sword
> Be drain'd! Let me embrace thee, Ajax.
> By him that thunders, thou has lusty arms;
> Hector would have them fall upon him thus.
> Cousin, *all* honour to thee!
>
> (IV.v. 119–37)

Another feature of this principle of linking parts which is emphasised in the speech, is that of kinship itself. Characters frequently refer to each other in the play in terms of their blood relationship (and blood, and its division into drops, occurs with great frequency). For instance, Ajax says, 'I came to kill thee, cousin' (IV.v. 139); Troilus complains to Hector, 'Brother, you have a vice of mercy in you' (V.iii. 37), and is later praised by Hector on the battlefield, 'O, well fought, my youngest brother!' (V.vi. 12); Cressida and Pandarus refer to each other as 'uncle' and 'cousin', 'niece' (I.ii. 43–4, 203), and so on.

But kinship is also emphasised through its antithesis by Thersites who is the source of so much verbal brilliance. When challenged by Hector on the battlefield — 'Art thou for Hector's match?/Art thou of blood and honour?' — his answer is both prompt and apt: 'No, no: I am a rascal, a scurvy railing knave: a very filthy rogue' (V.v. 26–9). Even more brilliantly he escapes death at the hands of Margarelon, a bastard son of Priam's, through claiming kinship through their very lack of kinship wholeness: 'I am a bastard too: I love bastards. I am bastard begot, bastard instructed, bastard in mind, bastard in valour, in everything illegitimate . . . Take heed: the quarrel's most ominous to us — if the son of a whore fight for a whore, he tempts judgement. Farewell, bastard.' (V.vii. 16–22)

In engineering his escape Thersites is also engaging in his characteristic activity of stripping everything and everybody down to bare essentials: Cressida is a 'whore' (V.iv. 24); Agamemnon is 'an honest fellow enough . . . but he has not so much brain as ear wax'; Menelaus 'his brother the bull . . . is both ass and ox' (V.i. 50–9). In response to being labelled a 'fragment' by Achilles he describes the latter as 'thou *full* dish of fool' (V.i. 8–9), subtly and ironically maintaining the contrast between part and whole. As for Ajax, he warns him that Achilles could 'pun thee into *shivers*' and threatens to anatomise him: 'I will begin at thy *heel*, and tell what thou art by *inches*, thou thing of no bowels thou.' (II.i. 40–52) The war itself is summed up succinctly: 'All the argument is a cuckold and a whore: a good quarrel to draw emulous factions, and bleed to death upon.' (II.iii. 74–6)

Moving to the epicentre of the play there are two speeches by Diomedes — uttered in response to Paris' question as to 'who in your thought deserves fair Helen best?' — which evaluate Helen in terms of what the pursuit of her has cost. Diomedes is perhaps the second most hard-headed and unromantic character in the play — Thersites bears the palm — and these speeches reveal a clear awareness of the lunacy of fighting a war over a faithless woman. What is particularly significant for present purposes is the way in which the whole calculation takes the form of contrasts and comparisons in terms of units: weight, number, quantity and proportion.

Diomedes.   Both alike:
  He merits *well* to have her that doth seek her,
  Not making *any* scruple of her soilure,
  With *such* a hell of pain and *world* of charge;
  And you *as well* to keep her that defend her,

Not palating the taste of her dishonour,
With *such a costly loss* of wealth and friends.
He, like a puling cuckold, would drink up
The *lees and dregs* of a flat tamed piece;
You, like a lecher, out of whorish loins
Are pleas'd to breed out your inheritors.
Both *merits pois'd*, each *weighs no less nor more*,
But he as thee, each *heavier* for a whore.

Paris.   You are *too* bitter to your country-woman.

Diomedes. She's bitter to her country: hear me, Paris —
For *every false drop* in her bawdy veins
A *Grecian's life* hath sunk; for *every scruple*
Of her contaminated carrion *weight*
A *Trojan* hath been slain. Since she could speak,
She hath not given *so many* good *words breath*
As for her *Greeks and Trojans* suffer'd death.

(IV.i. 55–75)

This devastating appraisal, which goes to the heart of the war and
makes the Trojan debate scene (II.ii.) appear almost like shadow
boxing, underlines the principles of comparing costs and benefits
in a detailed way. In the face of this analysis there is no way of
hiding from the realities by employing such vague moral absolutes
as honour or converting a faithless woman into a 'pearl'

Whose price hath launch'd above a thousand ships,
And turn'd crown'd kings to merchants.

(II.ii. 82–4)

Indeed this particular comparison is revealing. For Troilus the fact
that Helen has precipitated such action is itself a measure of her
worth. The launching of over a thousand ships endows her with a
proportionate value (though, ironically, in Troilus' own comparison the kings become devalued as they are transformed to
merchants). The romantic Troilus wants to see the world in terms
of wholes and absolutes; the experienced and sagacious Diomedes
insists on breaking everything down into fragments — even time.
What is relevant is not what happened before the fighting began,
but what has happened since. Moreover, she is the 'lees and dregs'
or leftovers, and every drop of her blood is 'false'; 'every scruple'
of her 'carrion weight' is 'contaminated'. (Shakespeare here links
the characteristic metaphors of disease, food, remnants, scraps or

fragments and references to birds.) Finally, Helen will contaminate Paris' offspring: he will produce a line of bastards, kinsmen to Thersites, not Hector.

Cressida, too, is a symbol of division and forms a significant part of the kinship web. She is the daughter of a traitor, and though she protests 'I have forgot my father' (IV.ii. 99), she also moves over to the Greeks as she forms part of a transaction in which she is used to 'buy' Antenor. Shortly before she and Troilus consummate their love she expresses anxiety arising from a sense of duality:

> I have a kind of self resides with you,
> But an unkind self, that itself will leave
> To be another's fool.
>
> (III.ii. 146–8)

Despite the uncertainty arising from this expression of duality, Cressida goes on to assert the completeness, wholeness and changeless nature of her love for Troilus in terms of units which are enormous or minute:

> Prophet may you be!
> If I be false, or swerve a *hair* from truth,
> When *time* is *old* and hath *forgot* itself,
> When *water-drops* have *worn the stones* of Troy,
> And *blind oblivion swallow'd cities up*,
> And *mighty states characterless* are *grated*
> To dusty *nothing* — yet let memory,
> From false to false, among false maids in love,
> Upbraid my falsehood.
>
> (III.ii. 181–9)

When Cressida learns that she must leave Troy to rejoin her father she again insists on the wholeness and purity of her love for Troilus and the grief she feels at parting:

> Why tell you me of moderation?
> The grief is *fine, full, perfect*, that I taste,
> . . .
> If I could temporize with my affection,
> Or *brew* it to a *weak* and *colder* palate,
> The like *allayment* could I give my grief.

88

My love admits no *qualifying dross*,
No more my grief, in such a *precious* loss.

(IV.iv. 2 – 10)

Here is the now familiar contrast between that which is whole or
pure and that which is diluted or contaminated.

Troilus' response dwells on the speed of their forced separation.
The whole speech conveys a sense of breathless and rough speed
('jostles', 'hastes', 'crams'). The long-drawn-out process of
finding each other with 'so many thousand sighs' is now mocked
by a separation which demands that the farewells which should be
as numerous as the 'stars in heaven' be snatched in a moment and
innumerable kisses be limited to one — and even that is to be
'distasted' with 'broken tears'.

And *suddenly*; where injury of chance
Puts back leave-taking, *jostles* roughly by
All time of pause, *rudely* beguiles our lips
Of all *rejoindure, forcibly prevents*
Our *lock'd embrasures, strangles* our dear vows
Even in the *birth* of our own *labouring breath*.
We *two*, that with *so many thousand* sighs
Did *buy* each other, must *poorly sell* ourselves
With the *rude brevity* and discharge of *one*.
Injurious Time now with a *robber's haste*
Crams his rich thiev'ry up, he knows not how;
As *many* farewells as be *stars in heaven*,
With *distinct* breath and *consign'd* kisses to them,
He *fumbles* up into a *loose* adieu,
And *scants* us with a *single* famish'd kiss
Distasted with the salt of *broken* tears.

(IV.iv. 32 – 47)

Here we have number, division, and fragmentation in abundance,
allied with the food imagery and culminating in the word 'tears'
which is so persistent in the play. (Indeed, the parts of the body are
enumerated endlessly in this play but the eyes most frequently and
most potently.)

These assertions of the wholeness of the love of Troilus and
Cressida and the pain of their hurried parting finds its counterpart
in the betrayal scene. As Cressida recognises her shifting affections
she murmurs to herself:

89

Troilus, farewell! *One eye* yet looks on thee,
But with my heart the *other eye* doth see.

(V.ii. 106–7)

Troilus, having seen all, stops to make a 'recordation . . . of *every syllable*' that has been spoken. But having witnessed Cressida's betrayal he has to absorb the evidence of his senses. Initially, he has to assert that there are two Cressidas:

This she? — No, this is Diomed's Cressida.
. . .
If there be *rule in unity itself*,
This is not she. O madness of discourse,
That cause sets up with and against itself!
Bifold authority! where reason can revolt
Without perdition, and loss assume all reason
Without revolt. This *is*, and *is not*, Cressid.
Within my soul there doth conduce a fight
Of this strange nature, that a thing *inseparate*
Divides more wider that the sky and earth;
And yet the *spacious breadth* of this *division*
Admits no orifex for a point as subtle
As Ariachne's *broken woof* to enter.
Instance, O instance! strong as Pluto's gates:
Cressid is mine, *tied* with the *bonds* of heaven.
Instance, O instance! strong as heaven itself:
The *bonds* of heaven are *slipp'd, dissolv'd*, and *loos'd;*
And with another knot, five-finger-tied,
The *fractions* of her faith, *orts* of her love,
The *fragments, scraps*, the *bits*, and greasy *relics*
Of her *o'er-eaten* faith are given to Diomed.

(V.ii. 136–59)

Here, then, what seemed incapable of division has become fragmented, the dissolution or fragmentation once more ultimately being expressed in terms of the food imagery. Interestingly, as Helen and Cressida are so often compared in the play, in each case they, or their love, are visualised as left-overs.

A few more scenes require comment in order to drive home the extent, intensity and significance of the process being analysed. Taking II.ii. first, Priam's speech opens the debate. What is especially significant is the way in which the costs of the war are itemised and their comprehensive nature made manifest:

> After so many *hours, lives, speeches spent,*
> Thus *once again* says Nestor from the Greeks:
> 'Deliver Helen, and *all damage else* —
> As *honour, loss of time, travail, expense,*
> *Wounds, friends,* and *what else dear* that is *consum'd*
> *In hot digestion* of this *cormorant* war —
> Shall be struck off.'
>
> (II.ii. 1 – 7)

This catalogue in itself ought to be enough to settle the debate in favour of ending the war. But Hector is required to carry the calculation and comparison even further:

> Since the *first* sword was drawn about this question
> *Every tithe* soul 'mongst *many thousand dismes*
> Hath been as *dear* as Helen — I mean, of ours.
> If we have lost *so many tenths* of ours
> To guard a thing not ours nor *worth* to us
> (Had it our name) the *value of one ten,*
> What merit's in that reason which denies
> The yielding of her up?
>
> (II.ii. 18 – 25)

Significantly, Troilus turns his back on the precision of arithmetic and insists on the impossibility of attempting to measure or weigh what is at stake:

>   Fie, fie, my brother:
> *Weigh* you the *worth* and *honour* of a king
> *So great* as our dread father's in a scale
> Of common *ounces?* Will you with *counters sum*
> The *past-proportionate* of his *infinite,*
> And buckle in a waist *most fathomless*
> With *spans* and *inches* so *diminutive*
> As fears and reasons? Fie for godly shame!
>
> (II.ii. 25 – 32)

After diverse interjections Hector returns to the simple but telling formula of costs and benefits:

Brother,
She is not *worth* what she doth *cost* the keeping.

(II.ii. 51–2)

When Hector reverses himself, having effectively won the debate in favour of ending the war, he foresakes calculation and comparison and couches his argument in terms of moral imperatives:

For 'tis a cause that hath no mean dependence
Upon our joint and several dignities.

(II.ii. 193–4)

Close analysis and insistence on measurement give way to incalculable generalisations — even though Hector has previously suggested that arithmetic has a place even in the sphere of theology:

'Tis mad idolatry
To make the service greater than the god;

(II.ii. 57–8)

Not only is the price already paid acknowledged, but the risk of the total annihilation of Troy, as predicted by Cassandra, is accepted. Here, then, Shakespeare is insistently drawing attention to the triumph of the irrational over the rational, and the way in which that comes about. It seems probable that Shakespeare's interest in this subject arose out of a probing of the question of why the participants, especially the Trojans, fought a destructive and long-drawn-out conflict for such an apparently trivial reason as a faithless woman. Clearly he was too intelligent not to have thought that there were perhaps more genuine reasons for the conflict, such as competition over trade etc., but he deliberately chooses to ignore such possibilities while at the same time making us powerfully conscious of trade and commerce through the imagery of the play. It would appear that Shakespeare wishes to focus attention on the way in which decisions can be made by intelligent men that clearly fly in the face of reason. In the debate scene the participants are carried towards a logical solution by means of quantification and comparison; they arrive at an irrational conclusion by insisting on adhering to values which they refuse to subject to calculation and comparison.

The nature of the relationship between personal attributes and evaluation is developed in II.iii where Agamemnon is being frustrated in his attempt to persuade Achilles to rejoin the battle. He is obliged to accept Patroclus as intermediary and attempts to convey to him a sense of inequality between Achilles' self-estimation and the general valuation of him:

> *Much attribute* he hath, and *much* the reason
> Why we *ascribe* it to him; yet *all* his virtues,
> Not virtuously on his *own* part beheld,
> Do in *our* eyes *begin* to lose their gloss —
> . . .
>   and you shall not sin
> If you do say we think him *over-proud*
> And *under-honest*, in *self-assumption greater*
> Than in the *note of judgement*; and *worthier* than himself
> . . .
>   Go tell him this, and add
> That if he *overhold his price so much*
> We'll *none* of him, . . .
>
>   (II.iii. 118–36)

Whilst awaiting an answer the emulous Ajax pushes Agamemnon into making a comparison between them:

> *Ajax.*   What is he *more* than another?
> *Agamemnon.* *No more* than what he thinks he is.
> *Ajax.*   Is he *so much*? Do you think he thinks himself a
>   *better* man than I am?
> *Agamemnon.* No question.
> *Ajax.*   Will you subscribe his thought, and say he is?
> *Agamemnon.* No, noble Ajax; you are *as strong, as valiant, as*
>   *wise; no less noble, much more gentle,* and *altogether*
>   *more tractable.*
>
>   (II.iii. 144–52)

Of course, Agamemnon thinks of them as equally unintelligent; the only attribute he desires in them apart from fighting prowess is tractability. What emerges so strongly from this scene is the inevitability of weighing qualities and valuing people for their particular attributes. Ironically, the very qualities possessed by Achilles and Ajax are not being used. The value of their service to the Greeks is zero or even negative (following Ulysses' view that by setting such a bad example Achilles stimulates insubordination and disaffection).

It is the desperate desire to draw Achilles back into the action that causes Ulysses to set a trap for him: to provoke him into believing that his reputation has declined far below his self-evaluation. Having pointed to the opposite movement of Ajax's reputation, Ulysses engages in generalisations which lead right back to the nature of time and reputation. At the conclusion of the Trojan debate Troilus exulted in Hector's determination not to let slip one jot of fame (II.ii. 203–7). But here Ulysses insists that fame too is subject to fragmentation and disintegration. Numbers, quantities, units of time and speed are the characteristic features of expression in these speeches:

> Time hath, my lord, a wallet at his back
> Wherein he puts *alms* for oblivion,
> A *great-siz'd* monster of ingratitudes.
> Those *scraps* are good deeds past, which are *devour'd*
> *As fast* as they are made, *forgot as soon*
> *As done.*
> . . .
> > Take the *instant* way;
> For honour travels in a strait so narrow
> Where *one* but goes abreast. Keep then the path;
> For emulation hath a *thousand* sons
> That *one* by *one* pursue; if you give way,
> Or hedge aside from the direct forthright,
> Like to an enter'd tide they *all* rush by
> And leave you *hindmost*;
>
> > > (III.iii. 145–60)

Finally, Ulysses presents a comprehensive list of the victims of time and applies the principle to the relative movements in the reputation of the two Greek heroes:

> > O let not virtue seek
> Remuneration for the thing it was;
> For beauty, wit,
> High birth, vigour of bone, desert in service,
> Love, friendship, charity, are subjects all
> To envious and calumniating Time.
> *One* touch of nature makes the *whole* world kin —

That *all* with *one* consent praise new-born gauds,
. . .
The present eye praises the present object:
Then marvel not, thou *great and complete* man,
That *all* the Greeks begin to worship Ajax,

(III.iii. 169–82)

The wholeness of humanity is apparent only in its fickleness. The
lesson for any hero, therefore, is constant action to renew his
reputation. This is the lesson Ulysses wishes Achilles to absorb,
but this argument has another implication: the quest to secure
permanent fame through action — which is what motivates Hector
and Troilus — is futile because all fame is fleeting. The existence
of the play itself, however, casts doubt upon that pessimistic view
of the nature of fame. The actions of the Trojans and Greeks did
live on in human memory and continue to do so. But Shakespeare's
play raises a further doubt: in all his historical plays he seems to be
acutely conscious of the impossibility of representing what really
happened; the audience is constantly pushed into asking: was it
really like this? In dealing with the Troy story, Shakespeare found
so many unpleasant features of Achilles that he could not weld the
amalgam into a heroic warrior. Shakespeare's Achilles is ultimately exposed as a brutal coward. Conversely, the much more
attractive portrait of Hector's human qualities that emerges from
the sources makes for a consistent character who is warm-hearted,
courageous and magnanimous. Shakespeare adopts these qualities
but underlines Hector's naïvety to the point where he becomes
wilfully irresponsible.

Ulysses' description of Achilles as 'thou great and complete
man' is designed to flatter, but in a sense he is complete. Ajax can
appear as a buffoon in one scene and as a generous and courteous
knight in another: he really is a man made up of diverse parts.
Achilles, however, is a tight knot of pride, envy and brutality; and
this is well brought out in the scene where the two great men meet.
One of the most striking features of the scene is the courtesy and
warmth with which all the Greeks welcome Hector with the single
and embarrassing exception of Achilles. Agamemnon's welcome is
couched in terms that obliterate both past and future: only the
present matters. Moreover, what he stresses is the wholeness of his
welcome: it is untouched by the smallest fragment of envy or
malice; the contrast in the speech between division and wholeness
is marked:

> Understand more clear:
> What's past and what's to come is strew'd with *husks*
> And *formless ruin* of oblivion;
> But in this *extant moment*, faith and troth,
> *Strain'd purely* from all hollow bias-drawing,
> Bids thee with *most divine integrity*
> From *heart of very heart*, great Hector, welcome.

(IV.v. 164 – 70)

Nestor's equally warm-hearted welcome is followed by a dialogue between Hector and Ulysses which again focuses on parts and numbers. Ulysses asks how Troy can stand 'When we have here her base and pillar by us?' (IV.v. 211) Hector comments on the number of Greeks and Trojans who have died since he 'first' saw Ulysses on his embassy to Troy. And as the tension mounts and the precarious reality of the war breaks through, Ulysses insists 'My prophecy is but *half* his journey yet'. Hector's reply underlines how the outcome will be a step-by-step process culminating in a moment of dreadful finality:

> The fall of *every Phrygian stone* will cost
> A *drop of Grecian blood*. The *end* crowns all;
> And that old common arbitrator, Time,
> Will *one day* end it.

(IV.v. 222 – 5)

The amicable embrace of these two adversaries (and a striking feature of this scene is the natural affinity between Hector and the Greeks which contrasts with the antagonisms within the Greek camp) is interrupted by Achilles' severing of decorum employing the familiar pattern of body parts and food imagery:

> Now, Hector, I have *fed* mine *eyes* on thee;
> I have with exact view perus'd thee, Hector,
> And quoted *joint* by *joint*.

(IV.v. 230 – 2)

In response to Achilles' invitation to feast his eyes on him, Hector satisfies himself with a mere glance which provokes Achilles to look on Hector a 'second time' and view him 'limb by limb'. This examination is followed by a metaphorical dismemberment of Hector:

Tell me, you heavens, in which *part* of his body
Shall I destroy him — whether *there*, or *there*, or *there* —
That I may give the *local wound* a name,
And make *distinct* the very *breach* whereout
Hector's great spirit flew?

(IV.v. 241–5)

Eventually Hector is goaded into a wild response which perpetuates the image of dismemberment:

For I'll not kill thee *there*, nor *there*, nor *there*;
But, by the forge that stithied Mars his helm,
I'll kill thee *everywhere*, yea, *o'er* and *o'er*.

(IV.v. 253–5)

Ironically, Hector is the one who is hacked 'o'er and o'er' though by the Myrmidons. The man who threatens violence when courtesy is called for runs away when he finds himself at the end of Hector's sword.

Finally, in the closing phase of the play the relation of parts to the whole and estimation of relative values appears in a particularly concentrated form. As Hector's family tries to dissuade him from fighting on the fateful day, he makes an assertion about human values:

Mine honour keeps the weather of my fate:
Life *every man* holds *dear*, but the *dear man*
Holds honour *far more precious-dear than life*.

(V.iii. 26–8)

Hector is, however, omitting something from the calculus: throughout the play he is seen as the prop of Troy. As Cassandra expresses the point to Priam:

He is thy crutch. Now if thou lose thy stay,
Thou on him leaning, and all Troy on thee,
Fall all together.

(V.iii. 60–2)

Hector is not only putting honour before his own life but before the lives of the whole city. The relationship of part to whole is made explicit. Achilles expresses the relationship cogently as he looks down on Hector's corpse:

So, Ilion, fall thou next! Come, Troy, sink down!
Here lies thy heart, thy sinews, and thy bone.

> (V.viii. 11–12)

Cassandra, as she foretells of Hector's wounds bleeding at 'many vents', insists on the true magnitude of the calculation, 'Thou dost *thyself* and *all our Troy* deceive' (V.iii. 90). Hector's high-sounding formula is specious because it is incomplete. It is spurious for another reason: the man against whom he fights, and permits to flee to safety, is not constrained by any such code. Hector's plaintive cry the second before he dies reveals a staggering naïvety: 'I am unarm'd: forego this vantage, Greek' (V.viii. 9). As the dismemberment of Hector takes place before our eyes we are presented with the mutilation implicit in war which has already been indicated in the passages previously quoted and in the memorable description of Achilles' defeated warriors fleeing from Hector:

Together with his *mangled* Myrmidons
That *noseless, handless, hack'd* and *chipp'd*, come to him
Crying on Hector.

> (V.v. 33–5)

The process of fragmentation, disintegration and unification is precisely illustrated at this point in the play. As Nestor observes Achilles and Ajax raging for revenge he comments tersely: 'So, so, *we draw together*' (V.v. 44). Perhaps the most vivid presentation in the play of the absurdity of the war, the refusal to make or act on rational calculation, occurs when Troilus storms into battle seeking the man who has displaced him in the affection of the faithless Cressida: 'I come to lose my arm, or win my sleeve' (V.iii. 96). What could be more foolish than to venture an arm for a besmirched love token? Once again we see the presentation of implicit calculation and the use of part to suggest the irrationality of the participants and the enterprise.

In gloating over the body of Hector, Achilles provides a powerful image of darkness descending on the scene, accentuating the sense of division which characterises the play and employing the pervasive food imagery:

The dragon wing of night o'er-spreads the earth
And, stickler-like, the army *separates*.
My *half-supp'd* sword, that *frankly* would have fed,
Pleas'd with this *dainty bait*, thus goes to bed.

> (V.viii. 17–20)

Clearly a fundamental aspect of division and separation is the division of the body into its constituent parts, a number of which have already been indicated. However, it is worth devoting some consideration to the frequency of the references to eyes, ears and tongues. Troilus begins his praise of Cressida by reference to her 'eyes' (I.i. 54); Ulysses refers to the 'med'cinable eye' of the sun (I.iii. 91); Aeneas seeks permission to present himself before the 'kingly eyes' of Agamemnon whom he seeks to distinguish 'from eyes of other mortals' (I.iii. 218–24); as Ulysses begins to reveal his scheme to Nestor the latter exclaims 'I see them not with my old eyes' (I.iii. 366) while Ulysses refers to the 'salt scorn' of Achilles' eyes (I.iii. 371); Agamemnon says of Achilles' virtues that they 'Do in our eyes begin to lose their gloss' (II.iii. 121); Ulysses arranges for the Greek leadership to snub Achilles so that he will be forced to wonder 'Why such unplausive eyes are bent, why turn'd on him' (III.iii. 43); Achilles acknowledges the paradox whereby men perceive the impact of their qualities and actions on other men by reflection:

> The beauty that is borne here in the face
> The bearer knows not, but commends itself
> To others' eyes; nor doth the eye itself,
> That most pure spirit of sense, behold itself,
> Not going from itself; but eye to eye oppos'd
> Salutes each other with each other's form;
>
> (III.iii. 103–8)

Here is a recognition of the social nature of human existence: no matter how individualistic men seek to be they are bound in by a web of connections and relationships: self has no meaning outside the fabric of relationships. A man knows what he is through the evaluation of other men. As Ulysses expresses the point, ostensibly acquired from the book he is holding,

> That no man is the lord of anything,
> Though in and of him there be much consisting,
> Till he communicate his parts to others;
> Nor doth he of himself know them for aught,
> Till he behold them form'd in the applause
> Where th'are extended;
>
> (III.iii. 115–20)

He goes on to point out, 'The present eye praises the present object' (III.iii. 180) so that reputation has constantly to be renewed. Hector asks Ajax to identify the leading Greeks for him with the exception of Achilles whom he is confident of discovering with his own 'searching eyes' (IV.v. 160). Cressida expresses her anxiety about the future by claiming 'more dregs than water, if my fears have eyes' (III.ii. 66). When Troilus is suffering from the emotional shock of observing Cressida's betrayal, Thersites asks, 'Will a swagger himself out on's own eyes?' (V.ii. 135). Hector asks Achilles 'Why dost thou so oppress me with thine eye?' (IV.v. 240) As Cassandra visualises Hector's death she observes the future event in the present saying, 'Look how thy diest: look how thy eye turns pale:' (V.iii. 81). The diseased Pandarus complains to Troilus, 'I have a rheum in mine eyes, too' (V.iii. 104 – 5). Finally, Troilus in describing the process of choosing a wife connects the eye and ear as vital instruments of judgement:

> My will enkindled by mine eyes and ears,
> Two traded pilots 'twixt the dangerous shores
> Of will and judgement —
>
> (II.ii. 64 – 6)

The references to ears are not as numerous as to eyes but they are interesting and ambiguous. Like the eyes they ought to be employed as critical instruments, but as Hector says to Troilus and Paris,

> pleasure and revenge
> Have ears more deaf than adders to the voice
> Of any true decision.
>
> (II.ii. 172 – 4)

Ulysses claims that Nestor 'Should with a bond of air,'

> knit all the Greekish ears
> To his experienc'd tongue —
>
> (I.iii. 66 – 8)

But if the Greeks are failing to pay due attention to Nestor, Andromache insists that Hector is deliberately failing to make use of a vital faculty:

When was my lord so much ungently temper'd
To stop his ears against admonishment?

(V.iii. 1-2)

Ulysses criticises Achilles for having been adversely affected
through paying too much attention to what has been said of him:

The great Achilles, whom opinion crowns
The sinew and the forehand of our host,
Having his ear full of his airy fame,
Grows dainty of his worth, and in his tent
Lies mocking our designs:

(I.iii. 142-6)

Thus eyes, ears, and tongues are vital faculties for comprehending
and communicating but only the intellect can put them to proper
use: praise may lead to conceit and arrogance; men may choose to
be deaf to arguments they find uncongenial; and tongues may be
used to slander and deceive.

In this play Shakespeare is concerned to probe the very centre of
the cause and conduct of the Trojan war. The play portrays the
relationships between the participants and their debates and
calculations. Some are deceived and are self-deceiving; others are
cold-eyed and perceptive. The sordid nature of the conflict is
widely acknowledged but it rolls on unremittingly to its desolate
conclusion. By the end of the play we are made more conscious
and more pessimistic about the way in which human beings handle
affairs. One of Shakespeare's methods in undertaking this exploration is a verbal patterning which is extraordinary in its insistence:
parts are compared with wholes: delineation, disintegration and
fragmentation constitute an integral part of the verbal structure;
and these features are frequently linked with the fabric of kinship
and with the imagery and association of food in its various forms,
especially remains. As attributes are separated and examined, so
too are the parts of the body continually presented to the senses as
objects of beauty, or as essential constituents of the functioning
whole or as broken or severed remnants. Even the trees have
knees: 'the splitting wind/Makes flexible the knees of knotted oaks'
(I.iii. 49-50). The hand has special significance but it is the eye
that is most frequently present — 'That most pure spirit of sense'
(III.iii. 106). Logic turned inside out finds its physical counterpart
in Ajax 'who wears his wit in his belly and his guts in his head'

(II.i. 75 – 6). If the eye has a symbolic significance as the organ through which we primarily apprehend and analyse the world outside ourselves, the droplet or tear is also of special importance. As we become conscious of disintegration, even time itself is fragmented. We encounter the ultimate emblem of dissolution in Patroclus' vivid figure: 'like a dew-drop from the lion's mane,/ Be shook to air' (III.iii. 223 – 4).

Another vital feature of the play is the abundance of references to the identity and nature of the characters in the play: some characters are analysed in depth by others; there are scores of references to the essential attributes of individuals; and impersonation is a favourite pastime. Jan Knott in his essay 'Amazing and Modern' states that 'In no other play of Shakespeare's, perhaps, do the characters analyse themselves and the world quite so violently and passionately.'[3] What, then, is the extent and function of the process of 'translating' the man, which appears to be one of the most distinctive features of this distinctive play? (It is significant that this word 'translate' is used by Ulysses to describe character assessment and analysis after the most extensive piece of character interpretation in the play (IV.v. 96 – 112).) For Kenneth Palmer, the problem of identification which characterises the play is connected with the question of value and values; he expresses the point by stating that 'the matter of right identification is also a matter of right valuation: that a man's self-knowledge is linked with knowledge of other men'.[4]

At the purely quantitative level there are over 200 references by characters to the qualities or attributes of themselves or others. These references range from one word insults to long speeches such as Ulysses' description of Troilus (IV.v. 96 – 109). After Ulysses delivers what appears to be an accurate and insightful analysis of Troilus, he reveals that he is only repeating what Aeneas has told him. Another striking feature of the play which is related to the frequency of character description or analysis is the prevalence of questions. Again at the purely quantitative level there are around 400 questions (more than in any other play in the canon) and only one scene does not contain a single question (V.viii.). Many of these questions relate to the identity of characters, ranging from the simplest enquiry — Who is it? — to the ambiguous — What is he? (About one-third of the questions are rhetorical.)

Frequently confusion or uncertainty of identity gives rise to laughter. For instance, there is the outstanding moment when

Pandarus identifies the great warriors of Troy, for the sake of his niece, Cressida, and then fails to distinguish Troilus from Deiphobus having previously suggested that Troilus is so remarkable as to be unmistakable. This momentary confusion gives rise to the characteristic comedy of the play but also raises the question which thereafter recurs in various forms: what are the distinguishing features of any individual? How does the appearance relate to the essence or inner man? How do different people see a given individual? What is the relationship between a man and his reputation? How closely does a man's view of himself conform to the public view of him? Is a man's nature fixed, or variable depending on the situation or context? Finally, what is the relationship between social values and individual action? It is through the process of proffered opinions, impersonation and abuse (not confined to Thersites) that Shakespeare insinuates these questions. In dealing with them we not only come to terms with issues of human and dramatic significance, but also journey to the heart of the play: why did the Trojan War take place and why was it allowed to proceed to such a destructive conclusion? What values animated the participants? Were the values actually shared and fixed or did they diverge and were they shifting? In seeking to answer these pressing and direct questions we are pushed to a deeper level of generality to explore human beings and the principles which they hold or extol.

In addition to the plethora of questions and issues of identity and character there is a great deal of business allocated to go-betweens or messengers. Even the Prologue acts as a go-between: stepping between the action and the audience it sets the scene and provides crucial descriptions of some of the major participants:

The *ravish'd* Helen, *Menelaus' queen,*
With *wanton* Paris sleeps.

(9-10)

Here is a description of Helen's condition (ravish'd), her true status (Menelaus' queen) and her temperament — she is wanton by association. Before considering other views of Helen it is worth noting that the Prologue contrasts the state of the combatants — 'fresh and yet unbruised Greeks' and 'expectation, tickling skittish spirits/On one and other side' — with the risks ('chance', 'hazard') and realities of war ('cruel war', 'ransack Troy'). Hence there is a gap between perceptions and reality. In I.ii. Pandarus and Cressida in discussing the colour of Troilus' face have a dialogue which raises a question about the interpretation of something which ought to be utterly straightforward but is not:

Pandarus. . . . for a brown favour for so 'tis, I must confess —
not brown neither —
Cressida. No, but brown.
Pandarus. Faith, to say truth, brown and not brown.
Cressida. To say truth, true and not true.

(I.ii. 93–8)

This comic exchange prompts the question of interpretation: if colour is a matter of doubt, what about more ambiguous matters? Later in the scene Pandarus attempts to persuade Cressida that Helen loves Troilus — which is false — in order to make her jealous so that she will reciprocate Troilus' love. Ironically, Cressida already 'loves' Troilus but is pretending not to. Again Pandarus is disproportionate in his dismissal of Achilles — 'A drayman, a porter, a very camel' (I.ii. 253) — whereas he represents Troilus as the quintessence of manhood: 'Why, have you any discretion? Have you any eyes? Do you know what a man is? Is not birth, beauty, good shape, discourse, manhood, learning, gentleness, virtue, youth, liberality and such like, the spice and salt that season a man?' (I.ii. 255–60) The rhetorical questions emphasise the tangibility and value of these attributes: nobody with eyes and understanding could possibly fail to recognise and appreciate their worth. Cressida responds with a joke (perpetuating the cookery imagery) because she is already powerfully attracted to Troilus, but still wishes to hold off for the present. However, these attributes are encompassed by the comprehensive list of elements which Ulysses insists are victims of 'envious and calumniating Time' (III.iii. 174). But the irony does not end there: for Cressida, knowing 'what a man *is*' amounts to something more limited and fundamental — the essence of a man lies in his sexuality.

This question of identity and the essence of man is posed interestingly by Cressida's father (whom she has 'forgot'). Calchas in seeking to persuade the Greeks to exchange Antenor for Cressida points out that he has acquired the name of traitor and that with this change of allegiance he has effectively lost his old identity. He has become 'As new into the world, strange, unacquainted' (III.iii. 12). He suggests that personal identity is not something that is portable: it is connected with and shaped by

104

specific circumstances: 'time, acquaintance, custom, and condition' (III.iii. 9). This loss of identity is underlined by Agamemnon who asks, 'What would'st thou of us, Trojan?' (III.iii. 17) He does not use Calchas' name, he is merely a Trojan; and yet he is no longer a Trojan either. In his quest for safety he has relinquished his identity. Ironically, the proposal which he proceeds to make transforms Cressida into a commodity: Antenor shall 'buy' his daughter. Quickly Diomedes is given the role of messenger thereby re-creating the structural device of question, identity, messenger.

Another perspective is provided by Ulysses who presents a vivid scene of Achilles lying on his bed entertained by Patroclus imitating the Greek leaders. Not only does Patroclus reduce them to ludicrous figures, pompous, bombastic and senile, but, as Ulysses points out, he robs them of their attributes and functions, thereby transforming them to superfluous nonentities:

> And in this fashion
> All our abilities, gifts, natures, shapes,
> Severals and generals of grace exact,
> Achievements, plots, orders, preventions,
> Excitements to the field, or speech for truce,
> Success or loss, what is or is not, serves
> As stuff for these two to make paradoxes.

> (I.iii. 178–84)

We are back with the question Pandarus posed for Cressida: 'Do you not know what a man is?' A man is identified by his attributes and function. Has Patroclus revealed part or all of the truth? Do these leaders appear closer to Patroclus' characterisation than to their portrayal in history or myth? Even if we accept the validity of Patroclus' perception, do we also accept his wholesale contempt for the *function* of leadership? Just as Patroclus has parodied Agamemnon and Nestor, Ulysses has exercised irony in his references to 'god Achilles' and 'Sir Valour'. Here we have a complex presentation of Ulysses describing and commenting on Patroclus' performance of parodying Agamemnon and Nestor (with the lively audience of Achilles), which serves to remind us that we are watching the depiction of these historical characters by yet another playwright and his actors. Hence we have an extended process of character identification, delineation and interpretation. Both in drama and life we seek truth, but translating the man is not a simple business. (Significantly, amateur dramatics has quite a currency in the Greek camp because Thersites — 'A slave whose gall coins slanders like a mint' (I.iii. 193) — also derides the leaders for the benefit of Ajax.)

The problem of identification is emphasised by Aeneas because he is incapable of determining which of the Greeks is 'that god in office, guiding men?' (I.iii. 230) Agamemnon's godlike qualities must relate purely to his function as he has nothing in his appearance to indicate his identity. It may be, of course, that as Hector later reminds Achilles, there is much more to a man than appearances suggest (IV.v. 239). In the case of Agamemnon, his initial unimpressiveness is underlined by Thersites who expresses the view that only if he were covered by running boils 'would come some matter from him' (II.i. 8). Thersites is interrupted at this point by the demands of Ajax and so proceeds to denounce the latter as a beast, a commodity, and as being emulous of and inferior to Achilles. Thersites then threatens to provide a detailed characterisation of Ajax — 'by inches' (II.i. 51). Although he is distracted from this task by the arrival of Achilles and Patroclus, he condemns the two famous warriors for being all muscle and no brain and identifies their real function: to be yoked 'like draught-oxen' and made to 'plough up the wars' (II.i. 108–9). Once Thersites leaves the scene Achilles is obliged to communicate the substance of the 'proclamation', and this leads to his implied assertion that he is the best of the Greeks and Ajax's rejection of the claim. Thus though neither is fighting the Trojans, each seeks the title of supreme warrior.

Abuse is by no means confined to Thersites. During the debate scene Helenus justifiably accuses Troilus of disdaining reason because he seems incapable of employing that faculty. In return Helenus is denounced as a coward. However, Troilus is forced into using reason by Hector's insistence that Helen has to be evaluated objectively.[5] Troilus seems incapable of very powerful reasoning but the metaphor which he attaches to Helen (a 'pearl') turns her into a commodity and 'crown'd kings to merchants'. Unintentionally he takes the dignity out of the debate: the Greeks are merchants and the Trojans 'thieves' (II.ii. 84–95). Helen is devalued in an argument intended to place her beyond valuation. Paris' interjection is quickly stifled by Priam who denounces him as 'one besotted on your sweet delights' (II.ii. 144). Nevertheless, he goes on to insist that she is a woman who surpasses all others. Consequently, when we finally encounter 'Nell' it is a moment of profound anticlimax: whatever her beauty she is woman devoid of admirable qualities. Even before we have the opportunity of assessing her true worth, Hector insists on the rightness of her return to the Greeks because of what she *is*: 'wife to Sparta's king' (II.ii. 184). Her intrinsic qualities and the cost of keeping her in loss of life are ultimately of secondary importance: what is crucial is her position or status in the law of nations. Having reached the crux of the matter, Hector makes his breathtaking about-turn relegating legal niceties to a footnote: she is merely a symbol upon which their honour rests. As Arnold Stein expresses the point, there is an 'absolute gap between the emptiness of Helen the person and the attributes she has demonstrably acquired as a symbol . . . Helen is a mere *casus belli*, an arrested symbol that the war has outgrown'.[6] Suddenly, even Troilus is prepared to see her decline in value from being priceless to worthless once Hector has handed him an argument for continuing the war.

Two things become clear during the course of this scene: keeping Helen cannot be justified by even a cursory examination of the losses to date; and, as Cassandra predicts — 'Our firebrand brother Paris burns us all' (II.ii. 111) — consideration of the possible future loss (the destruction of Troy) makes the retention of Helen totally irrational. However, while the capture of Helen may have caused the war, she is no longer the reason for its continuation. If Paris' appetite feeds off the thing that satisfies it (Helen's body) Hector and Troilus have insatiable appetites for honour. What is not clear from this point onwards is the extent to which both sides see Helen as irrelevant to the continuation of the conflict. The comments made about her are at all times derogatory because she can be blamed for starting the war. (In fact, she is no more than a pawn; it is the masculine values of the Greeks and Trojans who see her as a symbol and a *commodity*, something *owned*, which causes the war.) The most savage indictment of Helen is made by Diomedes in a scene in which the pressures exerted on identity and worth are powerful. Act IV opens with questions which relate to identity but then go deeper as Paris invites Aeneas to reiterate his complimentary comments on Diomedes' fighting qualities. The ensuing dialogue reveals the tension between the requirements of courtesy and the recognition of deadly rivalry. The conclusion is tense but suggests that these two men have detected a fundamental source of antipathy between them (which is surprising, given Aeneas' honeyed tongue and easy-going nature):

Aeneas. We know each other well.
Diomedes. We do, and long to know each other worse.

(IV.i. 31–2)

Paris then invites Diomedes to choose the worthier man between himself and Menelaus. But instead of praise he receives a crushing denunciation of himself ('like a lecher out of whorish loins') and Menelaus ('a puling cuckold'). Diomedes' contempt for Helen is expressed with devastating vigour and force:

> For every false drop in her bawdy veins
> A Grecian's life hath sunk; for every scruple
> Of her contaminated carrion weight
> A Trojan hath been slain. Since she could speak,
> She hath not given so many good words breath
> As for her Greeks and Trojans suffer'd death.

(IV.i. 70–5)

After this critique of Helen and her role it is impossible to dignify her with any semblance of worth or to see the Trojan War as less than monumental folly. The attack is all the more devastating for coming from a wide-eyed realist who does not have very high expectations of men or women — though Kenneth Muir argues that 'We may discount Diomedes' bitter attack, as that hard-boiled cynic is likely to be prejudiced.'[7] Paris' riposte in defence of Helen is feeble, but appropriately he falls into the idiom of commerce.

It is characteristic of the play that Diomedes has no sooner delivered his opinion of Helen, Paris and Menelaus than he is the subject of Ulysses' character assessment. When Agamemnon is unsure of Diomedes' identity, Ulysses provides a telling cameo in which external features exemplify the inner man:

> 'Tis he, I ken the manner of his gait:
> He rises on the toe; that spirit of his
> In aspiration lifts him from the earth.

(IV.v. 14–16)

The scene which follows Diomedes' translation of Helen (IV.ii.), though brief, is littered with questions (36 in all) which ultimately press on the true nature of Cressida. First Pandarus seeks to identify the messenger and the nature of his business; then Troilus and Cressida, in turn, fire questions at Pandarus to discover what is wrong. The following interchange is expressive of the character of the scene:

> *Cressida.* How now? What's the matter? Who was here?
> *Pandarus.* Ah, ah!
> *Cressida.* Why sigh you so profoundly? Where's my lord? Gone?
> Tell me, sweet uncle, what's the matter?
>
> (IV.ii. 80–4)

When Cressida discovers that she has been 'changed' for Antenor she protests that she has 'forgot' her father and knows 'no touch of consanguinity'. Her past connection with her father has been severed, and she protests to the gods that they 'make Cressid's name the very crown of falsehood/If ever she leave Troilus!' (IV.ii. 100–4) So after all the questions of the scene the audience is guided to the final question: what is Cressida? Is she capable of enduring all weathers or is she a tradeable commodity?

At their parting Troilus expresses his fears that Cressida will not be able to withstand the temptations of the Greeks. Perhaps her question suggests a hint of excitement about the possibility of being tempted: 'Do you think I will?' (IV.iv. 91). His answer is that he does not believe that she will willingly betray him. However, in response to her question about his fidelity Troilus replies with an interpretation of his character which is tellingly accurate:

> Who, I? — alas, it is my vice, my fault.
> Whiles others fish with craft for great opinion,
> I with great truth catch mere simplicity.
>
> (IV.iv. 100–2)

Troilus' passionate innocence is revealed immediately in his clash with Diomedes who is disdainful of his courteous requests: 'I'll nothing do on charge: to her own worth/Shall she be priz'd' (IV.iv. 131–2). Diomedes' treatment of Cressida (in contrast to his courtship of her in Chaucer, Lydgate and Caxton) implies a swift evaluation and one which is sharply at variance with that of Troilus'. Troilus has interpreted himself accurately but has misjudged Cressida. Diomedes knows himself and quickly gains a true estimation of Cressida. The scene ends on the question of value being raised by the messenger Aeneas, thus completing the familiar pattern of questions, interpretations of characters, and messengers (Diomedes and Aeneas).

If Agamemnon is short-sighted he does not need spectacles to see into Cressida: he begins the round of kissing which Cressida accepts without demur (indeed, she is so much at her ease that she is able to exercise her undoubted wit at the expense of Menelaus — a dog whom almost everyone sees fit to kick). It appears that Diomedes has 'found' Cressida at first glance (a clear case of lust at first sight) and her true nature is so apparent that she transforms the naturally verbose Nestor to being pithy: 'A woman of quick sense' (IV.v. 54). Only Ulysses scorns to kiss Cressida, and his sense of revulsion (precipitated by disgust at the misery resulting from the pursuit of Helen) is manifest in a speech which subjects Cressida and her kind to withering criticism:

> Fie, fie upon her!
> There's language in her eye, her cheek, her lip —
> Nay, her foot speaks; her wanton spirits look out
> At every joint and motive of her body.
> O, these encounterers, so glib of tongue,
> That give accosting welcome ere it comes,
> And wide unclasp the tables of their thoughts
> To every ticklish reader: set them down
> For sluttish spoils of opportunity
> And daughters of the game.
>
> (IV.v. 54–63)

Ulysses, then, assesses and classifies Cressida. Troilus has been completely deceived by her. He accurately summed up his own nature:

> I am as true as truth's simplicity,
> And simpler than the infancy of truth.
>
> (III.ii. 167–8)

But when he discovers Cressida's true nature he feels that all women are contaminated. His only way out of a denunciation of the whole of womankind is to assert that there are two Cressidas: his own and Diomedes'. Ulysses is more prosaic; seeing Cressida as representative of a type, his response to Troilus' outburst is 'What hath she done, prince, that can soil our mothers?' (V.ii. 133) During the course of the play Cressida is seen from several standpoints: engaging in bawdy banter with her servant Alexander and Pandarus (I.ii.); playing the 'coy' lover with Troilus (I.ii. 286–300); pledging her love to Troilus (III.ii.); parting from him in distress (IV.iv.); enjoying the attentions of the Greek leaders (IV.v. 19–53); succumbing to Diomedes — a scene made even more sordid by being observed by her deceived lover and Ulysses and by the bitter Thersites (V.ii.); and finally attempting to maintain her deception of Troilus in her letter to him (V.iii.). No other character in the play is scrutinised from so many vantage points. Troilus treats her as if she were a goddess (III.ii.), and Diomedes, although treating her as light stuff, nevertheless behaves like a true knight in sending Troilus' horse to her. Troilus risks his arm for the love token which she has besmirched and plays out in miniature the Helen–Paris (Trojans)–Menelaus (Greeks) triangle: he goes to lose his arm or win his sleeve: a comparison which highlights the absurdity of his action and that of the contending armies.

If the two women in the play are closely linked (and they are compared on several occasions), so too are the great heroes, Hector and Achilles. Both are referred to with great frequency throughout the play and they comment directly on each other. What is striking is that the epithets directed at Hector are unfailingly complimentary, whereas Achilles is usually seen in an unattractive light: his worth resides in his strength. The first comment on Hector is made by Alexander who refers to him as a man 'whose patience/Is as a virtue fix'd' (I.ii. 4–5), though he makes the generalisation by way of emphasising the unusual event of Hector being 'moved' as a consequence of being knocked down in the battle by Ajax. This glimpse of Hector reveals his steadfastness, while showing him capable of anger, but also suggests his vulnerability. Gradually the views expressed about Hector proclaim him as the very prop of Troy: unmatchable in battle (with the possible exception of Achilles), brave, warm-hearted, magnanimous and generous to the point of foolhardiness. However, before that state of knowledge is reached by the audience there is an interesting exchange between Pandarus and Cressida during which the former attempts to equate Troilus with Hector while Cressida denies the equation. In response to her assertion that 'there's no comparison' between the brothers, Pandarus asks: 'Do you know a man if you see him?' Cressida turns the question to a joke by answering, 'Ay, if ever I saw him before and knew him' (I.ii. 63–6). Cressida easily wins the combat of wit but the question remains in the air: do we recognise what a man really is without prior knowledge? And is the question meaningful without reference to specific criteria? Hector is a more powerful fighter than Troilus but he is too generous and naïve on the battlefield to live long. Troilus is correct to chastise Hector for failing to kill the adversaries he knocks down in the field: 'Brother, you have a vice of mercy in you,/Which better fits a lion than a man'. Hector's response, 'O, 'tis fair play' is aptly rejected by Troilus as 'Fool's play' (V.iii. 37–43).

Even Ajax who, for most of the play, seems devoid of generosity is almost transformed by Hector to a courteous knight, but knows that this degree of magnanimity does not suit with the times: 'Thou art too gentle and too free a man' (IV.v. 138). Only Achilles fails to recognise the true-hearted generosity of Hector. When Agamemnon speaks admiringly of Hector (who offers to accept conditions in the fight with Ajax) ''Tis done like Hector', Achilles' surly response is:

> But securely done,
> A little proudly, and a great deal misprizing
> The knight oppos'd.
>
> (IV.v. 73–5)

Likewise, when Hector makes the fatal error of permitting Achilles to escape, the latter's response involves a refusal to accept generosity: 'I do disdain thy courtesy, proud Trojan' (V.vi. 15). Hector, however, equally fails to interpret Achilles, to penetrate his soul, to see him for what he is, a ruthless coward. In a play which continually directs questions to the identity and nature of individuals and elicits innumerable comments and interpretations, Hector's naïvety at the point of death is breathtaking: 'I am unarm'd: forego this vantage, Greek' (V.viii. 9). The supreme warrior has been living in the past: Troilus knew; Ajax knew it — and on hearing of Hector's death insists, 'Great Hector was as good a man as he' (V.ix. 6). In this pattern of comparisons what does 'a good man' mean? The audience knows that in almost every respect Hector is better than Achilles. Achilles' only superiority lies in a willingness to put aside all principles of 'fair play' in order to murder the pillar of Troy. Judged in terms of effectiveness, there-fore, Achilles is the 'better' man. Thus the probing of the nature and qualities of individuals inevitably brings to the foreground the questions of value and worth which lie at the heart of the play.

It is significant that the most complete picture of Troilus is painted by Ulysses who speaks admiringly of him and by implication reveals that Troilus is even more formidable than Hector:

Not soon provok'd, nor, being provok'd, soon calm'd;
His heart and hand both open and both free;
For what he has he gives, what thinks he shows,
Yet gives he not till judgement guide his bounty,
Nor dignifies an impare though with breath;
Manly as Hector, but more dangerous;
For Hector in his blaze of wrath subscribes
To tender objects, but he in heat of action
Is more vindicative than jealous love.

(IV.v. 99 – 107)

This character analysis has, of course, come via Aeneas who knows Troilus 'Even to his inches' and did 'thus translate' him to Ulysses. It is clear that Ulysses admires an open-hearted and generous nature but recognises that in the real world, and certainly in the military arena, these qualities have to be subordinated to ruthlessness. Human qualities have to be assessed in context. In the world of love Troilus' judgement has been severely defective with the result that he gives himself totally to Cressida and receives in exchange 'no matter from the heart'. Troilus' judgement has also been shown to be singularly weak in the debate over the continuation of the war. Troilus, then, is perfectly adapted to the battlefield but ill-equipped for the council chamber. He is ideally suited for the role that the Greek leadership attempt to impose on Achilles and Ajax: to plough up the wars like 'draught-oxen' (II.i. 109).

Ironically, for most of the action of the play the two most powerful warriors in the Greek camp lie idle, and despite their limited 'intellectual armour' refuse to be goaded or cajoled into fighting by the combined brain-power of Agamemnon, Nestor and Ulysses. Thersites' terse commentaries appear to be accurate: 'Here's Agamemnon: an honest fellow enough, and one that loves quails, but he has not so much brain as ear-wax' (V.i. 50 – 2). Menelaus is totally beneath contempt and exhausts even Thersites' diminutives so that he is left to conclude, 'to be Menelaus I would conspire against destiny' (V.i. 62 – 3). The policy of the Greeks is aptly if irreverently summed up by Thersites: 'the policy of those crafty swearing rascals — that stale old mouse-eaten dry cheese

Nestor, and that same dog-fox Ulysses — is not proved worth a blackberry. They set me up in policy that mongrel cur Ajax, against that dog of as bad a kind Achilles; and now is the cur Ajax prouder than the cur Achilles.' (V.iv. 9–15) It would be completely mistaken to dismiss Thersites as a degenerate railer since he is so accurate in his pronouncements. If Ulysses has justly touched on Diomedes' arrogance and egotism, Thersites alerts us to another unattractive side of his nature. Diomedes is 'a false-hearted rogue, a most unjust knave' (V.i. 87–8). He has never been known to keep his word and so makes an appropriate partner for Cressida — 'the Trojan drab' (V.i. 96). Thersites' delight in words hardly justifies a rejection of his veracity. Moreover, he is not equally savage with all his victims. Nevertheless, Thersites has provoked the ire of many critics. Alvin Kernan, for example, reviles Thersites, wrongly, for believing himself subtle and intelligent and exhibiting hatred. There is a difference between contempt and hatred. This confusion may explain in part why Kernan fails to recognise the satiric nature of the play.[8] Likewise, F. McAlindon claims, 'Thersites is no nearer the truth than the "overlabour" of Aeneas'.[9] Una Ellis-Fermor expresses a contrary view and comments on the perception that Thersites guides us towards: 'mankind in his eyes is as incapable of worthy judgement as of worthy conduct . . . In the world he offers there is no stability in character, ideals, institutions, judgement, nor imagination itself.'[10] John Bayley makes the perceptive observation that 'A logical result of the play's time technique is the domination of Thersites, who seems at times virtually to "speak for" the play in a Brechtian sense, a sense unique in Shakespeare.'[11] Joyce Carol Oates expresses the view that 'it is certainly Shakespeare's belief, along with Thersites, that "all the argument is a cuckold and a whore"'.[12]

In II.iii. Thersites soliloquises on the worthlessness of Patroclus before Achilles enters and invites him to evaluate Agamemnon. In response to the question 'Come, what's Agamemnon?' Thersites replies by reference to function rather than character: 'Thy commander'. Thersites describes himself as Patroclus' 'knower' before claiming kinship with his auditors and Agamemnon as a fool. But by asserting that Patroclus is a 'fool positive' he tricks him into asking 'Why am I a fool?' only to supply the answer 'Make that demand of the Creator' (II.iii. 46–69). Not only has Thersites turned away from providing comic imitation of Agamemnon, but he has indicted Achilles, Patroclus and himself

— and by implication the entire Greek army. Moreover, he has forced a question on Patroclus which could profitably be asked by virtually all the characters who participate in the action. Right on cue the Greek leaders arrive with Ajax in tow, to interview Achilles, which draws from Thersites his summary of the whole business: 'Here is such patchery, such juggling, and such knavery! All the argument is a cuckold and a whore: a good quarrel to draw emulous factions, and bleed to death upon' (II.iii. 73–6). If self-knowledge, as well as an understanding of others, is rare in this play, Thersites emerges near the top of the class. The following self-portrait is not drawn simply to save his life when confronted by Hector: 'I am a rascal, a scurvy railing knave: a very filthy rogue' (V.iv. 28–9). Not only is Hector convinced of the 'quality' of Thersites but so is Priam's bastard son Margarelon when he is informed 'I am a bastard, too: I love bastards. I am bastard begot, bastard instructed, bastard in mind, bastard in valour, in every-thing illegitimate' (V.vii. 16–18). Thersites does not stop at this self-denigration but denounces both his own mother and Margarelon's as whores. At the very least he is willing to pursue the truth to its ugliest conclusion. Interestingly, his summary of the war is very close to the judgement of the love-sick Troilus in the opening scene of the play:

Fools on both sides, Helen must needs be fair
When with your blood you daily paint her thus.

(I.i. 90–1)

It is in the very scene where Troilus perceives the folly of the war that there begins a series of comparisons between Helen and Cressida. For Troilus, Cressida cannot be equalled — 'In whose comparison all whites are ink' (I.i. 56); Pandarus sees his niece as being at least as fair as Helen. Later, when Helen's servant describes his mistress as 'the mortal Venus, the heart-blood of beauty, love's visible soul', Pandarus immediately responds 'Who, my cousin Cressida?' The serving man's riposte, 'No, sir, Helen: could not you find out that by her attributes?' (III.i. 31–5) is unintentionally telling: he has enumerated *all* her qualities. By the time that the luxurious, indolent and self-indulgent Helen makes her appearance Cressida has already revealed herself as shrewd and witty, and, like Helen, taking delight in sexual sugges-tion. Both women are light stuff, but of the two Cressida is clearly the more artful and vivacious. If she rivals Helen in beauty she has all the potential for surpassing her in faithlessness. A. P. Rossiter's comment is perhaps the fairest of the wide-ranging assessments of Cressida: 'her passion is quite genuine (so far as that goes); so is her grief at her separation from Troilus. Only nothing is deep-rooted in her.'[13] Having seen and heard Helen it comes as no shock when she is transformed to 'Nell' by Paris. When he says 'I would fain have armed today, but my Nell would not have it so' (III.i. 132–3) there is no dram of sympathy for this besotted lover: the 'honey-sweet queen' at the centre of this sickly scene has nothing with which she can captivate this imperceptive and weak-willed man apart from her beauty, and even that feels over-ripe. Troilus' young passion is understandable and evokes sympathy; Paris' self-indulgent doting elicits contempt. His closing line of the scene is ambiguous, carrying a distinctly different significance for the audience from that which he intends to convey: 'Sweet, above thought I love thee' (III.i. 155).

This scene also contains a comic presentation of the theme of identity. Helen's servant leads Pandarus a merry dance by deliberately misunderstanding his questions. In answer to Pandarus' question 'You know me, do you not?' the servant replies ambiguously 'Faith, sir, superficially' (III.i. 9–10). He knows Pandarus 'slightly' but well enough (either by quick assessment or past experience) to know that he can make a fool of him. Additionally, Pandarus is such a light character that brief acquaintance is sufficient to plumb his depths. Alas, for Troilus he has already asked the question 'What Cressid is, what Pandar, and what we' (I.i. 99) without achieving a true assessment. Oates and Stein both make interesting suggestions about Troilus' perceptions and the reality of the situation. Stein claims that Troilus 'seems overrefined, as from an effort to spiritualise the sensual . . . She is underrefined . . . we notice a kind of gross directness barely disguised. She has a trick . . . of slyly provoking immodest jokes at which she then can be embarrassed.'[14] Oates comments, 'Troilus' tragedy is his failure to distinguish between the impulses of the body and those of the spirit. His "love" for Cressida, based upon a Platonic idea of her fairness and chastity, is a ghostly love without an object;' she goes on to add, 'he does not see that it is really a lustful love based upon his desire for her body . . . Troilus' youthful lust is a lust of innocence that tries to define itself in terms of the spiritual and the heavenly.'[15] If the shrewd Cressida does not exhibit self-knowledge she reveals an understanding of the position of women in relation to men:

Yet hold I off. Women are angels, wooing:
Things won are done; joy's soul lies in the doing.
That she belov'd knows naught that knows not this:
Men prize the thing ungain'd more than it is.
. . .
Then though my heart's content firm love doth bear,
Nothing of that shall from mine eyes appear.

(I.ii. 291 – 300)

While Cressida gives expression to a general truth she misjudges both Troilus and herself: he is genuinely lost in love, whereas she merely feels the youthful stirrings of physical passion.

The most comic example of the treatment of identity and character occurs when Aeneas seeking Agamemnon asks how may

A stranger to those most imperial looks
Know them from eyes of other mortals?

(I.iii. 222 – 3)

Agamemnon is understandably baffled. He is not accustomed to such courtesy and can only gasp 'How?' Clearly this raises the question of whether a commander necessarily looks like a leader. If the leader is a nonentity then he will probably be indistinguishable from his fellows. Evidently Aeneas has before him a group of men who appear equally impressive or unimpressive. He has, therefore, to press his questions further:

Which is that god in office, guiding men?
Which is the high and mighty Agamemnon?

(I.iii. 230 – 1)

Agamemnon is unsure whether Aeneas is being ironic or whether the Trojans are 'ceremonious courtiers'. This scene neatly highlights the question of identity and character. Does a man occupying a position of high status necessarily look imposing? Whether he does or not, is he in any way impressive? Agamemnon never appears impressive and Thersites' estimation of him seems right. His counterpart in the Trojan camp probably looks more imposing but apart from his shrewd chastisement of Paris appears merely as nominal leader of the Trojans. Hector is the true leader. Like Agamemnon, Priam is a cipher. If the Greeks have a leader it is Ulysses, though he does not possess the status of Hector who

117

represents both the head and arm of the Trojans. Achilles is the arm of the Greeks but has no voice in the managing of the war.

The scene in which the Greek head attempts to set the Greek arm in motion again probes the issue of identity and character. Does a man have an essence or is he merely the aggregation of his actions? If the latter then a man may be easily transformed: the triumph of Ajax over Hector will make him the supreme man and relegate the inactive Achilles to the second rank. The deliberate slighting of Achilles by the Greek leaders causes him to ask 'know they not Achilles?' Here he means 'Do they not recognise me?' However, his mind quickly turns to the issues of social recognition in the sense of respect:

> for men, like butterflies,
> Show not their mealy wings but to the summer,
> And not a man, for being simply man,
> Hath any honour, but honour for those honours
> That are without him — as place, riches, and favour:
> (III.iii. 78–82)

Having reached this state of apprehension Ulysses reinforces the conclusion by proposing — via the book that he is supposedly reading — that there can be no such thing as intrinsic worth because all esteem is the consequence of socially acclaimed action. Moreover, he adds the telling point that reputation has to be constantly renewed because Time quickly erases past achievement. Although Ulysses is deliberately attempting to seduce Achilles back into action there is no reason to believe that he is simply 'making up' a convenient line of argument. Ulysses is using a social generalisation which is sound and employing it for a practical purpose, but it presses hard against the issue of identity, character and recognition. Reputation or fame are precarious possessions — 'Prizes of accident as oft as merit' (III.iii. 83) — and may be acquired by men of little intrinsic moral worth. Antenor, who is reputed to have the finest wit in Troy, appropriately, says nothing. (This seems a particularly deft touch by Shakespeare for in Caxton, for instance, the wise Antenor 'spache moche'.)

The frequent references to value suggest a contrast between attempting to assess the moral worth of something compared with the value or price that emerges in the market place. It is the values associated with trade and commerce which prevail. When Diomedes denounces Helen, Paris retaliates with an example drawn from the sharp practice of commerce. Similarly, Ulysses, in pressing the case for Ajax as representative of the Greeks against Hector, once more draws on the practices of tradesmen who attempt to sell the customer shoddy goods and resort to producing the best wares only for insistent and discriminating buyers. In the world of this play men are constantly weighed by one another, and generally enjoy seeing their fellows undervalued or rated at a low price by others. When Cressida mischievously praises Achilles, Pandarus denounces him as 'A drayman, a porter, a very camel' (I.ii. 253). Significantly Pandarus dismisses the common soldiers — who fight without having a voice in the proceedings and do not have a single line in the play (they simply pass over the stage) — as 'Asses, fools, dolts, chaff and bran, chaff and bran; porridge after meat' (I.ii. 245–6). Perhaps the best example of devaluation occurs as the epilogue to Ulysses' degree speech when he describes Patroclus' ridicule of Agamemnon and Nestor in the 'pageant' which he provides for the highly amused Achilles. Moreover, Nestor reports that this drama is apparently rivalled in Ajax's tent where Thersites — 'a slave whose gall coins slanders like a mint' (I.iii. 193) is encouraged by Ajax:

> To match us in comparisons with dirt
> To weaken and discredit our exposure,
>
> (I.iii. 194–5)

Of course, the dramatic director, Ajax, is himself later the subject of Thersites' impersonation. He is described as being so transformed by pride that he mistakes Thersites for Agamemnon. As Thersites says: 'What think you of this man, that takes me for the general? He's grown a very land-fish, languageless, a monster. A plague of opinion' (III.iii. 261–3). Pride has made Ajax incapable of making the most obvious distinction, and the loss of this ability transforms a man to a monster — without judgement, language is superfluous, ineffective; he is indeed languageless. Overvaluation of self dislocates the individual from the society.

Whilst drunk with 'opinion' Ajax is exposed to the ridicule of Agamemnon, Nestor and Ulysses. He is puffed up to the point where he denounces the pride of Achilles and protests that he knows no taint of it:

Ajax.   What is he more than another?
Agamemnon. No more than what he thinks he is.

Ajax.	Is he so much? Do you not think he thinks himself a better man than I am?
Agamemnon.	No question.
Ajax.	Will you subscribe his thought, and say he is?
Agamemnon.	No, noble Ajax; you are as strong, as valiant, as wise; no less noble, much more gentle, and altogether more tractable.
Ajax.	Why should a man be proud? How doth pride grow? I know not what pride is.

(II.iii. 144–54)

This is a telling exchange that succinctly focuses on worth, evaluation and self-esteem. These giant heroes are valued for their fighting prowess but they are not admired, because they estimate men by a single quality which they happen to possess and are unaware of their deficiencies — pride and lack of intellect (Ajax is as wise = foolish, as Achilles). Moreover, the pressure of emulation is tangible in the dialogue: their actions are intended to gain them a position of pre-eminence rather than to commit themselves to the common cause. For them, war is a matter of personal glory, not sacrifice. (Significantly, Shakespeare drops Achilles' comment in Caxton where he articulates a preference for survival over quest of further glory on the battlefield.) Of course, the quality which Agamemnon genuinely admires and wishes they possessed is tractability. For the Greek leadership these men are merely human battering rams. Here again we have the identification ambiguity: Ajax means that pride is so alien to him that he knows no taint of it; but to his auditors it signifies that he can't even recognise his own pride. When Ajax describes Achilles as 'A paltry, insolent fellow!' Nestor comments in an aside 'How he describes himself!' (II.iii. 209–10) The whole scene rises to a crescendo of ridicule as Ajax is exposed as possessing the very qualities which he attributes to Achilles and which he professes to despise. The Greek leaders have so completely beguiled the simple-minded Ajax that Ulysses concludes the process by saying:

Thank the heavens, lord, thou art of sweet composure;
Praise him that gat thee, she that gave thee suck;
Fam'd be thy tutor, and thy parts of nature
Thrice fam'd beyond, beyond all erudition;

(II.iii. 240–3)

After proceeding to the just praise of Ajax's physical attributes,

Ulysses concludes by proclaiming Ajax the intellectual equal of Nestor:

> Here's Nestor,
> Instructed by the antiquary times —
> He must, he is, he cannot but be wise;
> But pardon, father Nestor, were your days
> As green as Ajax', and your brain so temper'd,
> You should not have the eminence of him,
> But be as Ajax.
>
> (II.iii. 250–6)

Ulysses' irony is intended to expose Ajax to the full blast of ridicule. However, there is another question raised by this example: is Nestor really wise despite his antiquity? From what has been seen of Nestor it would require very little intelligence to equal his. Ulysses' crucial line is revealing, 'He must, he is, he cannot but be wise'. There is no evidence of his wisdom, merely an implied appeal to an equation between age and wisdom. Indeed, it is remarkable that Nestor can have lived so long and have gained so little understanding. When Ajax meekly asks Nestor 'Shall I call you father?' his simplicity provokes laughter, but in a play in which relationships are so frequently mentioned the choice of adopted father for Ajax is appropriate rather than ludicrous.

Nestor also has a connection with Hector, having fought with his grandfather, and so he is able not only to assess Hector's martial qualities in terms of the present age, but also in comparison with his own ancestors:

> I knew thy grandsire,
> And once fought with him: he was a soldier good;
> But by great Mars, the captain of us all,
> Never like thee.
>
> (IV.v. 195–8)

The generous Nestor draws a distinction between seeing Hector in armour (the soldier) and seeing the man:

> And I have seen thee pause, and take thy breath,
> When that a ring of Greeks have sharp'd thee in,
> Like an Olympian wrestling. This have I seen,
> But this thy countenance, still lock'd in steel,
> I never saw till now.
>
> (IV.v. 191–5)

He implies a distinction between the war machine and the man behind it. Nestor feels an excitement at coming face to face with the hero and is evidently delighted when Hector embraces him — 'Let me embrace thee, good old chronicle' (IV.v. 201). Here is a mutual respect: Hector is put in direct touch with history and Nestor clasps heroic destiny in his arms; they are flesh and emblems. The sense of excitement at seeing and talking with the unarmed Hector is general, but the duality of Hector is maintained throughout the scene. Ulysses continues the pattern by saying:

I wonder now how yonder city stands
When we have here her base and pillar by us?

(IV.v. 210–11)

However, after reminding Hector of his embassy and his prophesy of the destruction of Troy, Ulysses addresses him with the respect and warmth of a friend, 'Most gentle and most valiant Hector, welcome'. These two have an easy relationship despite possessing a full understanding of their situation, which makes the intrusion of Achilles all the more distasteful:

Now, Hector, I have fed mine eyes on thee;
I have with exact view perus'd thee, Hector,
And quoted joint by joint.

(IV.v. 230–2)

Hector's initial response to Achilles' pride and arrogance is to examine him only briefly, but when he insists on viewing Hector as a victim, the latter responds:

O, like a book of sport thou'lt read me o'er;
But there's more in me than thou understand'st.
Why dost thou so oppress me with thine eye?

(IV.v. 238–40)

Apart from Achilles the Greeks behave with respect towards Hector because of his achievements on the battlefield and because he is a generous and courteous human being. Achilles, despite having earlier spoken of possessing a 'woman's longing' to see Hector 'in his weeds of peace' (III.iii. 236–8), seeks only an adversary. He thinks that he can assess the warrior from what he sees before him, but that is an illusion. There is more in Hector than can be seen with the eye. His substance is more formidable than his limbs. There is an intangible quality to a man which at best is within easy reach only of the discerning eye.

Achilles' behaviour is so out of place that the Greeks are embarrassed and even Ajax steps in with a courteous word to restrain Hector — 'Do not chafe thee, cousin' — before chastising Achilles. At one level this is a natural tension arising from a realisation by the two men that it is their fight which will eventually determine the outcome of the war, but it also focuses attention on the question of the essential man and those attributes which make him admired or feared. Clearly, Achilles is merely a bully: a nonentity without his physical strength. What he reveals of his nature here is sufficient to prepare the audience for his final act of duplicity. Indeed, before the meeting with Hector, Achilles is planning to secure an advantage over his rival by giving him excess wine:

> I'll heat his blood with Greekish wine tonight,
> Which with my scimitar I'll cool tomorrow.
> Patroclus, let us feast him to the height.

> (V.i. 1–3)

Despite Achilles' reputation as a fighting machine, there are no descriptions of his performance on the battlefield, in contrast with the colourful accounts of Hector's prowess and magnanimity, and he is only twice seen fighting: on the first occasion he retires from the fight with Hector even though he is a fresh man fighting a tired one; and on the second he appears like a gang leader as his Myrmidons slay Hector in a brutal and cowardly manner. He then follows this despicable act by trailing Hector's corpse around the battlefield: a savage and shameful act, but one which epitomises the man. Instinctively Troilus refers to him as a murderer and a coward although he does not know the circumstances of Hector's death.

But if Achilles appears near the foot of the ladder of human worth in this play, Hector does not stand close to the top. He has gambled the survival of Troy in pursuit of honour and has hopelessly misjudged the values that animate the arena in which he excels. Excess of generosity costs him his life. Northrop Frye makes the interesting point that 'One word frequently associated with Hector is "live"': he dislikes killing people unless they are enemies of a type that fall within his strictly defined heroic code, and the contrast with Achilles, examining Hector and gloating with such pleasure over the idea of killing in itself, is a sharper form of the contrast between the romantic and realistic worlds'.[16] Though he is warm-hearted and generous he is not above hunting a man for his armour. The glittering armour covers a rotten body, just as the heroic language covers a rotten cause, and as ideas of romantic love obscure sexual licentiousness. Ultimately Hector must be judged a fool and the young 'Trojan ass' Troilus has learned nothing. Gazing into the eyes of defeat he rages for ultimate destruction; having been deceived by Cressida he turns off Pandarus with contempt:

> Hence, broker-lackey! Ignomy and shame
> Pursue thy life, and live aye with thy name!
>
> (V.x. 33–4)

But he has not learned to distinguish between types of women; he has become totally disillusioned. All the questions about identity, character and values create a picture of human folly on a grand scale. Distaste for the ostensible cause of the war cannot prevent both sides from pursuing a costly, futile and destructive struggle. The course of the war finally turns on the relative 'strength' of the two strongest battering rams. Ironically, the muscle power that is so necessary to the Greek triumph is viewed with contempt by the leaders. Moreover, one of the Greeks' best fighters is half-Trojan. It is not surprising that the dominant imagery of the play relates to animals, cooking, eating and regurgitation.

If the physical takes precedence over the intellectual in the war story, the same can be said of the 'love' stories. The urgent drives of sex and luxury obliterate signs of finer feelings. Troilus is dedicated to both Cressida and the war but his failure to join his mental faculties with his passion ensures the annihilation of his love and his city. One of the ways in which the play conveys a sense of the inadequacy of intellectual power and genuine social values is through the abundance of messengers. This is part of the indirection of the action. Pandarus is, of course, the professional go-between, but Ajax needs Thersites to read the proclamation; Aeneas spends most of his time trudging between two camps; Diomedes is sent for Cressida; Achilles will not be spoken to by his own general but has messages transmitted by his friend Patroclus; and news of Hector's death is carried through the field by Achilles' Myrmidons. The leaders of the two armies never meet to discuss the war. Yet in the midst of all this to-ing and fro-ing there are dire warnings about the outcome. Cassandra is unequivocal; Calchas has already predicted the future, and the play is littered with references to omens and destiny. Men recognise the reality of the past and the future but cannot summon the will to shape the future by hard intellectual endeavour. Greeks and Trojans are truly the prisoners and fools of time.

Finally, how do we connect the love story and the war story? What does an understanding of the identification process do to clarify the nature of this connection? The war is scrutinised by several characters and is perhaps best summed up by Diomedes and Thersites. Hector and Troilus have already condemned the war and justify it essentially on the grounds that it affords the opportunity of acquiring 'honour'. Likewise, the love story is commented upon both directly and indirectly: Diomedes' advances to Cressida are immediate; the evaluation of her by the Greek leaders is instantaneous; and Troilus, Ulysses and the ubiquitous Thersites all view her betrayal. Thus the emptiness of the justification for the war is exposed — Helen is 'not worth what she doth cost the keeping' (II.ii. 52) — and the faithlessness of Cressida is perceived before the betrayal and the betrayal itself observed. Put crudely, the love affair and the war are both a sham. So, too, are the characters. They are all scrutinised and commented upon by other characters and the conclusions are invariably unflattering. Perhaps the most attractive character is Hector but he lets himself down twice — once during the debate and secondly when he chases and kills a man for his armour. Moreover, his failure to comprehend the nature of the world in which he lives costs him his life. In fact, his failure is the greatest in the play because his responsibility is the greatest and he betrays it, not through cowardice but through folly. Joyce Carol Oates mis-guidedly claims that once Hector 'relinquishes the "game" of chivalry, he relinquishes his own right to be treated like a human being'.[17] His fatal error occurs prior to the armour incident: it happens when Hector chivalrously lets Achilles live. The fact that Hector becomes even more vulnerable through acquisitiveness is simply another irony in the situation. He dies, paradoxically, through both *fulfilling and violating* his code.

Hector has to be judged not only as a soldier — a role in which he is supreme — but as a leader and decision-maker. His counter-parts in the Greek camp are notably ineffective, even Ulysses the most attractive and clear-sighted of them. The catastrophe of the annihilation of Troy, Shakespeare implies, was not a matter of fate or destiny — though the references to predictions are numerous — but the consequences of human action and inaction. We see a civilisation moving inexorably towards the precipice but lacking the imagination and will to turn back. By exposing and interpreting characters with such frequency and deliberation, Shakespeare enables us to witness the process of the calamity with singular clarity. We know the nature of the participants and many of them know each other. We see only the people at the top: leaders and warrior heroes, but we perceive the consequences for the voiceless. Antenor, one of the shrewdest minds in Troy, says nothing, presumably because he possesses sufficient knowledge of the people who matter, to know that comment would be futile. In this play Shakespeare seems at pains to deny the significance of amorphous social forces, and portrays actions as the outcome of personal qualities and interactions. Troy does mirror Ulysses' picture of the ordered social and cosmic hierarchies: the common men must steadily bleed and eventually endure mass slaughter because their leaders lack compassion, wisdom and will. The Greeks, too, despite their ultimate victory, are ravaged and desolated by the war — though they did not constitute the historic symbol that Troy embodied for Shakespeare's audience. Ironically, had Thersites been made the General, as he is momentarily by Ajax, the Greeks would have sailed home early leaving behind them the 'Grecian whore' and the 'Trojan drab'.

Before examining the leading metaphors and similes in the play it is worth noting two examples of the subtly delicate imagery which connect the key elements. Early in the play Alexander tells Cressida how Hector has been so angered by being knocked down in battle by Ajax that he can't wait to get back into action:

> And like as there were husbandry in war,
> Before the sun rose he was harness'd light
> And to the field goes he, where every flower
> Did as a prophet weep what it foresaw
> In Hector's wrath.

(I.ii. 7 – 11)

First there is a comparison and contrast between the labour that forms part of the life-giving process of producing food with the life-destroying activity of war. Second, there is the astonishingly delicate image of flowers weeping at the prospect of mutilation

126

and death. Typical of this play is the disjunction between action and response: the flowers weep in anticipation of what will happen just as Cassandra invites the Trojans to weep before Troy is destroyed. Frequently future events are predicted or visualised, and in the latter case the future imaginatively becomes the present as when Cassandra describes Hector's death to him before he sets out to fight on the fateful day (it is so vivid, with the future being described in the present tense, that Hector, too, sees himself die before the event).

The second example occurs late in the play when Nestor provides a thrilling description of Hector wreaking havoc among the Greeks.

> There is a *thousand* Hectors in the field;
> Now *here* he fights on Galathe his horse
> And *here* lacks work: annon he's *there* afoot,
> And *there* they fly, or die, like scaled sculls
> Before the belching whale; then is he *yonder*,
> And *there* the strawy Greeks, ripe for his edge,
> Fall down before him like a mower's swath.
> *Here, there*, and *everywhere*, he leaves and takes,
> Dexterity so obeying appetite
> That what he will he does, and does *so much*
> That proof is call'd impossibility.
>
> (V.v. 19-29)

Once more there is the image of the farmer, but the actions of this 'mower' are not life-enhancing but life-destroying. Here we have a sense of incongruity through the 'unnaturalness' of the association of the mower with the soldier. Again there is incongruity through evidence or proof being denied: Hector seems to be 'everywhere'; his deeds are so astonishing that they simply can't be the work of one man — there are a 'thousand Hectors in the field'. Finally, there is the central image of appetite which elicits a response proportional to its own enormity.

Appetite is a central concern in *Troilus and Cressida*: both honour and sexual gratification are greedily sought. Pandarus portrays the whole process of courtship in terms of baking and cautions Troilus lest he burn his lips (I.i. 15-26). At the other extreme Ulysses depicts the all devouring nature of gross appetite as 'an universal wolf'.

> Then everything includes itself in power,
> Power into will, will into appetite,
> And appetite, an universal wolf,
> So doubly seconded with will and power,
> Must make perforce an universal prey,
> And last eat up himself.

(I.iii. 119–24)

Here is a paradox which is typical of the play: appetite is so all consuming that it devours itself. As Thersites says of Troilus and Diomedes when he loses sight of them on the battlefield:

> I think they have swallowed one another. I would laugh at that miracle; yet in a sort lechery eats itself.

(V.iv. 33–5)

Agamemnon insists that 'He that is proud eats up himself' (II.iii. 156). Another aspect of an excess of eating is regurgitation and even the troops leaving the Grecian ships are perceived in terms of being disgorged (Prologue, line 12). Pandarus describes the common soldiers following the heroes as 'chaff and bran; porridge after meat' (I.ii. 245–6). Nestor sees the emulation of Ajax and Achilles as the bait to goad them into action:

> Two curs shall tame each other: pride alone
> Must tar the mastiffs on, as 'twere their bone.

(I.iii. 391–2)

Troilus, anticipating the consummation of his love with Cressida, says:

> Th'imaginary relish is so sweet
> That it enchants my sense: what will it be
> When the wat'ry palate tastes indeed
> Love's thrice-repured nectar?

(III.ii. 17–20)

But his use of food imagery is more characteristic of the play when he experiences betrayal by Cressida:

> The fractions of her faith, orts of her love,
> The fragments, scraps, the bits, and greasy relics
> Of her o'er-eaten faith are given to Diomed.

(V.ii. 157–9)

Appetite is seldom natural in this play: it is excessive and focuses on scraps or dregs ('the remainder viands' (II.ii. 71) is another of Troilus' expressions) and the sickness or regurgitation which follows, such as Achilles' complaint:

> I have a woman's longing,
> An appetite that I am sick withal,
> To see great Hector in his weeds of peace,
>
> (III.iii. 236 – 8)

One of the few examples in the play of not eating to excess is packed with irony as Achilles says of his sword which has been plunged into Hector's corpse:

> My half-supp'd sword, that frankly would have fed,
> Pleas'd with this dainty bait, thus goes to bed.
>
> (V.viii. 19 – 20)

Disease imagery occurs early in the play and runs right through from the 'open ulcer' of Troilus' heart in the opening scene (I.i. 53) to Pandarus' sickly complaint about his aching bones in the epilogue which concludes with the word 'diseases'. In between, disease imagery has pervaded the play reaching its apogee in Thersites' colourful denunciation of Patroclus:

> Now the rotten diseases of the south, the guts-griping, ruptures, catarrhs, loads o'gravel i'th'back, lethargies, cold palsies, raw eyes, dirt-rotten livers, whissing lungs, bladders full of impostume, sciaticas, lime-kilns i'th'palm, incurable bone-ache, and the rivelled fee-simple of the tetter, take and take again such preposterous discoveries!
>
> (V.i. 16 – 23)

Again, body references and imagery abound, ranging from the metaphorical dismemberment of Cressida by Troilus — 'Her eyes, her hair, her cheek, her gait, her voice' (I.i. 54) — and the desired division of Ajax by Hector (IV.v. 119 – 35) through to the literal mutilation of the Myrmidons 'That noseless, handless, hack'd and chipp'd' (V.v. 34) run to Achilles for help. The eye — 'That most pure spirit of sense' (III.iii. 106) — is given a special place in the play. The upside-down nature of the world is epitomised by Ajax 'who wears his wit in his belly and his guts in his head'

(II.i. 75–6). Animal imagery is also pervasive and most strikingly men are equated with animals, especially the physical giants of Greece, Ajax and Achilles, who are used like 'draught-oxen' to 'plough up the wars' (II.i. 108–9). Alexander likens Ajax to the lion, the bear and the elephant (I.ii. 19–21); Ulysses describes him as a 'horse' (III.iii. 126); Pandarus dismisses Achilles as a 'camel' (I.ii. 253); Thersites denounces Patroclus as a 'whoreson indistinguishable cur' (V.i. 27–8), ridicules Paris as a 'dog', Menelaus as a 'bull' and describes himself and Margarelon as bears (V.vii. 10–19); Thersites also describes Menelaus as both 'ass and ox' (V.i. 59). When he gets into his stride Ajax and Achilles are described as curs, Troilus as an 'ass' and Ulysses as a 'dog-fox' while Nestor is depicted as a 'mouse-eaten dry cheese' (V.iv. 6–15). But animal references are not limited to abuse. As the retreat is sounded after the death of Hector, Achilles' comment 'The dragon wing of night o'er-spreads the earth' (V.viii. 17) provides a powerful image of darkness descending on the battlefield while simultaneously presaging the long night which will culminate in the destruction of Troy.

Imagery of trade and commerce is used frequently and to great effect in bringing down all ostensible values to market prices, as in Troilus' description of Helen:

Is she worth keeping? — Why, she is a pearl
Whose price hath launch'd above a thousand ships,
And turn'd crown'd kings to merchants.

(II.ii. 82–4)

Every reference to trade depicts it as an activity in which men behave deviously. As Ulysses comments to Nestor in advocating the choice of Ajax over Achilles as an opponent to face Hector:

Let us like merchants
First show foul wares, and think perchance they'll sell:
If not,
The lustre of the better shall exceed
By showing the worse first.

(I.iii. 358–62)

Cressida becomes an item of merchandise, as Calchas says that the Trojan prisoner Antenor can be used to 'buy' his daughter (III.iii. 28). When Diomed has delivered his devastating assessment of Helen to Paris the latter responds:

> Fair Diomed, you do as chapmen do,
> Dispraise the thing that they desire to buy;
> But we in silence hold this virtue well,
> We'll not commend, that not intend to sell.

(IV.i. 76–9)

Thus the imagery of trade is used to reinforce the undermining of proclaimed values. This is a world of market transactions and sharp practice masquerading as high-principled conflict. Only Hector fails to recognise the social reality that lies behind the façade of chivalric rhetoric.

In an intriguing essay Raymond Southall devotes particular attention to the nature and function of imagery in the play. He argues that Troilus 'almost invariably thinks of Cressida with his belly; beginning as a tasty titbit yet to be enjoyed she ends as a piece of left-over meat' and goes on to suggest that 'the whole of the play is busily reducing life to the demands of the belly'.[18] Southall sees this imagery as serving Shakespeare's purpose to expose the essential underlying nature of the new value system which had gained ascendancy by the close of the sixteenth century. 'Ulysses's contention that "appetite" is "a universal wolf" (I.iii.) touches the very quick of Shakespeare's conception of the spirit of capitalism as a force which reduces life to the mere satisfaction of the appetites.'[19] Moreover, he perceives a close connection between the imagery of appetite and the disease imagery. Citing Ulysses' diagnosis of the 'envious fever' which thwarts the Greeks (I.iii. 132–5) and Thersites' description of Agamemnon's imagined boils (II.i. 2–9) Southall concludes that 'disease is closely associated with the appetites and infects the blood and only gradually makes its presence felt'.[20] Likewise he focuses sharply on the 'vocabulary of trade' which he sees as expressing 'the central preoccupations of the play'.[21] Trading, bargaining, and dealing dominated interpersonal relations for the first time, so that the ethic to which men responded was not that espoused by the church but that which existed in the market-place. Southall quotes John Wheeler, Thomas Nashe and Thomas Dekker in support of his claim about the nature and force of the prevailing acquisitive and manipulative sensibility. Even the great theme of Time, which is so significant in the play, Southall sees as being integral to the dominant conception of appetite. Quoting Troilus' famous lines:

Injurious Time now with a robber's haste
Crams his rich thiev'ry up, he knows not how;
As many farewells as be stars in heaven,
With distinct breath and consign'd kisses to them,
He fumbles up into a loose adieu,
And scants us with a single famish'd kiss
Distasted with the salt of broken tears.

(IV.iv. 41–7)

Southall goes on to claim that

> The thematic function of Time here is simply to define the
> sensibility of Troilus and, consequently, that of the play:
> Time is appetitive, sensual and limiting — Time with 'haste
> Crams his rich thiev'ry up . . . And scants us with a single
> famish'd kiss, Distasted . . .'; more especially, Time is
> lecherous — 'He fumbles up into a loose adieu'; there can be
> little doubt as to the dominant sense of the ambiguous word
> 'loose' (cf. 'loose woman').[22]

Part of the richness and density of the play is that there is a good
deal to be said for this argument, but it is incomplete in terms of
the treatment of Time. Time is perceived as an arbiter by Hector
in his dispute with Ulysses. When the latter claims that his
prophesy 'is but half his journey yet' Hector responds:

                    and modestly I think
The fall of every Phrygian stone will cost
A drop of Grecian blood. The end crowns all;
And that old common arbitrator, Time,
Will one day end it.

(IV.v. 217–25)

Time in this context is seen as neutral, standing outside the hurly-
burly of human affairs. When Hector embraces Nestor who 'hast
so long walk'd hand in hand with Time' (IV.v. 202) he is put in
touch with the past by means of a man who is capable of making a
direct comparison between Hector and his grandfather.
Agamemnon in welcoming Hector attempts to create a present
which is cocooned from past and future:

What's past and what's to come is strew'd with husks
And formless ruin of oblivion;

> (IV.v. 165 – 6)

Ulysses in attempting to seduce Achilles back into the fighting warns how Time erases past endeavours and achievements so that only present actions count:

> O let not virtue seek
> Remuneration for the thing it was;
> For beauty, wit,
> High birth, vigour of bone, desert in service,
> Love, friendship, charity, are subjects all
> To envious and calumniating Time.
> . . .
> The present eye praises the present object:

> (III.iii. 169 – 80)

Here time is portrayed as anything but neutral; it is active, eagerly seeking to destroy. But is Time all powerful and does Ulysses believe what he says? If the philosophical perspective is accepted then even fame won in battle is so ephemeral as to be hardly worth fighting for. The quest for distinction becomes a treadmill. Thus while Ulysses' argument is of questionable value to his purpose it serves to slow the pace of the play and invite a response to the contemplation of the nature of Time which transcends the immediate considerations. Time, then, is not simply subservient to other themes but constitutes a major concern of the play. What is Time? Is it something abstract and neutral or an active participant in human affairs which inflicts itself on men's consciousness? Cressida visualises a process of atrophy which encompasses everything including Time:

> When time is old and hath forgot itself,
> When water-drops have worn the stones of Troy,
> And blind oblivion swallow'd cities up,
> And mighty states characterless are grated
> To dusty nothing —

> (III.ii. 183 – 7)

Ulysses tells Nestor

133

I have a young conception in my brain:
Be you my time to bring it to some shape.

(I.iii. 311 – 12)

Here time is seen as a shaper of the embryo. Again he cautions
Achilles that

The providence that's in a watchful state
. . .
Do thoughts unveil in their dumb cradles.

(III.iii. 195 – 9)

And in several other places in the play there is a sense of things
moving from conception or infancy through to maturity or decay.
Time is seen as one of the key concepts in the human imagination:
it is an abstract tool, but because of human awareness of the limit
of terrestrial existence imposed by time it becomes a Protean
character on the stage of life; demon of the imagination and
impregnable enemy, it has to be defeated through the immorality
of fame or procreation. The theme is clearly too great to be
confined in the way Southall suggests, but it may well operate as
he claims in the context to which he refers. There can be little
doubt that Shakespeare was very conscious of the social and
economic changes taking place in his society and that these
developments find expression in the play. Consequently Southall's
essay provides a useful insight into an important dimension of the
drama. What is open to question is the validity of his argument
that Shakespeare is providing a critique of the new system and
expressing a preference of the older order with its greater emphasis
on personal relationships. Nevertheless, Southall's conclusion is of
considerable interest:

> The distinctively Shakespearian activity in the play, then,
> assesses the weakening of feudal relations that had taken place
> during the sixteenth century by bringing to bear upon a world
> of romance and chivalry (the world of the Trojan War as
> traditionally presented by medieval and Elizabethan writers)
> the powers of personal and social corruption inherent in the
> appetitive spirit of capitalism.[23]

Troilus and Cressida is not only the richest in imagery of the problem
plays, it is the most brilliantly versatile of all Shakespeare's plays.

It is not surprising that many critics see it as standing apart from *All's Well* and *Measure for Measure*. Its satire and irony are so subtle and powerful, and its central concern with mighty antagonists manoeuvring towards mutual destruction is so full of significance for the modern world that appreciation of the play continues to grow. During the last few years all three problem plays have been staged very effectively by the RSC with *All's Well* and *Troilus and Cressida* receiving high acclaim. Whatever the problems associated with these plays, it is clear that they are enormously enjoyable in the theatre, offering rich possibilities for directors and actors. In the 1985 Stratford production of *Troilus and Cressida* Juliet Stevenson played Cressida as a victim of war, being manhandled by the Greeks on entering their camp and only gradually acquiring the facility to stand up to them. Ulysses' acid comment on her was the result of being humiliated when he 'begg'd' a kiss. (She snapped her fingers and indicated that he should fall to his knees.) Menelaus appeared as a blockhead, part of the Greek leadership, but remaining a despised nonentity always in the background. As Ulysses began his famous 'Order' speech the slow-witted Agamemnon raised his eyes to the ceiling signalling that his 'intellectual' colleague was at best loquacious and at worst a windbag. Paris emerged as the most distasteful and self-indulgent character in the play, egotistic and self-important. Thersites firgured as a Geordie waiter and provided high comedy of astonishing brilliance. The decaying mansion which constituted the set epitomised the decadence that characterised the play. The golden Achilles was unkempt and surly, a degenerate to whom murder came naturally. Set in the period of the Crimean War the production had both swords and guns. The killing of Hector took the form of a firing squad, emphasising both his helplessness and naïvety.

One of the most fascinating scenes of this enormously rich and resonant production was III.i. The scene reeked of decadence. As disaster drew ever closer the audience were afforded a view of night life in the recesses of Troy: high-spirited debauchery constituted the essence of a scene which possessed two moments of poignancy: coarse gaiety was fractured for a second when Helen rested her forehead on Pandarus' chest and gave expression to a terrible anguish with the line 'this love will undo us all./O Cupid, Cupid, Cupid!' (III.i. 105–6) As the scene closed Paris was luxuriating in the garish Helen's beauty while she conveyed a sense of impotent desolation as she gazed beyond him to the audience and the world outside.

The suave, straw-hatted Pandarus occupied a central position in the production, opening the play by sitting at a table sipping wine and reading his paper and concluding by rising from the piano, pale, gaunt and half-blind. This jaunty voyeur goes out on a joke, more pathetic than tragic. Kenneth Muir has recently commented that 'Pandarus is one of the few' characters not motivated by 'self-interest',[24] but the Stratford production revealed Pandarus deriving enormous vicarious pleasure from the courtship of the young lovers (even joining in the embraces) and tingling with pleasure as he applauded Hector's physical prowess — and in doing so he formed a vital element in the pattern of incongruity which characterises the play. The destruction of Troy, like the collapse of other civilisations, contains much that is absurd and foolish. In Shakespeare's tragedies men's failures possess a grandeur that is moving; in *Troilus and Cressida* we are conscious of the unforgivable folly and incompetence of mankind: there is no consolation of failed greatness and Shakespeare intended none. For all its brilliant comedy *Troilus and Cressida* ends on a bleak note. As Pandarus left the stage in the Stratford production he turned suddenly to see the piano playing itself. The effect was to create a vision of artefacts remaining after the makers had destroyed themselves. This interpolation provided an image full of resonances for the modern audience. As one theatre critic commented on the concluding moments, 'If any one character sums up the mood of this production it is the Pandarus of Clive Merrison . . . who finally sits picking out a wistful tune on the piano as the lights of battle blaze and as structured society disintegrates. I found this a chilling moment: an unforgettable image of a collapsing civilisation.'[25]

All three problem plays have provoked vigorous debate and posed serious difficulties of interpretation. But whereas with *All's Well* and *Measure for Measure* the areas which have stimulated critical response can be clearly delineated, *Troilus and Cressida* has produced bewilderment and incomprehension. Theatregoers and critics have continued to ask such fundamental questions as: what *kind* of play is it? What is Shakespeare attempting to achieve? Consequently *Troilus and Cressida* offers the critic an unusual challenge. Despite the emergence of some valuable recent criticism, as the play has become increasingly appreciated, it still remains an enigma, creating an intense sense of bewilderment and perplexity. As Kenneth Palmer succinctly makes the point in his penetrating essay:

Part of the difficulty of coming to terms with *Troilus* derives
from a simple fact: that the structure, the language, the tone
of the play — even the possible methods of acting any given
scene — are all likely to be, in themselves or in relationship,
ambivalent. It seems an odd thing to say, since Shakespeare's
dramatic technique relies heavily in most of the plays upon
the juxtaposition of similar or opposed attitudes or actions, so
that the audience may make a comparative judgement. But in
Troilus it is more than usually difficult to determine one's
response either to the single phenomenon or to the resultant
of the things compared. The whole play seems designed at
once to invite and to frustrate judgement: to insist upon the
relative at the expense of the absolute.[26]

This is precisely why the play offers such rich opportunities for
actors, directors and critics. The play invites reinterpretation and
reassessment of characters. What kind of person is Cressida? She
can be played convincingly in a number of ways ranging from a
daughter of the game to a victim of war. What sort of character is
Ulysses? Is he unsuccessful manipulator or intellectual leader?
Evidently Shakespeare intends to provoke a close questioning of
the nature and meaning of character: the perpetual commenting
on individuals and the insistent character evaluations heighten
awareness of the difficulty of determining what is the true nature of
a man or woman and the slippery nature of the concept of
character. Questions abound in this play as in no other play of
Shakespeare's. As characters probe and question aspects of their
social universe and their inner selves everything is subjected to
calculation, and separation into constituent parts. As the world of
Shakespeare's audience was becoming dominated by the language
and perceptions of trade and commerce so this play calls forth the
need for impersonal evaluations in order to reach logical conclusions. Against this process is set the human desire to act in conformity with predetermined desires and values. Troilus believes in
an all-consuming passionate love to the extent that he initially
denies the evidence of his senses: Cressida divides into two so that
the cheap one belongs to Diomedes. The Trojan appetite for
honour is so insatiable that seven years' destruction and the
prospect of annihilation cannot quell their ardour. Honour is
above measurement. Once that view is accepted there is no room
for rational argument. Throughout the verbal structure of the play
there is an insistence on measuring, calculating, evaluating,

questioning and testing. Both human ideals and appetites seek to evade this analysis, to stand above the petty concerns of the commerce of everyday life. All positions and all answers, the play implies, are tentative. The quest for absolutes is as natural as the endeavour to satisfy appetites, but as the latter frequently leads to excess, regurgitation and disease, so the headlong pursuit of moral absolutes can lead to destruction or even extinction. No wonder *Troilus and Cressida* is seen as Shakespeare's most disturbing and most modern play. Time itself is relative: we seek immortality in a world which affords only fleeting existence; all monuments decay and collapse; but that is not a reason for despair. Rather it should provoke a recognition that Time is not a single element or concept: it is both an expression of the imagination and a practical tool to be used in the process of living.

Notes

1. See Kenneth Muir (ed.), *Troilus and Cressida* (Oxford Shakespeare, Oxford, 1985), p. 8.
2. The relationship between the drama and the changing social and economic circumstances of Elizabethan and Jacobean society first received close critical scrutiny by L. C. Knights in his seminal book *Drama and Society in the Age of Jonson* (Chatto and Windus, London, 1937; Peregrine Books, 1962). One of the most recent and illuminating studies is that of Jonathan Dollimore, *Radical Tragedy: Religion, Ideology and Power in the Drama of Shakespeare and his Contemporaries* (Harvester Press, Brighton, 1984). Another interesting discussion of this question is to be found in Raymond Southall's essay, '*Troilus and Cressida* and the Spirit of Capitalism' in Arnold Kettle (ed.), *Shakespeare in a Changing World* (Lawrence and Wishart, London, 1964).
3. Jan Knott, 'Amazing and Modern' in Priscilla Martin (ed.), *Troilus and Cressida* (Casebook Series, Macmillan, London, 1976), p. 144.
4. Kenneth Palmer (ed.), *New Arden Shakespeare: Troilus and Cressida* (Methuen, London, 1982), p. 75.
5. Several critics have discussed at length the question of value which is so central to the debate scene. Some of the most illuminating comments are to be found in: Terence Eagleton, *Shakespeare and Society* (Chatto and Windus, London, 1970), pp. 24–6; Una Ellis-Fermor, 'The Universe of Troilus and Cressida' in Priscilla Martin (ed.), *Troilus and Cressida*, pp. 71–81.
6. Arnold Stein, 'The Disjunctive Imagination' in Martin (ed.), *Troilus and Cressida*, p. 189.
7. Kenneth Muir, 'Troilus and Cressida' in Kenneth Muir and Stanley Wells (eds), *Aspects of Shakespeare's 'Problem Plays'* (Cambridge University Press, Cambridge, 1982), p. 100.
8. Alvin Kernan, 'The Satiric Character of Thersites' in Martin (ed.),

Troilus and Cressida, pp. 96 – 9.

9. F. McAlindon, 'Language, Style and Meaning' in Martin (ed.), *Troilus and Cressida*, p. 209.

10. Una Ellis-Fermor, 'The Universe of *Troilus and Cressida*' in Martin (ed.), *Troilus and Cressida*, p. 79.

11. John Bayley, 'Time and the Trojans' in Martin (ed.), *Troilus and Cressida*, p. 228.

12. Joyce Carol Oates, 'Essence and Existence' in Martin (ed.), *Troilus and Cressida*, p. 175.

13. A. P. Rossiter, '*Troilus* as "Inquisition"' in Martin (ed.), *Troilus and Cressida*, p. 104.

14. Stein, 'The Disjunctive Imagination' in Martin (ed.), *Troilus and Cressida*, p. 187.

15. Oates, 'Essence and Existence' in Martin (ed.), *Troilus and Cressida*, p. 178.

16. Northrop Frye, 'The Ironic Vision' in Martin (ed.), *Troilus and Cressida*, p. 184.

17. Oates, 'Essence and Existence' in Martin (ed.), *Troilus and Cressida*, p. 169.

18. Raymond Southall, '*Troilus and Cressida* and the Spirit of Capitalism' in Arnold Kettle (ed.), *Shakespeare in a Changing World*, pp. 225 – 6.

19. Ibid., p. 227.

20. Ibid., p. 230.

21. Ibid., p. 226.

22. Ibid., p. 227.

23. Ibid., p. 231.

24. Muir (ed.), *Troilus and Cressida* (Oxford Shakespeare), p. 34.

25. Michael Billington, 'False Love Proves True', *Guardian*, 27 June 1985.

26. Palmer (ed.), *Arden Shakespeare*, p. 84.

4

Virtue and Honour in *All's Well that Ends Well*

A striking feature of *All's Well* is the way in which the play opens by specifying relationships and engaging the theme of virtue as an intrinsic quality which may be complementary to or in conflict with nominal status. In the opening line of the play the Countess expresses sorrow at the imminent departure of Bertram, but does so by emphasising the fundamental nature of family bonds: 'In delivering my son from me, I bury a second husband'. Bertram acknowledges his debt of affection to his dead father but counter-balances it with his duty to the King and his 'subjection' (line 5). However, this statement of Bertram's is to sound like a hollow formula in the light of his later disregard of the King's authority. No sooner has Bertram expressed himself formally than Lafew speaks of the King as a 'husband' to the Countess and 'father' to Bertram: formal bonds are to be affective ties. Lafew's confident reassurance to the Countess is based on knowledge of the King's virtue and her desert: 'He that so generally is at all times good must of necessity hold his virtue to you, whose worthiness would stir it up where it wanted, rather than lack it where there is such abundance' (I.i. 7–10).

The pattern is continued a few lines later with the first reference to Helena. She too has lost a father and has become the adoptive daughter of the Countess. Before extolling her virtues the Countess makes a remarkable statement about Helena's gifted father. Although, as Lafew comments, 'he was skilful enough to have liv'd still, if knowledge could be set up against mortality' (I.i. 28–9) the Countess describes him as one 'whose skill was almost as great as his honesty' (I.i. 17–18). Immediately there is a weighing and balancing of admirable qualities: if this man was

140

famous as a physician he must have been a man of total integrity for his honesty to surpass his skill. The implication is that honesty is valued even above life-saving skills. Characteristic of the problem plays is the way in which we plunge into a consideration of values.

The relationship between inherited qualities and education is developed by the Countess in her praise of Helena: 'I have those hopes of her good that her education promises her dispositions she inherits — which makes fair gifts fairer' (I.i. 36–8). Where skills and talents are cultivated but are at the disposal of an 'unclean mind' they are not to be admired. Rather, 'they are virtues and traitors too' (I.i. 40). The suggestion that talent and honesty do not always go together is followed by an awareness that integrity is not necessarily inherited. The Countess' farewell to Bertram expresses hope rather than certainty that he will prove worthy of his breeding:

> Be thou bless'd, Bertram, and succeed thy father
> In *manners* as in *shape*! Thy *blood* and *virtue*
> Contend for empire in thee, and thy *goodness*
> Share with thy birthright!
>
> (I.i. 57–60)

The Countess is aware that Bertram is on the brink of being tested for the first time in his life. His inexperience is revealed in her plea to Lafew:

> 'Tis an unseason'd courtier; good my lord,
> Advise him.
>
> (I.i. 67–8)

If the hope but uncertainty of inherited qualities is suggested by the Countess' speech, along with an awareness of the need for education and experience to bring intrinsic qualities to fruition, the idea of the child as preserver of the parent's reputation is brought out by Lafew's farewell to Helena: 'Farewell, pretty lady; you must hold the credit of your father' (line 75). It is ironic that Helena's tears are not for her famous father because she has already forgotten him. Indeed, the impression made by Bertram on her imagination is so powerful that it has erased all other images. Helena's soliloquy, in which she gives vent to her adoration of Bertram, possesses an ease and fluency which contrasts with the compacted speeches that precede it: analysis of concepts and values gives way to free flowing verse which is expressive of Helena's idealised love of Bertram:

> I am undone; there is no living, none,
> If Bertram be away; 'twere all one
> That I should love a bright particular star
> And think to wed it, he is so above me.
> In his bright radiance and collateral light
> Must I be comforted, not in his sphere.
> Th' ambition in my love thus plagues itself:
> The hind that would be mated by the lion
> Must die for love. 'Twas pretty, though a plague,
> To see him every hour; to sit and draw
> His arched brows, his hawking eye, his curls,
> In out heart's table — heart too capable
> Of every line and trick of his sweet favour.
> But now he's gone, and my idolatrous fancy
> Must sanctify his relics.
>
> (I.i. 82–96)

The immediate effect of this speech is to create a sense of surprise or incongruity. Helena's 'idolatrous fancy' seems strikingly at odds with Bertram's cold and detached comment to her 'Be comfortable to my mother, your mistress, and make much of her' (I.i. 73–4). Not only are they separated by a social gulf, but Bertram seems unaware of her as a young woman. Moreover, there is nothing in the early exchanges to suggest why Bertram should attract such admiration — other than the fact that he is a handsome young man. That Helena is not just a silly young girl is made clear by her shrewd assessment of Parolles: she recognises that he is a 'liar', 'fool' and 'coward', but rather than feeling contemptuous towards him she implies that these qualities don't create an altogether unattractive character. Helena quickly routs Parolles in a battle of wits which reveals an ease of manner that enables her to cope admirably with his bawdy talk and self-importance. It is her resilience and strength of character which are manifested in the closing speech of the scene:

> Our remedies oft in ourselves do lie,
> Which we ascribe to heaven; the fated sky
> Gives us free scope; only doth backward pull

Our slow designs when we ourselves are dull.
. . .
The mightiest space in fortune nature brings
To join like likes, and kiss like native things.

(I.i. 212–19)

Here Helena expounds a philosophy to underpin her action.
Leaving everything to heaven often serves as a pretext for
inaction; and frequently seemingly disparate things are brought
together and conjoined. If the audience feels any scepticism at this
stage it is not about her determination to be active but rather about
the worth of Bertram. Has this young woman so idealised the
object of her love that he will not prove worth the effort? Significantly, her enthusiastic description of him is confined to physical
characteristics: the comments of the Countess have been sufficient
to create an awareness of the possibility of a discrepancy between
intrinsic and extrinsic qualities. Moments later the King directs
the attention of the audience back to this duality with its potential
for conflict:

> Youth, thou bear'st thy father's face;
> Frank nature, rather curious than in haste,
> Hath well compos'd thee. Thy father's moral parts
> Mayest thou inherit too!

(I.ii. 19–22)

The King hopes rather than assumes that Bertram will inherit his
father's qualities.

When the King recalls Bertram's father he conveys a genuine
sense of loss: there is no feeling of respectful sentiment being the
due of the dead, but rather a picture is created of a man
remarkable for humour, tact and humanity. And when the King
reaches the climax of his praise it comes as something of a surprise:
his greatest virtue was an ability to communicate so easily with
men of all social levels that they felt comfortable with him, indeed
as if they were dealing with their social equal:

> Who were below him
> He us'd as creatures of another place,
> And bow'd his eminent top to their low ranks,
> Making them proud of his humility
> In their poor praise he humbled. Such a man

Might be a copy to these younger times;
Which, followed well, would demonstrate them now
But goers backward.

                                        (I.ii. 41–8)

The quality for which Bertram's father is most praised will be
found most markedly absent in Bertram. But the King's speech
suggests that Bertram should find it easier to shine as a consequence of the falling away in the present generation. The King
undoubtedly creates a sense of two distinct eras, with the present
being inferior to the former. While this could easily appear to be
part of the traditional expression that things are no longer what
they were, there is a feeling that the King is not merely responding
as a ageing man idealising the past. One of the minor links
between the problem plays is criticism of the obsession with the
new-fangled: Ulysses makes the point in *Troilus and Cressida*
(III.iii. 175–6); and so too does the disguised Duke in *Measure for
Measure* (III.ii. 217–20). Here the King attributes the view to
Bertram's father:

       'Let me not live,' quoth he,
    'After my flame lacks oil, to be the snuff
    Of younger spirits, whose apprehensive senses
    All but new things disdain; whose judgements are
    Mere fathers of their garments; whose constancies
    Expire before their fashions.'

                                        (I.ii. 58–63)

Just as in the opening scene the fathers of Bertram and Helena are
linked, the King turns to ask how long it has been since the death
of the physician who was 'much fam'd' (I.ii. 71). The King's
welcome to Bertram is concluded in a manner which expresses the
emotional bond which binds them through the father-friend:

              Welcome, count;
    My son's no dearer.

                                        (I.ii. 75–6)

So it is that both scenes focus sharply on human qualities through
recollections of Bertram's father and the father of Helena.

While the question of Bertram's worth remains open, Helena's
virtue is placed beyond question. On hearing of Helena's love of

Bertram the Countess makes clear her estimation of her adopted daughter.

> Her father bequeath'd her to me, and she herself, without other advantage, may lawfully make title to as much love as she finds; there is more owing her than is paid, and more shall be paid her than she'll demand.
>
> (I.iii. 97 – 101)

Moreover, the Countess insists that her feelings towards her adopted daughter are as great as those for her natural son. In expressing this feeling Shakespeare has the Countess employ his favourite source of imagery: horticulture (also used at a critical moment in *Measure for Measure* but virtually absent from *Troilus and Cressida*):

> I say I am your mother,
> And put you in the catalogue of those
> That were enwombed mine. 'Tis often seen
> Adoption strives with nature, and choice breeds
> A native slip to us from foreign seeds.
>
> (I.iii. 137 – 41)

This reference to 'foreign seeds' is critical, because for Bertram there can be no question of social equality between people of unequal descent. Whereas the Countess enthusiastically accepts Helena as her own, and eagerly embraces the prospect of her marriage to Bertram, and the King praises Bertram's father for his natural humility which enabled men of inferior birth to feel that they were being treated as equals, Bertram appears to have total contempt for such values. He exhibits a powerful sense of social superiority. However, before revealing his attitude in this important sphere Bertram expresses an enthusiasm for the value of military honour. He fears that he will be forced to stay at court 'Till honour be bought up' (II.i. 32).

When he is chosen by Helena he is not only vigorous in expressing his dislike of the proposal, but is positively insolent in responding to the King's question:

> Know'st thou not, Bertram,
> What she has done for me?

> Yes, my good lord,
> But never hope to know why I should marry her.
>
> (II.iii. 108–10)

Here is a clear breach of decorum which Bertram reiterates before going on to make the basis of his defiance clear:

> I know her well:
> She had her breeding at my father's charge —
> A poor physician's daughter my wife! Disdain
> Rather corrupt me ever!
>
> (II.iii. 113–16)

A great deal of special pleading has been made on Bertram's behalf — he is immature, too shocked to respond more cautiously, bitterly disappointed at being deprived of the excitement of being a young man at court and going off to the wars, etc. — but Shakespeare could hardly have made this character's feelings more explicit and unambiguous. To marry someone of Helena's social standing would be to suffer dishonour regardless of her personal qualities. Clearly for Bertram, unlike the King and his mother and father, status is everything; personal qualities are irrelevant. The King's reply constitutes a philosophical generalisation but is also a gentle attempt to persuade Bertram that he is mistaken:

> 'Tis only title thou disdain'st in her, the which
> I can build up. Strange is it that our bloods,
> Of colour, weight, and heat, pour'd all together,
> Would quite confound distinction, yet stands off
> In differences so mighty. If she be
> All that is virtuous, save what thou dislik'st —
> A poor physician's daughter — thou dislik'st
> Of virtue for the name. But do not so.
> From lowest place when virtuous things proceed,
> The place is dignified by th'doer's deed.
> Where great additions swell's and virtue none,
> It is a dropsied honour. Good alone
> Is good, without a name; vileness is so:
> The property by what it is should go,
> Not by the title. She is young, wise, fair;
> In these to nature she's immediate heir,
> And these breed honour; that is honour's scorn

Which challenges itself as honour's born
And is not like the sire. Honours thrive
When rather from our acts we them derive
Than our foregoers. The mere word's a slave,
Debosh'd on every tomb, on every grave
A lying trophy, and as oft is dumb,
Where dust and damn'd oblivion is the tomb
Of honour'd bones indeed. What should be said?
If thou canst like this creature as a maid,
I can create the rest. Virtue and she
Is her own dower; honour and wealth from me.

(II.iii. 117 – 44)

The King's response to Bertram is astonishing for its powerful insistence that assessment of human worth must be made in terms of character and action ('is', 'deed', 'breed', 'acts', all operate to generate a sense of action) rather than by means of social status or breeding. Starting at the fundamental physiological level the King makes a statement of fact that blood cannot be distinguished in terms of social status. Hence when the term 'blood' is being used as a means of making social distinctions it is operating as a metaphor not as a description of physiological reality. The King argues that the comparison must be between actions regardless of the status of the actors. He then goes one step further: high social standing cannot transform a bad action into a good deed. Finally, he insists that Helena has derived outstanding qualities from nature, which she may transmit to the next generation and so produce genuine honour, as opposed to the honour of title unsupported by virtuous character.

It is difficult to think of another speech in the whole of Shakespeare which sets forth this 'democratic' argument with such force and clarity. It is all the more remarkable coming from the King: a man who owes his position to inheritance of title. The argument does not necessarily undermine the principle of inheritance, the existence of an aristocracy or a hierarchical society, but it does imply that title and high status require virtuous behaviour — honour goes with actions not title — and that there should be no barrier to upward social mobility: not every virtuous and beautiful young woman can become a countess, but when she is chosen by a nobleman or is endowed with wealth (as Helena is by the King) there is no possible justification of citing humble birth as a means of casting doubt on the acceptability of such a marriage. The King in Shakespeare's source material does have momentary qualms about the marriage on social grounds; Shakespeare's King is unequivocal in his dismissal of the values enunciated by Bertram. Bertram's answer to the King's speech is surprising. When he insists, 'I cannot love her nor will strive to do't' (II.iii. 145), not only is he rejecting the social ethos advanced by the King, but he is also denying a vital social principle in his society: his duty to his monarch. The King reminds Bertram of this but not before Helena has attempted to relinquish her reward and the King has insisted that fulfilling his side of the bargain is a matter of honour:

> My honour's at the stake, which to defeat,
> I must produce my power. Here, take her hand,
> Proud, scornful boy, unworthy this good gift,
> That dost in vile misprision shackle up
> My love and her desert; that canst not dream
> We, poising us in her defective scale,
> Shall weigh thee to the beam; that wilt not know
> It is in us to plant thine honour where
> We please to have it grow. Check thy contempt;
> Obey our will which travails in thy good;
> Believe not thy disdain, but presently
> Do thine own fortunes that obedient right
> Which both thy duty owes and our power claims;
> Or I will throw thee from my care for ever
> Into the staggers and the careless lapse
> Of youth and ignorance; both my revenge and hate
> Loosing upon thee in the name of justice,
> Without all terms of pity. Speak. Thine answer.
>
> (II.iii. 149–66)

Only after Bertram has been warned that he will have no significant place in the court life of his society does he submit to the King's demand. What in the source material was a private transaction behind closed doors is in Shakespeare's play a public occasion which is embarrassing and humiliating to all three participants. Bertram's retreat is anything but dignified and stems quite clearly from a recognition of his own dependence on the King's favour:

> Pardon, my gracious lord; for I submit
> My fancy to your eyes. When I consider

What great creation and what dole of honour
Flies where you bid it, I find that she, which late
Was in my nobler thoughts most base, is now
The praised of the king; who, so ennobled,
Is as 'twere born so.

(II.iii. 167 – 73)

Having reiterated his pledge to provide Helena with a handsome
dowry (one that will make her more than Bertram's equal in terms
of wealth) the King warns Bertram that his fortunes are inextri-
cably tied to Helena:

As thou lov'st her
Thy love's to me religious; else, does err.

(II.iii. 182 – 3)

Clearly the King has less than total confidence in Bertram's
willingness to be a 'good' husband without a strong incentive.

Thus, like the debate scene in *Troilus and Cressida* which begins
with Priam setting out the costs of the war and the Greeks' offer of
peace, and ends with Hector's astonishing turn about, this public
occasion conveys a feeling of the perversity of human nature. As
Hector sets forth an irrefutable case for ending the war before
joining ranks with Troilus in the pursuit of 'honour', so too in this
scene is there a feeling that Bertram has bowed to necessity but
remains unconvinced of the validity of the social principles
enunciated by the King. And what of Helena? The problem for the
audience is to comprehend how she will be able to retain her
feeling of love for Bertram after the treatment she has received in
this scene. Can she still idolise him?

When Helena next appears it is to be informed by Parolles that
she has to forgo the consummation of her marriage because
Bertram has urgent business elsewhere. Helena's response is one
of simple acceptance: 'In everything I wait upon his will'
(II.iv. 52). Before Helena receives the remainder of her instructions from Bertram — to return to Rossillion where he will join her
in two days — the audience has had the opportunity of seeing
Parolles thoroughly exposed by Lafew, while being accepted as a
worthy confidant by Bertram. Even after Lafew has insisted that
'the soul of this man is his clothes' (II.v. 43 – 4), Bertram remains
convinced that Parolles 'is very great in knowledge, and
accordingly valiant' (II.v. 7 – 8). Bertram, then, is singularly

undiscerning: he lacks the ability to see through even such a transparent character as Parolles.

Bertram's attitude to Helena is one of contempt: as she advances to receive her instructions from him his terse comment is 'Here comes my clog' (II.v. 53). He then proceeds to lie to her and in response to her tentative plea for a kiss he dismisses her coldly. After making all possible allowances for Bertram's disappointment it is difficult to feel any sympathy for him. His behaviour towards Helena is callous. However, even after receiving the next blow — the riddling letter informing her that Bertram will never accept her as his wife until she has his ring and a child fathered by him — Helena expresses no antagonism towards Bertram. Rather she suffers great anxiety on his part and a sense of guilt that she has caused him to court danger in the wars:

> Poor lord, is't I
> That chase thee from thy country, and expose
> Those tender limbs of thine to the event
> Of the none-sparing war?
> . . .
> Whoever shoots at him, I set him there;
> Whoever charges on his forward breast,
> I am the caitiff that do hold him to't;
> And though I kill him not, I am the cause
> His death was so effected.
>
> (III.ii. 102–16)

The contrast between the reactions of Helena and the Countess is striking. The Countess is direct in her chastisement of her son:

> Nothing in France until he have no wife!
> There's nothing here that is too good for him
> But only she, and she deserves a lord
> That twenty such rude boys might tend upon
> And call her, hourly, mistress.
>
> (III.ii. 78–82)

Moreover, she claims that honour is not interchangeable: the sum of honour cannot be augmented if it is lost in one sphere and gained in another: 'tell him that his sword can never win/The honour that he loses' (III.ii. 93–4). Ironically, when Bertram does return from the war the honour he has gained in battle does serve him well in gaining quittance for his treatment of Helena.

It is not merely Helena's tender care for Bertram which is so marked but the whole speech is delivered in a highly romanticised vein; she is still in love with what sounds like an ideal or idealised young man rather than the insensitive character who has treated her with contempt. There seems nothing selfish in Helena's love; her own bruises she can bear with equanimity; it is the prospect of Bertram suffering that she cannot endure. And yet, though her ostensible reason for leaving home is to encourage Bertram to return, Helena is soon in Florence on Bertram's doorstep planning yet again to win him. Although Helena's chief goal is to see Bertram safe and comfortable she is unable to quell her longing for him. Shakespeare has headed off any antagonism towards her by the Countess' comment that:

> What angel shall
> Bless this unworthy husband? He cannot thrive,
> Unless her prayers, whom heaven delights to hear
> And loves to grant, reprieve him from the wrath
> Of greatest justice.

(III.iv. 25–9)

This attitude is reinforced by the ladies of Florence who are full of admiration for Bertram's appearance but dislike his treatment of his wife and the attempt to seduce Diana. It is the young virgin herself who insists on placing moral considerations in the final estimation of a man: 'if he were honester/He were much goodlier' (III.v. 79–80). Likewise, Mariana in cautioning Diana against Bertram states: 'the honour of a maid is her name, and no legacy is so rich as honesty' (III.v. 12–13). Bertram, in contrast, sees honesty as Diana's only failing: 'That's all the fault' he replies in answer to the comment 'But you say she's honest' (III.vi. 107–8). Here is the topsy-turvy world of the dashing young nobleman: he gives his all on the battlefield to heap up honour, but in order to satisfy his lust is prepared to ruin a poor young virgin. In a play overflowing with references to worth and honour Shakespeare has created an awareness of the incongruities between scales of values. When Helena puts her proposal of the bed-trick before the widow she has to persuade her that there can be no question of improper behaviour. Despite her poverty the widow is proud of her ancestry claiming 'And would not put my reputation now/In any staining act' (III.vii. 6–7). In contrast to the reticence of the widow

Helena has no doubt that Bertram will surrender his family ring in
payment for Diana's virginity:

> Now his important blood will naught deny
> That she'll demand; a ring the country wears
> That downward hath succeeded in his house
> From son to son some four or five descents
> Since the first father wore it. This ring he holds
> In most rich choice; yet, in his idle fire,
> To buy his will it would not seem too dear,
> Howe'er repented after.

(III.vii. 21–8)

It is ironic that a man who stood first against marriage on the
principle of high birth should be willing to part with a symbol of his
family's honour for an hour of sexual gratification with a woman
whom he disdains as a human being. The ring is of far greater
symbolic significance than the drum ostensibly sought by Parolles.
But the drum is merely a pretext for action that will win esteem;
Parolles' difficulty is to acquire the symbol without risking his life.
Unlike Bertram who possesses physical courage in abundance,
Parolles is a natural coward. As he ruminates on his dilemma, one
of the eavesdropping lords asks the question, 'Is it possible he
should know what he is, and be that he is?' (IV.i. 44–5) Rather
than promoting a contempt for Parolles' brazenness, this comment
rather creates an awareness of his self-knowledge. At no point in
the play does Bertram ever display such a sense of insight into his
own character: from first to last he appears to think of himself as
an admirable fellow. Moreover, Parolles' exposure is highly comic
as he unwittingly participates in a dialogue with his fellows. His
vice is revealed in an atmosphere of amusement, whereas
Bertram's exposure takes place in a formal situation which is
untouched by comic elements. When Parolles is 'captured' his outburst is poignant as well as comic:

> O, let me live,
> And all the secrets of our camp I'll show,

(IV.i. 83–4)

Parolles' disgrace, as a soldier, is total. But when set beside
Bertram's calculated wooing of Diana his response is understandably human. In the light of his later denunciation of Diana,

Bertram's courtship is cynical in the extreme. Dismissing the ties of his enforced marriage he pledges undying love to the woman whom he intends to use:

> I was compell'd to her, but I love thee
> By love's own sweet constraint, and will for ever
> Do thee all rights of service.
>
> (IV.ii. 15–17)

As Diana wards him off Bertram's vows become more pressing; he insists:

> And my integrity ne'er knew the crafts
> That you do charge men with.
>
> (IV.ii. 33–4)

No doubt, Bertram is a novice in this activity but he presses his case as persuasively as a seasoned seducer. Initially he refuses to part with his ring, but once Bertram recognises that it is the essential currency for the purchase of Diana's 'honour' he willingly accedes to her demand:

> Here, take my ring;
> My house, mine honour, yea, my life be thine,
> And I'll be bid by thee.
>
> (IV.ii. 51–3)

He is even prepared to anticipate the death of Helena as he promises marriage to Diana in the event of his wife's demise.

It might be argued that this behaviour is very natural for a handsome young man sojourning in foreign parts, but in the very next scene his peers discuss Bertram's action with extreme distaste. They criticise him both for his treatment of Helena and for his seduction of Diana:

> He hath perverted a young gentlewoman here in Florence, of a most chaste renown, and this night he fleshes his will in the spoil of her honour;
>
> (IV.iii. 13–15)

The response of the First Lord on hearing of Bertram's escapade is to reflect ruefully on the nature of mankind: 'As we are ourselves, what things are we!' (IV.iii. 18–19) The Second Lord is eager to dispose of any suggestion that he is Bertram's confidant: 'Let it be forbid, sir! So should I be a great deal of his act' (IV.iii. 43–4). Finally, when he is informed of Helena's death the Second Lord has no doubt about Bertram's reaction to the news: 'I am heartily sorry that he'll be glad of this' (IV.iii. 61).

What becomes clear from this dialogue is that Bertram's behaviour is not characteristic of his fellows and that his treatment of Helena and his seduction of Diana are deplored by young men who admire him in many other ways. The Second Lord weighs Bertram's acquisition of honour in the military sphere with his loss of honour outside it: 'The great dignity that his valour hath here acquir'd for him shall at home be encount'red with a shame as ample' (IV.iii. 65–7). The response of the First Lord mitigates criticism of Bertram by generalising about human nature: 'The web of our life is of a mingled yarn, good and ill together; our virtues would be proud if our faults whipp'd them not, and our crimes would despair if they were not cherish'd by our virtues' (IV.iii. 68–71). Bertram's exuberant entrance comes as a shock, especially as the dialogue between the two lords has revealed that on receipt of a letter from his mother Bertram had 'chang'd almost into another man' (IV.iii. 4). Rather than appearing contrite Bertram enumerates his evening's actions culminating with a boast about his seduction of Diana and the possibility of having made her pregnant: 'I mean, the business is not ended, as fearing to hear of it hereafter' (IV.iii. 93–4).

Bertram's sense of self-satisfaction is diminished only when he discovers that Parolles has made a comprehensive confession. His immediate reaction is one of fear lest Parolles has revealed something unpleasant about him. As the blindfolded Parolles is put through his paces Bertram expresses no embarrassment about having been taken in by 'the gallant militarist' (IV.iii. 137). After Parolles has denigrated the First Lord in the most extreme terms the latter is able to comment, 'He hath out-villain'd villainy so far that the rarity redeems him'. Bertram, in contrast, who has been relatively unscathed by Parolles' calumnies, can only respond testily: 'A pox on him! He's a cat still' (IV.iii. 264–6). While he awaits judgement Parolles determines to give up the futile pretence of military valour: 'I'll no more drumming. A plague of all drums! Only to seem to deserve well, and to beguile the supposition of that lascivious young boy, the count, have I run into this danger' (IV.iii. 288–91). Even under the duress of imagined capture and interrogation Parolles has been unable to stop his tongue running away with him, but the experience has been enough to persuade him to discard any further military pretentions. He is set on the path to reform as far as his nature will allow. Once the humiliation is complete, far from creeping away in shame Parolles looks reality in the face, accepts himself as he is, and the new role which he must seek:

> Yet am I thankful. If my heart were great
> 'Twould burst at this. Captain I'll be no more,
> But I will eat and drink and sleep as soft
> As captain shall. Simply the thing I am
> Shall make me live.
> . . .
> Rust, sword; cool, blushes; and Parolles live
> Safest in shame; being fool'd, by fool'ry thrive.
> There's place and means for every man alive.
> I'll after them.
>
> (IV.iii. 319–29)

In this engaging soliloquy Parolles, stripped bare, seems to breathe a sigh of relief that his acting days are over. Henceforth he can be himself, a copper coin passing as small change rather than current gold. But before he can secure his new position he serves another function. Lafew blames him for having mislead Bertram, describing him as 'a snipp'd-taffeta fellow . . . whose villainous saffron would have made all the unbak'd and doughy youth of a nation in his colour' (IV.v. 1–4). Typically Parolles is described by reference to his extravagant clothing and the link is forged between the clothing and food by means of saffron which was used to colour both. But despite Parolles' bad influence on Bertram the audience can't take Lafew's rationalisation at face value. As Lafew goes on to inform the Countess that the King has agreed to a marriage between his daughter and Bertram, the scene has all the flavour of an exercise designed to restore social harmony and reintegrate Bertram into the community. Helena is remembered and described movingly by the Countess — 'If she had partaken of my flesh and cost me the dearest groans of a mother I could not have owed her a more rooted love' (IV.v. 10–12) — mingling imagery of growth, consanguinity and value. But the pursuit of the growth imagery by Lafew soon spills over into joking with Lavatch — the kind of response characteristic of funerals where an attempt is made to return to the moving current of life while recognising the numbing impact of loss through death. Thus Shakespeare provides a scene in which the loss of Helena is recognised but the way is prepared for Bertram to re-establish himself. No one really believes that his misdemeanours are all attributable to the influence of Parolles, but it provides an adequate social cover.

As Helena is laid to rest there is a characteristic glance at the past when the Countess says of Lavatch, 'My lord that's gone made himself much sport out of him; by his authority he remains here' (IV.v. 61 – 2). That brief comment contains a number of resonances: the disparity between father and son is called to mind: Lavatch has really outlived his credit — the Countess makes an effort to engage Lavatch so that he may feel that he still has a part to play in the household. Lafew possesses the sympathy of the older generation and affords Lavatch the opportunity of exhibiting his wit. Helena is the only character who appears to have a totally congenial relationship with Lavatch: they are comfortable with each other, and in her company his humour is less contrived. For instance, Helena enjoys his effortless deflation of Parolles (II.iv. 17 – 35). In contrast Bertram and Lavatch have nothing to say to one another. The favourite of the father has no rapport with the son. When Lavatch announces the arrival of Bertram he does so in a way that suggests the patch on his face may be intended to cover a blemish which is the consequence of venereal disease rather than a battle scar. Although this could be an example of weak humour it also has a touch of malice which Lavatch displays on at least one other occasion. These little touches suggest that Lavatch is no admirer of Bertram's.

Thus the whole scene, which prepares for the arrival of Bertram and the tangled conclusion, is characteristic of the quiet scenes of this play: it is full of suggestion and atmosphere, and it is arguable that no other play of Shakespeare's so effectively conveys a sense of atmosphere: of place and time and mood. Here is Shakespeare at his most delicate and subtle, adopting a style which is uniquely fitted to this play.

As we encounter Helena, the widow and Diana there is both a quickening of pace and a sense of weariness: time and effort pervade a scene which commences with a speech by Helena that embodies these features and employs the growth imagery in a way which is both simple and utterly genuine:

But this exceeding posting day and night
Must wear your spirits low. We cannot help it;
But since you have made the days and nights as one
To wear your gentle limbs in my affairs,
Be bold you do so grow in my requital
As nothing can unroot you.

(V.i. 1 – 6)

As everyone moves towards Rossillion for the final drawing
together there is strong emphasis placed on valuation and re-
evaluation. Parolles confesses his poor worth to Lafew and receives
in exchange a jovial assessment of his character and a promise of
security: 'though you are a fool and a knave you shall eat'
(V.ii. 50). Likewise the King sums up Helena's worth and
Bertram's actions:

We lost a jewel of her, and our esteem
Was made much poorer by it; but your son,
As mad in folly, lack'd the sense to know
Her estimation home.

(V.iii. 1 – 4)

The effect of the discussion which ensues between the King, Lafew
and the Countess is to pose another possible conclusion to the play.
There is bitterness in the King's reflection on Bertram's past
action but a recognition of the necessity of restoring social
harmony. The mother forgives her son, the King his subject and
Lafew is instrumental in creating a new family alliance. The past
casts a shadow, but the nature of life is such that social cohesion
has to be continually re-created. Bertram appears to have inherited
none of his parents' virtues but he has inherited a position and so
must be brought inside once more. Even so, while recognising the
social reality the King conveys the impression of forcing himself to
forgive Bertram, always referring to the penitent as 'him' rather
than as the 'count' as he does when welcoming Bertram so warmly
and generously in I.ii. where he equates him with his son. The
King's inability to be wholehearted in his forgiveness is made clear
in his first speech to Bertram:

I am not a day of season,
For thou may'st see a sunshine and a hail
In me at once. But to the brightest beams

Distracted clouds give way; so stand thou forth;
The time is fair again.

(V.iii. 32–6)

This speech also takes up the theme of time which is developed
strongly by the King in response to Bertram's apology:

All is whole
Not one word more of the consumed time;
Let's take the instant by the forward top;
For we are old, and on our quick'st decrees
Th'inaudible and noiseless foot of time
Steals ere we can effect them.

(V.iii. 37–42)

Here is an example of the kind of outward movement into a
generalisation about time that occurs so powerfully in *Troilus and
Cressida*. But a great deal of the poignancy resides in the King's
awareness that his life is drawing to a close. His line 'All is whole'
is particularly significant in the context of the problem plays: here
is the characteristic desire to see relationships or ideals as standing
firm against human frailty or dishonesty. His diction is striking for
its simplicity, and there is a stark contrast between his simple
question to Bertram 'You remember/The daughter of this lord?'
(V.iii. 42–3) and the latter's elaborate response:

Admiringly, my liege. At first
I stuck my choice upon her, ere my heart
Durst make too bold a herald of my tongue;
Where, the impression of mine eye infixing,
Contempt his scornful perspective did lend me,
Which warp'd the line of every other favour,
Scorn'd a fair colour or express'd it stol'n,
Extended or contracted all proportions
To a most hideous object. Thence it came
That she whom all men prais'd, and whom myself
Since I have lost, have lov'd, was in mine eye
The dust that did offend it.

(V.iii. 44–55)

Nowhere in the play is there the slightest suggestion that
Bertram had been attracted to Lafew's daughter. Moreover, he

has never evinced an excess of modesty which he claims impeded him from making his feeling known to the young woman. At this moment Bertram has available to him several ways of accepting the young woman with good grace and acknowledging his poor treatment of Helena, but he chooses to practise deception — and does it with style: falsity and dishonesty seem to come naturally to this character. The speech contains the conventionalised features of falling in love and also a glimpse of the body parts so characteristic of *Troilus and Cressida*: 'heart', 'eye', 'tongue'. Artificial and insincere as this speech is, it is accepted by the King with alacrity because it is perceived as an attempt by Bertram to acknowledge and excuse his past guilt while moving forward with enthusiasm to embrace his new position in society. Even so, the King underlines the inadequacy of a sorrow that comes too late in a speech which points strongly in the direction of the romances:

> but love that comes too late,
> Like a remorseful pardon slowly carried,
> To the great sender turns a sour offence,
> Crying, 'That's good that's gone.' Our rash faults
> Make trivial price of serious things we have,
> Not knowing them until we know their grave.
>
> (V.iii. 57–62)

When Bertram hands over his ring to Lafew in a symbolic gesture of joining the two families it is, no doubt, with a good deal of relief as the references to Helena must soon cease. His sense of shock is all the more marked, therefore, when he is challenged successively by Lafew, the King and his mother about how he obtained the ring from Helena. For once Bertram is innocent, but in providing an explanation of how he acquired it Bertram not only lies easily, but also conveys an account which places him in the best possible light:

> You are deceiv'd, my lord; she never saw it.
> In Florence was it from a casement thrown me,
> Wrapp'd in a paper which contain'd the name
> Of her that threw it. Noble she was, and thought
> I stood ingag'd; but when I had subscrib'd
> To mine own fortune, and inform'd her fully
> I could not answer in that course of honour
> As she had made the overture, she ceas'd

In heavy satisfaction, and would never
Receive the ring again.

(V.iii. 92 – 101)

Two elements stand out in this part of the scene: first Bertram's
plausibility: he lies with such facility and spontaneity; second, how
quickly the King thinks the worst of him, even suspecting Bertram
of murder. The King's newly rekindled suspicions are expressed in
a way that is characteristic of the play. Though the meaning is not
obscure the mode of expression calls attention to itself through its
knotted quality:

My fore-past proofs, howe'er the matter fall,
Shall tax my fears of little vanity,
Having vainly fear'd too little.

(V.iii. 121 – 3)

After receiving Diana's letter the King is ready to express to the
Countess his conviction that Helena has been the victim of foul
play. But rather than reject any suggestion that Bertram could be
involved in such an act her response is, 'Now justice on the doers!'
(V.iii. 153) Nobody, it seems, has any confidence in Bertram; they
are willing to believe him worse than he is. Are they merely
responding naturally to the strange 'facts' or are they giving
expression to their true estimation of this young man? Lafew
quickly withdraws the offer of his daughter and Bertram is under
fire from all sides as Diana makes her accusation. At this point
there must surely be a good deal of audience sympathy for
Bertram, but Shakespeare quenches it with astonishing speed.
First, Bertram defends himself with brazen arrogance:

Let your highness
Lay a more noble thought upon mine honour
Than for to think that I would sink it here.

(V.iii. 178 – 80)

Then in response to Diana's direct accusation Bertram behaves in
the most despicable way possible, adopting an approach that has
been the age-old standard response of scoundrels who have
seduced or raped young women over the centuries:

160

> She's impudent, my lord,
> And was a common gamester to the camp.
>
> (V.iii. 186–7)

Is it possible that someone able to adopt this stratagem is really capable of being transformed into a 'good' man or a romantic hero? Here is the gentleman of noble birth, who cannot bring himself to contaminate his blood by marriage to a physician's daughter, resorting to the most ignoble behaviour in order to preserve his reputation as a gentleman. Could any audience fail to be disgusted by Bertram's behaviour? And could they, within minutes, accept his reformation and pledge of future love? If that is the intention of the dramatist he has certainly pushed Bertram's infamous behaviour to the absolute limit.

When Diana produces Bertram's ring, the Countess makes it very clear how greatly it has been valued as a symbol of family loyalty:

> Of six preceding ancestors, that gem
> Conferr'd by testament to th'sequent issue,
> Hath it been owed and worn.
>
> (V.iii. 195–7)

This is not a romantic comedy formula but a declaration of Bertram's disregard of family connection. The man who insists on his inherited status is prepared to relinquish an important symbol in order to secure sexual gratification — and with a woman for whom he feels contempt.

As Parolles is called for as a witness the parallel between his trial and Bertram's becomes evident. But whereas the former provoked laughter and pity, the latter produces distaste and contempt. It is all the more ironic, therefore, that Bertram is genuinely outraged at the thought of Parolles being called as witness. His language reveals that he has no conception of his own dishonesty and contemptible behaviour:

> He's quoted for a most perfidious slave
> With all the spots a'th'world tax'd and debosh'd,
> Whose nature sickens but to speak a truth.
>
> (V.iii. 204–6)

This is arrogance and moral blindness on a grand scale. But

Bertram has not finished degrading himself in an attempt to slip out of what he appears to conceive of as a little local difficulty: he denigrates Diana still further:

> Certain it is I lik'd her
> And boarded her i'th'wanton way of youth.
> She knew her distance and did angle for me,
> Madding my eagerness with her restraint,
> . . .
> and in fine
> Her inf'nite cunning with her modern grace
> Subdu'd me to her rate; she got the ring,
> And I had that which any inferior might
> At market-price have bought.
>
> (V.iii. 209–18)

Once more the question of value becomes part of the structure of the speech. As a consequence of her infinite cunning, Bertram protests, he was persuaded to accept her '*rate*' and thereby obtained what any '*inferior*' might have secured at mere '*market-price*'. Deeply embedded in the structure of the problem plays is an awareness of value in its various manifestations. One of the ironies of this speech, apart from Bertram's total disregard for the truth, is the assumed superiority of the speaker at the very moment when his estimation in the eyes of virtually everyone else has reached the lowest level. For Bertram, his social status insulates him against ignominy. He does not believe that actions make the man. Parolles makes the point succinctly in response to the King's question about whether Bertram loved Diana: 'He did love her, sir, as a gentleman loves a woman . . . He lov'd her, sir, and lov'd her not' (V.iii. 243–5). That is to say, he *said* he loved her, made love to her, but did not love her. That is precisely the category of 'gentleman' to which Bertram belongs. Yet, when Helena emerges to resolve the seemingly irresolvable confusion Bertram is unhesitating in his response. In reply to Helena's

> 'Tis but the shadow of a wife you see;
> The name and not the thing.

Bertram's uncharacteristically simple protestation is:

Both, both. O pardon!

(V.iii. 301 – 2)

When she claims that she has fulfilled the requirement of his letter
Bertram becomes the model lover:

If she, my liege, can make me know this clearly
I'll love her dearly, ever, ever dearly.

(V.iii. 309 – 10)

Or has Bertram seen a means of saving himself and responded
with his usual adroitness?

W. W. Lawrence comments, 'Critical explanations have
nowhere shown wider divergence than in regard to this play, nor
have the points at issue ever been more sharply marked.'[1] But for
his own part Lawrence feels totally comfortable about Bertram's
redemption: he suggests 'Bertram's sudden change of heart was a
convention of medieval and Elizabethan story, which must be
expected to follow Helena's triumph' and adds, 'there is no
implication that their after life would be anything but happy'.[2]
Lawrence rests his case on the force of the convention and the
constraint which it imposed on Shakespeare; he 'was not free, as is
a dramatist or novelist of today, to make such sweeping changes in
the meaning of traditional stories, in situations made familiar to
people by centuries of oral narrative'.[3] Although Lawrence
provides a 'solution' to the problem that troubles so many critics
and theatregoers he still sees the play as a failure:

the imagination of the dramatist has seldom been kindled, or
his sensibilities aroused. A curious hardness and indifference
are often evident. There are flashes of tenderness and fineness, as in the portraiture of Helena and the Countess, but
these are all too rare . . . He relied for effect, not on emotion
or truth to life, but on the familiarity and popularity of the
story, and upon the theatrical effectiveness of individual
scenes. And this, I think, is why the modern reader, who has
no feeling for the traditions of story, and who cannot judge
from the stage effects, finds *All's Well* highly puzzling.[4]

The last comment indicates that the difficulties of the play are
associated specifically with the play on the page rather than the
play on the stage. Nevertheless, Lawrence implies that *All's Well* is

not a very good play, and to be enjoyed it must be observed from the standpoint of an Elizabethan without any thought being given to verisimilitude. Neither of these arguments stand up to close examination: why did Shakespeare go to so much trouble to complicate the traditional story by making Bertram so unattractive? As G. K. Hunter argues, 'If personal reconciliation is really the end of this scene, we can only say that Shakespeare has been extraordinarily clumsy.'[5] Secondly, despite the problem of interpreting the conclusion, this play is now recognised as a great theatrical success. Neither is it a second class piece of work nor enjoyable simply in the naïve way of Lawrence's assumed Elizabethan playgoer. The enormously successful RSC production of 1981, for example, attests to the fineness of the play and its popular appeal. That production preserved the ambiguity by having Bertram and Helena walk off the stage side-by-side but with their hands not quite touching. The chilling thought remained that Bertram had used another ploy to save himself and that Helena, for all her personal qualities, was destined to endure a thoroughly miserable marriage. Yet the possibility of genuine happiness occurring after initial embarrassment and uncertainty was retained.

Philip Edwards, however, is unequivocal in his final evaluation of the reconciliation and the inadequacy of the play:

> The treatment of Parolles shows us a scoundrel changed by shame into a new recognition of himself and a new way of life. Bertram is not so treated. Helena never saves Bertram. He is unredeemable: Shakespeare could not save him. It is not a matter of failing to write the lines that would have changed the soul of the play: it is a matter of not being able to force one's conscience to alter a character whose alteration would be, simply, incredible. Angelo's alteration in *Measure for Measure* is an entirely different matter: he has all the resources for change, the depth of being, that the shallow Bertram never has. In *All's Well*, the unconvincing words, asking pardon and promising love, are all that can be wrested from the figure Shakespeare has created. Anything further would be falseness and he surely knew it. He has driven the play to a fold it cannot enter, and he refuses to make it enter. That is the failure. But why the obstinacy of the character of Bertram? Has Shakespeare 'accidently' created the wrong figure for his story? The obstinacy is in humanity as Shakespeare saw it before it is in his dramatic fiction. Given a

providence, given a whole world of family honour to guide him, given the angel-like wife to safeguard him from the consequences of his actions, the imbued irresponsibility, selfishness and shallowness of a Bertram remain intact.[6]

Shakespeare originally intended to create harmony and reconciliation but his own integrity stood in his way, Professor Edwards insists:

Shakespeare's honesty has then, in a way, wrecked the play: the final harmony is in fact discordant. The need he felt to tune that discord is seen in the composition of *Measure for Measure*. Yet to have wrecked the play as a comedy is still to have produced a work which speaks out even more truth than the completed circle could have shown. There is a consolation somewhere in the failure to bring off the consolation for the audience. Shakespeare has met the challenge he gave to his own earlier comedies, and wrought a form of comedy which would be more inclusive of the facts of evil. He refuses, at the last minute as it were, to believe that he can contain the facts within the form: if the play disappoints, we are surely deeply impressed by the sense of struggle and by the honesty of the craftsman who tries to bring the deep hopes of the soul into the images of art, and finds them countered by the even deeper doubts.[7]

This is a fascinating conclusion. Edwards refuses to resort to evasion; he recognises the power of this play yet ultimately he detects incongruity, the source of which is the disparity between Shakespeare's original intention and his achievement. However, Edwards claims that Shakespeare learned from this experience, so that *Measure for Measure* does not fail in the same way. In contrast to Bertram's reformation Professor Edwards claims, 'The penitence of Angelo and the reception of the new man into the society of the play is convincing and moving.'[8] Yet many theatregoers and critics find Angelo's penitence and reform just as difficult to believe in as Bertram's. So perhaps Shakespeare failed twice in the same way. The alternative explanation is that Shakespeare achieved precisely what he intended in both cases: the subversion or disruption of the romantic comedy ending. But why should he do this? What was he trying to achieve? Dowden felt that Shakespeare must have been experiencing some kind of mental breakdown during the period when he was writing these plays. This dubious conclusion at least has the merit of recognising that there is something peculiar about the problem plays. What Shakespeare did was to invent a new form, and that is one reason why the ambiguous terms dark comedies and tragicomedies are not useful as descriptive labels for these plays. They provide a familiar structure which embrace elements antithetical to that structure. It is as if Shakespeare sought to insinuate a questioning about certain aspects of life by creating a questioning of the form in which that life is embodied. The kinds of epithets associated with the problem plays are 'analytical', 'perplexing', 'puzzling'. In this sense Shakespeare achieved his objective. The Trojan war and the love story of Troilus and Cressida presented him with a unique opportunity for creating a play which evaded all existing classifications while enabling him to disturb his audience with profound questions about human values and the operation of human society. But that play did not exhaust the range of questions Shakespeare wanted to raise. His next step, in *All's Well*, was to adopt the structure of comedy but employing two endings: the ending of fairy tale which satisfies one kind of human desire, and an ending which points in an entirely different direction. Hence the blending of fairy tale with an intense sense of realism. In real life Helena could be mistaken about Bertram. But rather than present an outright denial of romantic comedy Shakespeare does something much more disconcerting: the audience is left pondering the possible scenarios beyond the end of the play. As they pursue these possible ends they spontaneously revert to consideration of the action which precedes the resolution of the drama. Not even Shakespeare's tragedies produce the intense analytical reflection that these plays provoke, nor do the problem plays allow the consolation of tragedy. Despite the destruction, cruelty and pain encountered in the tragedies, consolation is gained through an awareness of our common humanity. We cut through the fibrous strata to the very centre of human *being*. The problem plays deal with a broader and in one sense more superficial range of human thoughts and actions. In real life there is little heroism or grandeur: men struggle to establish values and institutions. These continually come under pressure from the chaotic stream of human action which contains a great deal of weakness, folly, greed, envy, self-deception, egotism, and pettiness. A large part of the social world depicted and *suggested* by Shakespeare in the problem plays bears close kinship with Brueghel's paintings.

While some men and women seek to purify life, to establish firm principles and values, others use existing values and institutions as props to be used for their own ends or as barriers to be negotiated. Bertram accepts the concepts of social hierarchy and nobility of birth while simultaneously rejecting their concomitant of obligation. He accepts fighting as a means of asserting personal worth and acquiring honour because it is congenial to him, but rejects the principle of honourable behaviour towards women. Self-gratification is his guiding principle, and it remains open whether Bertram will continue happily on his way, simply using the protection of a good wife as a cover. What sort of master will Bertram make? The question would have occurred more readily to some members of Shakespeare's audience than to a contemporary one. After three hours of observing the nasty little egotist, could anyone really feel that here is a man who will retain the tolerant and good-humoured regime established by his father and continued by his mother? Whereas in Shakespeare's plays it is generally misleading to stray beyond the confines of the play world, in the problem plays there is positive invitation to explore the adjacent territory. Shakespeare seems to be saying 'if this was the world of romantic comedy, this is how the play would end; but consider these events in the light of human experience and contemplate the probable outcomes'. This open-endedness makes its appearance in the contemporary novel. John Fowles's *The French Lieutenant's Woman*, for example, provides three clear options. Shakespeare provides an indeterminate and amorphous range of possibilities. Moreover, the consideration of likely scenarios arising from the conclusion of *All's Well* provokes a more intense re-examination of the preceding events than occurs in Fowles's novel. Fowles is adopting a traditional narrative form imitative of writers like Hardy and attempting to subvert it. He pursues his objective not by parodying the traditional narrative technique but by utilising it with great tact and sensitivity. At one level the book is a very fine nineteenth-century novel. But it is also a contemporary novel inviting a reappraisal both of the novel form and of the nature of social values and personal responses. Fowles and other contemporary novelists like him are doing very much what Shakespeare is doing with fable and folk tale in *All's Well*.

An important aspect of this question has been perceived by Nicholas Brooke who, in his insightful commentary on the play, focuses on the finely balanced and precisely articulated relationship between realism and folk tale. Shakespeare, argues Brooke, takes the established convention of the folk tale but locates it firmly within a realistic setting. In consequence the language moves between rhyming couplets applicable to fairy tale and terse, precise, prosaic expression which conveys a strongly naturalistic feeling. Brooke suggests that 'What *All's Well* does, is to take that familiar [folk tale] material and look at it in a very unfamiliar way.'[9] He goes on to draw an illuminating comparison between what Shakespeare is doing in this play and what Caravaggio does in his picture of Mary Magdalene.

> What Caravaggio has done is to take the familiar iconography and view it with a wholly unfamiliar naturalism, which projects an entirely new image. His Mary is neither crude whore nor glorious saint, but a quiet and plausible girl, very much alone. Once that is seen the painting becomes extraordinarily interesting; and its interest is generated, not by the naturalism alone, but by the juxtaposition of that with the traditional mythology. That is almost exactly the achievement I am attributing to Shakespeare in *All's Well*: not a simple naturalism, but a consistently naturalistic presentation of traditional romance magic.[10]

Brooke's comments go a long way towards creating an understanding of the connections between the romantic and naturalistic elements in the play and to the way in which Shakespeare has adopted a specific patterning and structuring of the language in order to keep these elements in balance. As Brooke himself expresses the point:

> I have already claimed for this play a distinctive and very distinguished language . . . so far from being a play that falls apart, it has a controlled unity of a kind rare even in Shakespeare. Its unity is conditioned by its tone; by the refusal ever to let it move beyond the limits which that defines.[11]

In contrast G. K. Hunter maintains that 'There is a general failure in *All's Well* to establish a medium in verse which will convey effectively the whole tone of the play.'[12] This view has rightly been criticised by Brooke who points out that 'the play's characteristic medium is precisely this uniquely bare language which excludes decoration and so makes all imagery, or any romantic valuation of experience, evidently superfluous'.[13] Brooke carries the argument further by stressing that the function of the naturalism of the language is that 'It continually delivers the shock of actuality into the context of anticipated fiction', and he adds, 'But the naturalism of the speech is not merely bluntness. It has the quality too of the reticence of natural speech.'[14] Thus the quality of incongruity which is so detectable is a very deliberate feature of this play operating at every level and being powerfully mediated through the language.

So far, no attempt has been made to analyse Helena. Her goodness is verified through the comments of the Countess, Lafew and the King. But because her virtue is to be taken for granted, rather than to be subjected to close psychological scrutiny, her relationship with Bertram forms a crucial part of the incongruity which informs the play, the connection between fairy tale and reality. As Rossiter comments:

Helena is (mainly) a fairy-tale, 'traditional' story-book female, who is 'good'; and we should no more inquire into the details than into those of her honeymoon . . . The problematic element remains, because this sentimental fairy-tale 'Good One' is conjoined with a realistic, real-life 'Bad 'Un'; and the two particles in this mysterious, alleged unity exist in not merely different orbits, but orbits in different systems. This produces a state of mixed feelings, in which the fairy-tale solution we might like to believe in (and are adjured to by the title, and by the 'historical method' interpreters) is in conflict with the realistic, psychological exposure — which is very much more convincing.[15]

And so we come full circle. The rock on which all criticism ultimately alights (or founders) is the consummation. Rossiter, like Edwards, expresses the view that the incongruity is the consequence of Shakespeare failing to complete the intended design. As he puts it,

In *All's Well* there are 'disparities of experience' (thought and feeling) which fail to reach 'amalgamation'. The play came from an unresolved creative mind, in which sentimentality tried to balance the scepticism, and deliberately not seeing far enough (the fairy-tale element), tried to write off the results of seeing too far through (the 'realist' or tragic-comic inquiry into mankind).[16]

It is worth citing the response of one or two other critics in order
to convey just how pervasive is the anxiety and dissatisfaction with
the conclusion of this play. Roger Warren, for example, sums up
the feelings of many critics and theatregoers when he suggests that
'The most extraordinary feature of *All's Well*, surely, is the
curiously unsympathetic portrait of its hero.'[17] But he quite rightly
sees this as deliberate on Shakespeare's part:

> By the standards of ordinary romantic heroes, Bertram is a
> 'failure', but as a consistent character he is brilliantly
> successful, so much so that I think we must assume that
> Shakespeare meant him that way, and that the worrying effect
> is intentional.[18]

It is the very realism of the characterisation of Bertram that
explains the intensity of the antagoism which he has aroused.
Tillyard, for example, comments that 'The irony and the truth of
Helena's situation are that with so much intelligence and so firm a
mind she can be possessed by so enslaving a passion for an
unreformed, rather stupid, morally timid, and very self-centred
youth.'[19]

Here then is the enigma: it is difficult to see Bertram as a man
worthy of Helena's love or capable of becoming worthy of her
love. Roger Warren explores the Sonnets in order to suggest the
source of Shakespeare's feeling towards the story. He concludes
his discussion by commenting

> I think that he made Helena so intense, and presented her
> beloved with such relentless honesty, because he had some-
> thing especially personal to say about the power of love to
> prevail over all 'alteration' and humiliation, even if it proved
> less easy to show matters ending well in dramatic than in non-
> dramatic terms.[20]

Despite the intelligent and insightful nature of the argument we
once more see the critic driven back from offering an explanation
from within the drama. The implication is that whatever Shakespeare was aiming at he did not quite succeed.

One of the few critics who feels satisfied with the romantic interpretation of the play is Robert Smallwood. In his perceptive study
he suggests that the play 'concludes in gaity and in hope for the
future, though not in the triumphant joy of more unequivocally

romantic comedy'.[21] Thus even a critic who finds the behaviour of Bertram forgivable, and has a strong sense of his positive qualities, feels obliged to register a note of caution. Although Smallwood believes that 'The affection which Bertram is capable of inspiring in those around him is remarkable'[22] and that 'his heart, ultimately, is "great", or at least has the potential for greatness',[23] he insists that 'the play ends, and is meant to end, not in fully achieved happiness, but in hope'.[24] It is difficult to find a critic who argues his case more cogently, but even after reading this persuasive essay it is impossible to be convinced for long of Bertram's potential greatness or humanity.

Clearly the majority of critics of this play feel a sense of unease with the resolution. Rossiter and Edwards come out boldly in claiming that Shakespeare failed to fulfil his original intentions though they see the play as flawed rather than as a failure. Few perceive the ambiguity as intended and fewer still are satisfied with it. The argument advanced here is that Shakespeare was in complete control of his material and the ambiguity was fully intended. Following his artistic, though not necessarily popular, success of *Troilus and Cressida*, Shakespeare deliberately used the structure of romantic comedy to create an intense awareness of the moral and social values raised and to provoke an examination of the dramatic mode in which they are expressed. When Boas coined the term 'problem plays' he was being more insightful than he realised. These plays are profoundly concerned with problems of values and human attachments, and these are matters which concern not only the great and powerful, but all mankind.

Notes

1. W. W. Lawrence, *Shakespeare's Problem Comedies*, 3rd edn (Penguin, Harmondsworth, 1969), p. 43.
2. Ibid., p. 48.
3. Ibid., p. 73.
4. Ibid., pp. 78–9.
5. G. K. Hunter (ed.), Introduction to the *New Arden Edition of 'All's Well'* (Methuen, London, 1967), p. liv.
6. Philip Edwards, *Shakespeare and the Confines of Art*, 2nd edn (Methuen, London, 1972), pp. 114–15.
7. Ibid., p. 115.
8. Ibid., p. 115.
9. Nicholas Brooke, 'All's Well that Ends Well' in Muir and Wells (eds), *Aspects of Shakespeare's 'Problem Plays'* (Cambridge University Press,

Cambridge, 1982), p. 16.
10. Ibid., p. 17.
11. Ibid., p. 20.
12. Hunter (ed.), *New Arden Shakespeare*, p. lix.
13. Brooke, 'All's Well' in Muir and Wells (eds), *Aspects of 'Problem Plays*, p. 12.
14. Ibid., p. 13.
15. A. P. Rossiter, *Angel with Horns*, 4th edn (Longman, London, 1970), p. 100.
16. Ibid., p. 105.
17. Roger Warren, 'Why Does It End Well? Helena, Bertram and the Sonnets' in Muir and Wells (eds), *Aspects of 'Problem Plays'*, p. 48.
18. Ibid., p. 44.
19. E. M. W. Tillyard, *Shakespeare's Problem Plays*, 3rd edn (Penguin, Harmondsworth, 1970), p. 112.
20. Warren, 'Why Does It End Well?' in Muir and Wells (eds), *Aspects of 'Problem Plays'*, p. 56.
21. R. L. Smallwood, 'The Design of All's Well that Ends Well' in Muir and Wells (eds), *Aspects of 'Problem Plays'*, p. 41.
22. Ibid., p. 38.
23. Ibid., p. 41.
24. Ibid., p. 42.

5

Order and Authority in
Measure for Measure

One of the essential qualities of the stories upon which Shakespeare draws for *All's Well* and *Measure for Measure* is that they are fables which set forth a series of events that are to be taken as given. Even when the precise details differ, as for instance between Cinthio's play and his novella, psychological interrogation is not invited. Their essential purpose is to present a moral. Though the design of the story or drama is intended to maintain the reader's interest, the writer neither attempts psychological exploration nor encourages the reader to do so. Shakespeare draws on the sense of fascination aroused by these enduring fables and uses them to explore both human psychology and social institutions. So it is that audiences and critics experience a sense of incongruity or a duality between the clarity and simplicity of the story and the density and complexity of the dramatic presentation. This tension, between the unidimensional quality of the fable and the multidimensional nature of the social and psychological conflicts, is felt most keenly at the moment of resolution: 'and they lived happily ever after' attaches itself very naturally to the fable; the intensely realistic exploration of human nature, including its most unsavoury aspects, calls forth a questioning and sceptical response from the audience. We can enjoy the fable and its lesson, which is clear and unequivocal, but find ourselves drawn less cheerfully into a range of psychological and social issues which do not admit of comfortable solutions.

Quite apart from the dramatic possibilities precipitated by his source material, Shakespeare would have been acutely aware of the contemporary significance attaching to sexuality and law. Despite the wide ranging investigation of the bearing on the play of such matters as theology and judicial procedures, scant attention has been devoted to the running debate over the role of civil law in matters of sexual morality.[1] The essential question was whether sexual misdemeanours should be brought within the purview of the legal system or left to the discretion of ecclesiastical authorities. This debate culminated in legislation in 1650. The consequences of this Act and the arguments which preceded it have been analysed with admirable clarity by Keith Thomas, who comments:

> If any single measure epitomises the triumph of Puritanism in England, it must surely be the Commonwealth's act of 10 May 1650 'for suppressing the detestable sins of incest, adultery and fornication'. This was an attempt, unique in English history, to put the full machinery of the state behind the enforcement of sexual morality. Spiritual misdemeanours were reclassified as secular crimes and severe penalties prescribed for behaviour which had previously been left to the informal sanctions of neighbourly disapproval or the milder censures of the ecclesiastical courts. Incest and adultery became felonies, carrying sentence of death without benefit of clergy. Fornication was punished by three months in gaol, followed by a year's security for good behaviour. Brothel-keepers were to be whipped, pilloried, branded, and gaoled for three years; for a second offence the penalty was death.[2]

If the legislation of 1650 seems to have little bearing on what Shakespeare was writing during the first few years of the century, it is worth quoting one more sentence from Keith Thomas: 'Although owing its final passage to the special circumstances of the newly established republic, anxious to conciliate the Presbyterians and fearful of sectarian licence, it represented the culmination of more than a century's legislative pressure.'[3] It is not surprising, then, that Shakespeare's interest was kindled by the story which he found in Cinthio and Whetstone and with which he was probably familiar from other sources. Because of the relevance of the contemporary debate, Shakespeare's play immediately acquires a great deal of social significance. Claudio's plight is not merely a requirement of the plot but a situation which could become a social reality for Shakespeare's audience.

The contemporary relevance of this issue probably encouraged Shakespeare to intensify and vivify the low-life element of the

drama which he found in Whetstone's play. The inversion is significant. Whetstone's corrupt officials are expunged; sexual licence
is much more pervasive, and clearly uncontrollable. The implication is that when such laws bite, the victims will invariably be the
mildest of offenders as they are less skilled and practised in the art
of evasion. Moreover, the sexual drive is so elemental and potent
that even the establishment of a totalitarian society is incapable of
exercising control over the activities of its citizens. Pompey mischievously responds to Escalus' assertion that fornication will no
longer be tolerated, by asking: 'Does your worship mean to geld
and splay all the youth of the city?' (II.i. 227-8) Lucio likewise
insists on the inevitability of lechery: 'the vice is of great kindred;
it is well allied; but it is impossible to extirp it quite, friar, till
eating and drinking be put down' (III.ii. 97-9).

Not only is sexual impropriety inevitable because of man's
nature, but it will be manifested in prostitution because it gives
rise to the possibility of financial gain. The social reality is such
that even those who wish to live by means of legitimate activities
may be unable to do so. *Measure for Measure* portrays a whole
stratum of individuals who operate in an environment where
gaining a livelihood calls for guile and dexterity. The implication is
that severe legislation is of little use in such circumstances. Significantly, the only alternative employment available to Pompey is
that of executioner. And as the Provost reminds the professional
hangman who expresses his distaste for being given a bawd as an
assistant, 'you weigh equally: a feather will turn the scale'
(IV.ii. 28-9). Ironically, the social esteem accorded the man who
takes on the task of executing wrongdoers is on a par with that of
the individial who turns sexual desire to profit.

Neither Angelo nor Isabella are concerned with the reality that
encompasses the social world of Pompey and Mistress Overdone.
Isabella seeks an unsullied existence in a nunnery; Angelo is
prepared to deal out punishment to people as if they were capable
of steely discipline rather than being frail creatures of flesh and
blood. Rather than confront reality they seek to escape from it.

When Angelo falls he descends far below Pompey and the
traders in flesh: what he attempts is sexual violation and judicial
murder. When confronted with his crimes his conscience is so
weak that he resorts to lies to save himself. Pompey's manoeuvres
and equivocations, when he is being tried by Escalus, seem dignified in comparison — and comparison is surely intended by the
dramatist. Moreover, dishonesty and low dealing are not new to

Angelo. He has broken his pledge of marriage to Mariana and slandered her in order to justify his own breach of promise. What is new to Angelo when he encounters Isabella is not moral corruption, but lust. This self-deceiver who possesses not one spark of compassion for Claudio or Julietta appears less capable of reform than Pompey, and certainly possesses less humanity. Pompey is merely carried along with the current, making his way as best he can in a world that affords him few choices; Angelo deceives Mariana, revels in his reputation for self-discipline, takes pleasure in inflicting punishment and gives free rein to his newly discovered lust. Not content to rest there he is prepared to execute a man who is innocent in comparison with himself in order to avoid retribution, and finally to lie brazenly when confronted by Isabella.

What are the social implications of the implicit comparison between Angelo and such disreputable characters as Pompey and Mistress Overdone? Angelo stands for a regime characterised by rigorous discipline. Effectively he determines to establish order and morality through the tyranny of law. Pompey and his clique intend to operate in the 'black economy' regardless of the institutional changes which take place around them. The stews may bubble all the more vigorously through their participation but they are not capable of reforming or corrupting society. Their existence and way of life is a comment not on lax laws or judicial procedures, but of weaknesses inherent in human beings and the failure of their social superiors to create a better world. The real threat to society comes from Angelo: his world view is so confined and his conception of mankind so narrow that he is the embodiment of totalitarianism. Shakespeare is not making some glib point about striking a careful balance between rigour and compassion: he is exploring the nature and application of the conception of the disciplined society. Angelo before he experiences lust is the quintessential disciplinarian. The implications of such values are revealed vividly in the terror of the young man who falls victim to them. Claudio's speech expresses the newly experienced realisation of death which is simultaneously personal and universal:

> Ay, but to die, and go we know not where;
> To lie in cold obstruction, and to rot;
> This sensible warm motion to become
> A kneaded clod;

(III.i. 117–20)

It is astonishing that after such a vivid realisation of death Isabella can respond to Claudio's plea — to give herself to Angelo to save his life — with such violence. She exhibits all the contempt for human frailty that characterises Angelo. Isabella may possess a purity of spirit, but it is not of this world. To save her brother's life through committing such a sin, she argues, would constitute 'a kind of incest' (III.i. 138), and goes on to cast doubt on her mother's fidelity before concluding that Claudio is not guilty of a slip but possesses an ingrained vice.

Of course this seeming callousness in large part reflects Isabella's fear of sexual violation. Her repressed sexuality is suggested in her interview with Angelo when she asserts:

Th'impression of keen whips I'd wear as rubies,
And strip myself to death as to a bed
That longing have been sick for, ere I'd yield
My body up to shame.

(II.iv. 101–4)

Isabella, then, is as frightened as Claudio. But the very recognition of his right to make such a plea to her causes her to denounce him in the harshest terms because she could only meet his request by plunging herself into an action from which she recoils in terror. The paradox is that both Angelo and Isabella insist on a purity in the world: he must be free to impose the harshest penalties without let or hindrance; she must be free from any threat of physical violation or moral contamination. They are both idealists of sorts, but their idealism cannot encompass social reality. Both suffer severe shock when they have to face unpleasant facts. Angelo's cry of anguish is genuine: 'Blood, thou art blood' (II.iv. 15). Isabella's horror at Angelo's proposal and Claudio's plea for her acceptance of it shake her to the foundations. She is provided with an honourable escape from the impasse, but it involves participating in the real world where even Mariana's love is not free to find expression without the exercise of duplicity. Angelo discovers that the power of lust totally transcends anything that he has previously experienced and surpasses even his capacity for self-control. But what does the acquisition of self-knowledge do to these characters?

Angelo discovers that once he has fallen he cannot simply change course without suffering disgrace or even facing execution. The strong advocate of resoluteness is incapable of such moral courage. If Angelo eventually becomes a reformed character, it is the consequence of others saving him from his intended actions and the love of the remarkable Mariana. But there is no clear intimation of what the new Angelo will be like. He does not utter a word after admitting to Escalus that his impending execution is deserved. All that the dramatist provides is an indication of Angelo's sense of relief at escaping death:

> By this Lord Angelo perceives he's safe;
> Methinks I see a quickening in his eye.
>
> (V.i. 492–3)

Likewise, Isabella remains mute after making her plea for Angelo's life. Does the Duke's marriage proposal come as a complete surprise to her? If so, is she shocked? Or has she learned that the world needs all the virtue it can obtain and that she can make a greater contribution to humanity through engaging fully in an active life than in confining herself to the spiritual purity attainable in the nunnery? The latter interpretation seems the more probable, but it is not possible to demonstrate that this is the genuine or intended conclusion. There is a clear suggestion that though sex is a potent force it need not lead to whoring and prostitution — though such things are inevitable — and that the physical side of love requires no apology: indeed, its opposite, sexual repression, is anything but wholesome. It is significant that the loveliest speech in the play is delivered by Lucio to Isabella when he informs her of Claudio's situation:

> Your brother and his lover have embrac'd;
> As those that feed grow full, as blossoming time
> That from the seedness the bare fallow brings
> To teeming foison, even so her plenteous womb
> Expresseth his full tilth and husbandry.
>
> (I.iv. 40–4)

This speech encompasses the process of nature in all its fecundity and sees man as an integral part of it.

The contrast to this portrayal of man as part of bounteous nature is Lucio's description of Angelo:

> a man whose blood
> Is very snow-broth; one who never feels
> The wanton stings and motions of the sense;

But doth rebate and blunt his natural edge
With profits of the mind, study and fast.

(I.iv. 57–61)

Here is a man who refuses to recognise his natural passions. Not
content with that, he intends to direct the rest of erring humanity
along the same narrow path. Consequently the institution of law
which was designed for the protection of human beings, in his
hands becomes the 'hideous law' (I.iv. 63). Just as Angelo finds
the exercise of justice too lax, so Isabella finds the discipline of a
nunnery too mild:

Yes, truly; I speak not as desiring more,
But rather wishing a more strict restraint
Upon the sisters stood, the votarists of Saint Clare.

(I.iv. 3–5)

Both these characters are extremists seeking to supress what they
perceive to be the inferior and degrading aspects of human nature.
Isabella wishes to cut herself off from a social universe which is
soiled; Angelo is intent on cleaning it up. Paradoxically these
puritanical characters are drawn together through an action of
Angelo's against which Isabella finds it difficult to argue. When
told of the circumstances of Claudio's arrest, Isabella's first
reaction is to feel a sense of impotence: 'My power? Alas, I doubt'
(I.iv. 77). Here is a woman who has mentally disengaged herself
from the world. When pressed into action by Lucio — a licentious
scoundrel and slanderer — Isabella immediately expresses her
reluctance to plead for clemency in such a case:

There is a vice that most I do abhor,
And most desire should meet the blow of justice;
For which I would not plead, but that I must;
For which I must not plead, but that I am
At war 'twixt will and will not.

(II.ii. 29–33)

Hence the famous debate scene commences with the antagonists
sharing values which appear to be at variance with those of
virtually the whole of Vienna. Seconds before Isabella makes her
opening speech Angelo has given his instructions for dealing with
Julietta in a tone which leaves little doubt about his dispostion:

See you the fornicatress be remov'd;
Let her have needful, but not lavish means;

(II.ii. 23–4)

Angelo is not only a man of extreme views but someone who enjoys wielding power. His response to Isabella's apologetic opening is terse: 'Well: the matter?' (II.ii. 33) The contrast between these speeches and the Provost's aside could not be more marked: 'Heaven give thee moving graces!' (II.ii. 36) He invokes heaven to assist in securing a pardon for Claudio. Evidently he does not share the extreme views of Angelo or Isabella on the nature of the crime.

If Isabella's preamble is unpromising, her argument that Angelo should condemn the fault but not her brother is positively feeble. Amazingly, when Angelo quite rightly rejects her argument Isabella is prepared to leave: 'O just but severe law!' (II.ii. 41) Ironically, Claudio's life-line is provided by the disreputable Lucio who pushes Isabella into renewing her appeal. Once Isabella sets forth the claim for mercy her passion is kindled: and it is only when that happens that the force of her intellect is brought to bear on the case. It is as if the suppression of her natural impulses has obstructed the power of her mind. A second before Isabella launches on the upward curve of her passionate appeal Lucio upbraids her with the words, 'You are too cold' (II.ii. 56). It is the release of her natural energies and impulses which carries her forward in an unrelenting quest to save Claudio.

Isabella claims that there is no quality that more becomes the judge or ruler than mercy. She moves forward naturally from the proposition that were their roles reversed Angelo would not find Claudio so severe, to the Christian argument that spiritual salvation is dependent on the mercy of God. Angelo seeks to evade the force of this argument by claiming impotence and detachment: 'It is the law, not I, condemn your brother' (II.ii.80). This is, of course, manifestly false as Angelo has unfettered power to invoke the full rigour of the law or to mitigate it.

When Angelo insists that Claudio is to be executed the next day, Isabella responds even more passionately. There is a note of desperation in her claim that Claudio is not prepared for death; then she puts forward the argument that it is unfair that one man should die for a crime which is widely committed but goes unpunished — quite rightly implying that the law in such circumstances becomes arbitrary, merely making an example of unlucky victims. Angelo's response is invalid in this particular case: he argues that the sin of fornication would be less common had the law been used to make examples of wrongdoers. Whatever the general case for deterrence it manifestly does not apply in the case of fornication. Interestingly, Angelo's riposte is embodied in language redolent of the cycle of birth and death: 'conceiv'd, 'hatch'd and born', 'successive degrees', 'live', 'end' (II.ii. 97–100).

Finally, Isabella begs Angelo to be pitiful, but the quality of pity has been wholly submerged in him in his quest to discard his animal nature. Angelo's cold response calls forth the full flood of Isabella's indignation — a quality which she has sought to quell through the discipline of the nunnery:

> Could great men thunder
> As Jove himself does, Jove would ne'er be quiet,
> For every pelting petty officer
> Would use his heaven for thunder; nothing but thunder.
> Merciful Heaven,
> Thou rather with thy sharp and sulphurous bolt
> Splits the unwedgeable and gnarled oak,
> Than the soft myrtle. But man, proud man,
> Dress'd in a little brief authority,
> Most ignorant of what he's most assur'd —
> His glassy essence — like an angry ape
> Plays such fantastic tricks before high heaven
> As makes the angels weep; who, with our spleens,
> Would all themselves laugh mortal.
>
> (II.ii. 111–24)

Isabella has moved so far during her assault on Angelo's position that rather than requiring nudges from Lucio she receives his enthusiastic approval along with that of the Provost. Her final thrust is to ask Angelo that he seek within himself to see whether he has contemplated Claudio's crime. If he has, she insists, he cannot condemn Claudio. Ironically, it is Isabella who unintentionally provokes Angelo's desire. From this moment, clearly recognised by Angelo in the line 'She speaks, and 'tis such sense/That my sense breeds with it' (II.ii. 142), he has no excuse for condemning Claudio. As Angelo recognises, in a soliloquy which gives full expression to his bewilderment and anguish, he has so successfully suppressed his emotions that when sexual desire breaks loose in him he is undone.

                                        Can it be
That modesty may more betray our sense
Than woman's lightness? Having waste ground enough,
Shall we desire to raze the sanctuary
And pitch our evils there? O fie, fie, fie!
What dost thou, or what art thou, Angelo?
Dost thou desire her foully for those things
That make her good? O, let her brother live!
Thieves for their robbery have authority,
When judges steal themselves. What, do I love her,
That I desire to hear her speak again?
And feast upon her eyes? What is't I dream on?
O cunning enemy, that, to catch a saint,
With saints dost bait thy hook! Most dangerous
Is that temptation that doth goad us on
To sin in loving virtue. Never could the strumpet
With all her double vigour, art and nature,
Once stir my temper: but this virtuous maid
Subdues me quite. Ever till now
When men were fond, I smil'd, and wonder'd how.

                                    (II.ii. 168–87)

Angelo's awakening evokes a good deal of sympathy, but that is
soon dissipated during his second encounter with Isabella. He is
both calculating and brutal in the way in which he makes his
demand for her body in return for Claudio's reprieve. When
Angelo was grave and bloodless he required everyone else to conform to his view. Now that he is bent on gratifying his sexual
desire he seeks to strip away any claim to virtue or purity: women
are creatures of base passions who merely affect reticence; their
function is to satisfy men's needs:

                          Be that you are,
That is, a woman; if you be more, you're none.
If you be one — as you are well express'd
By all external warrants — show it now,
By putting on the destin'd livery.

                                    (II.iv. 133–7)

As Angelo relinquishes all semblance of honour, Isabella responds
with spirit and dignity. Yet, left alone with Angelo's demand ring-
ing in her ears she is adamant that no brother could desire a sister

to sacrifice her honour to save his life. Isabella has discovered a
good deal about the nature of the world in a short space of time,
but her unequivocal conclusion is chilling:

> Then, Isabel live chaste, and brother, die:
> More than our brother is our chastity.
>
> (II.iv. 183–4)

All sorts of religious and moral arguments can be advanced to
justify her position, but nevertheless it seems deficient in charity.

No sooner has Isabella expressed her conviction so forcibly than
we encounter a frightened young man in the condemned cell: the
taste of fear, which so obviously infects Claudio, brings all moral
formulas into question. Confronted by death Claudio quite
naturally has little sense of certainty attaching to any philosophy or
principle. The Duke underlines the fragility and insignificance of
mankind, but his speech can do nothing to ease the journey to the
axeman's block. His bleak account of the nature of life rolls on to a
conclusion that at an intellectual level makes the loss of life seem
unimportant:

> Thou hast nor youth, nor age,
> But as it were an after-dinner's sleep
> Dreaming on both; for all thy blessed youth
> Becomes as aged, and doth beg the alms
> Of palsied eld: and when thou art old and rich,
> Thou hast neither heat, affection, limb, nor beauty
> To make thy riches pleasant. What's yet in this
> That bears the name of life? Yet in this life
> Lie hid moe thousand deaths; yet death we fear
> That makes these odds all even.
>
> (III.i. 32–41)

Claudio's immediate rejoinder to this stark philosophical perspective is:

> To sue to live, I find I seek to die,
> And seeking death, find life.
>
> (III.i. 42–3)

But he feels a quickening of his pulse when Isabella arrives.
Claudio's response to Isabella's picturesque announcement that he

is to be executed the following day is telling:

> Is there no remedy?

Isabella's reply is intended to quell Claudio's anxious hope:

> None, but such a remedy as, to save a head
> To cleave a heart in twain.

The effect is to create a belief in Claudio that there may be some hope of salvation, so that his desperation is intensified:

> But is there any?
>
> (III.i. 60–2)

As Isabella reveals that there is a means of escape but one that is unacceptable, Claudio punctuates her drawn out disclosure of the circumstances with a series of short lines expressive of hope, fear, anguish and impatience until he bursts out with 'Let me know the point' (III.i. 72). Isabella's consciousness of Claudio's intense fear of death, and her counterbalancing fear of violation, causes her to attempt to make it impossible for her brother to beg her sacrifice to save his life:

> O, I do fear thee, Claudio, and I quake
> Lest thou a feverous life shouldst entertain,
> And six or seven winters more respect
> Than a perpetual honour. Dar'st thou die?
> The sense of death is most in apprehension;
>
> (III.i. 73–7)

As the Duke in his Friar's habit recommends acceptance of death on the basis of the worthless nature of life, so Isabella rests her case on the value of honour over life. When she goes on to reveal Angelo's true character and the nature of the offer he has made, Claudio is sufficiently shocked to insist 'Thou shalt not do't' (III.i. 102). But Isabella evidently feels a sense of guilt about being unwilling to make the necessary sacrifice as she then insists:

> O, were it but my life,
> I'd throw it down for your deliverance
> As frankly as a pin.
>
> (III.i. 103–5)

Despite Isabella's religious convictions and the nature of her chosen vocation, she does not express her objection to giving herself to Angelo in theological terms. It is Claudio, as his resolve weakens and he searches for a means of staying alive, who refers to the matter of sin. He casts doubt on the severity of the sin of fornication and admits his fear of death: 'Death is a fearful thing' (III.i. 115). Isabella does not respond by setting forth the theological implications of such a sin but rather points to the dishonour Claudio would incur by paying for his life by means of her sacrifice.

Claudio's response is frighteningly human. Through his eyes we experience for the first time the dreadful fears of death; the terror felt by a young man who has visualised his earthly extinction. At the end of this agonising speech Claudio begs his sister to sacrifice herself with an argument which is simultaneously rational and a rationalisation:

> Sweet sister, let me live.
> What sin you do to save a brother's life,
> Nature dispenses with the deed so far
> That is becomes a virtue.
>
> (III.i. 132–5)

Isabella still fails to contradict the validity of his argument but instead breaks into a hysterical denunciation directed at her brother's lack of manhood. The speech is infused with references to sexuality but devoid of any hint of theological implications:

> O, you beast!
> O faithless coward! O dishonest wretch!
> Wilt thou be made a man out of my vice?
> Is't not a kind of incest, to take life
> From thine own sister's shame? What should I think?
> Heaven shield my mother play'd my father fair:
> For such a warped slip of wilderness
> Ne'er issued from his blood.
>
> (III.i. 135–42)

This is not cold-blooded inhumanity, but panic; not a fear of committing sin, which she never mentions, but a subconscious fear of violation that finds expression in her explicit references to incest and adultery. Indeed, poor Claudio's sexual misdemeanour, and his frightened plea for his life to be redeemed by his sister's sacrifice, leads Isabella to denounce him as licentious:

> Thy sin's not accidental, but a trade;
> Mercy to thee would prove itself a bawd;

> (III.i. 148–9)

What is intriguing in this exchange is what it reveals about Isabella's attitude towards sexuality: as Angelo perceives no distinction between the procreation of an illegitimate child and murder, so Isabella quickly relegates her brother to the level of Pompey. Shakespeare seems to have presented two characters whose fear of sexuality has led to suppression of natural feelings to such an extent that their vision is distorted. For Isabella, fornication is an act that she can't bring herself to name; Angelo once vested with power immediately resurrects a statute dealing with sex.

Even when she has calmed down, Isabella informs the Duke that she has no intention of agreeing to Angelo's proposal: 'I had rather my brother die by the law, than my son should be unlawfully born' (III.i. 188–90). Here again the objection is not theological, but social. This remarkable feature of Isabella's response to her situation has received inadequate attention from scholars because they have frequently assumed that her objections are theological. (And there is some evidence for that view in her confrontation with Angelo.) But this is a characteristic of the problem plays; at key moments major characters employ arguments that are surprisingly or completely unexpected. The King in *All's Well* subordinates the principle of heredity to human goodness and Hector in *Troilus and Cressida* is responsible for the perpetuation of the war having delivered a critique which makes its continuation indefensible.

What Shakespeare does in the prison scene is to generate an intense awareness of the desperate desire of human beings to hang on to life in the face of any countervailing pressures, be they theological, philosophical or social. The will to live asserts itself; and just as surely the potency of sexual energy will prevail in the face of the most draconian laws. Thus a critical feature of the play is the tension which exists between order and control on the one hand, and energy and anarchy on the other. No sooner has Isabella left the stage than Pompey appears making a complaint which underlines this tension: ''Twas never merry world since, of two usuries, the merriest was put down, and the worser allowed by order of law' (III.ii. 6–8). Pompey protests that the profit (procreation) arising from usury is tolerated whereas procreation resulting from lechery is restrained. But the speech contains an irony of which Pompey is unaware. Interest rates in excess of 10 per cent (the maximum allowed under the statute of 1570) were not the consequence of official connivance but the result of economic pressures which asserted themselves over theological misgivings. Shakespeare is well aware that pressures against moral injunctions and legal constraints are not confined to the sphere of sexuality but manifest themselves powerfully in other areas where human passions are strong. Few human drives are stronger than acquisitiveness. Indeed, Shakespeare links these two elements very firmly in depicting the world of Pompey and Mistress Overdone. These are professional dealers in sex as opposed to Lucio who is licentious. But if the vitality of this underworld of sexual activity is inevitable, at no point does it appear less than thoroughly distasteful. The Duke sums up the nature of Pompey's activities when he chastises him for profiting from lechery:

> Say to thyself,
> From their abominable and beastly touches
> I drink, I eat, array myself, and live.
> Canst thou believe thy living is a life,
> So stinkingly depending? Go mend, go mend.
>
> (III.ii. 22–6)

Nevertheless, at the very moment that Pompey is carried off to prison the worldly Lucio insists the nature of lechery is such that 'it is impossible to extirp it quite, friar, till eating and drinking be put down' (III.ii. 98–9). So long as lechery exists there will be people who profit by it, no matter how many laws are passed.

Profit is a key term in this play: it constitutes a distinguishing mark between the actions of the disreputable and the honourable. When Pompey describes the inmates of the prison as well-known clients of Mistress Overdone, he goes on to enumerate their activities. These involve illegal profiteering or fraud, commencing with Master Rash who is in jail for engaging in the common crime of making part of a loan in commodities, which are either of poor quality or out of fashion, so that the real rate of interest greatly exceeds the legal maximum of 10 per cent. At the other extreme from this kind of activity is the Duke's proposal to Isabella:

Whereto if you'll a willing ear incline,
What's mine is yours, and what is yours is mine.

(V.i. 533–4)

In contrast to the wholehearted nature of the Duke's declaration of love for Isabella, is the gradual exposure of Angelo: he attempts to hide behind his office and reputation in order to save himself and has already devalued Mariana by claiming that her reputation had been called into question. The whole process is preceded by Angelo's contemplation of his crime and the question of status and evaluation.

This deed unshapes me quite; makes me unpregnant
And dull to all proceedings. A deflower'd maid;
And by an eminent body, that enforc'd
The law against it! But that her tender shame
Will not proclaim against her maiden loss,
How might she tongue me! Yet reason dares her no,
For my authority bears so credent bulk
That no particular scandal once can touch,
But it confounds the breather.

(IV.iv. 18–26)

Thus Angelo bases his security on his commanding position and Isabella's fear of besmirching her reputation. He hides behind his authority and believes she will be equally eager to conceal her loss of honour. Although expressing regret about Claudio's death, he justifies it on the grounds that the young man's sense of dishonour, through gaining reprieve by means of his sister's loss of honour, would drive him to revenge. Angelo feels remorse, but rather than losing his grip on things his calculations are cynically precise.

If Angelo seems momentarily to waver, the weakness of his conscience soon becomes manifest. The Duke greets him with commendations which ought to discomfort him. When confronted by Isabella's accusation, Angelo is astonishingly cool:

My lord, her wits I fear me are not firm.
She hath been a suitor to me for her brother,
Cut off by course of justice.

(V.i. 35–7)

Angelo's suavity is in sharp contrast to Isabella's passion which crashes forward on a series of clauses that are logical but knotted. (Interestingly, she is now capable of uttering the word 'fornication'.) The Duke in asserting scepticism and disbelief creates a number of clear opportunities for Angelo to confess. Indeed, the situation is structured precisely to ensure that Angelo has these clear invitations to give way, to be overcome by a sense of guilt. One speech by the Duke is aimed directly at Angelo's conscience:

> First, his integrity
> Stands without blemish; next, it imports no reason
> That with such vehemency he should pursue
> Faults proper to himself. If he had so offended,
> He would have weigh'd thy brother by himself,
> And not have cut him off.
>
> (V.i. 110–15)

Still Angelo remains impassive, his conscience untouched so that the Duke is obliged to press on with the torment of Isabella by giving orders for her to be taken to prison.

Angelo absorbs the further praise of Friar Peter and the Duke and accepts the offer of being judge in his own case. It might be argued that Angelo has been struggling with his conscience as he remains silent after his initial denunciation of Isabella, but as soon as Mariana removes her veil and accuses him Angelo reveals the full force of his mendacity: the chief reason he cites for his betrayal of Mariana is that 'her reputation was disvalu'd/In levity' (V.i. 220–1). He is the very man who 'disvalu'd' her reputation in order to escape from his commitment when her brother was lost at sea and she ceased to be a profitable investment. Morally, Angelo seems several steps below Pompey. This speech, which refers back to events which occurred five years previously, is concluded with the line 'Upon my faith and honour' (V.i. 223). When he speaks those words it is impossible not to draw a parellel between the extravagant and pointless calumnies of Lucio and the straightforward marketing of sexuality by Pompey and see them as open and innocuous by comparison. What seems clear is that the Angelos of the world are able to get away with a tremendous amount of dishonesty. When he finally turns with full force on Mariana, Angelo appears both callous and vicious:

> I did but smile till now:
> Now, good my lord, give me the scope of justice.

My patience here is touch'd: I do perceive
These poor informal women are no more
But instruments of some more mightier member
That sets them on. Let me have way, my lord,
To find this practice out.

(V.i. 232–8)

As Angelo plumbs the depths of cynicism he is prepared to make
use of Lucio's testimony against the disguised Duke and even calls
on Lucio to help restrain the mysterious Friar. As the Duke
emerges from his disguise there can be no doubting the genuine
nature of his contempt for Angelo as a man who has abused his
authority, betrayed the trust invested in him, and denigrated
honest people in a ruthless fashion. Angelo is not even referred to
by name:

We'll borrow place of him. Sir, by your leave.
Hast thou or word, or wit, or impudence,
That yet can do thee office?

(V.i. 360–2)

It is only now, when it is absolutely clear that lies and evasions are
of no further use that Angelo admits his guilt and seeks death. He
still has the possibility of equivocation over his engagement to
Mariana, but in response to the Duke's question, 'Say: wast thou
e'er contracted to this woman?' his answer is brief and clear: 'I
was, my lord' (V.i. 373–4).

Angelo's fall, it must be remembered, is unique in magnitude
but not in kind. It is clear that his treatment of Mariana is well
known to the Duke before the action of the play begins, and his
evaluation of Angelo is such that he expects him to behave badly
when given sole command. The Duke has detected something
rotten in Angelo that needs to be exposed before he has the opportunity of exercising unfettered control over people. As the Duke
prepares his controlled experiment he confides in the Friar:

Lord Angelo is precise;
Stands at guard with Envy; scarce confesses
That his blood flows; or that his appetite
Is more to bread than stone. Hence shall we see
If power changes purpose, what our seemers be.

(I.iii. 50–4)

This speech suggests that the Duke has not only detected a strain of dishonesty in Angelo, but that he has discerned a powerful capacity for self-deception: Angelo is playing up to a role which is designed to convince himself, as well as others, but the price paid is repression. There is a marked contrast between the attributes of the two men. Angelo can, under the intense emotional pressure of recognising his lust for Isabella, confess to himself, 'yea, my gravity,/Wherein — let no man hear me — I take pride' (II.iv. 9–10). The Duke, Escalus avers, is 'One that, above all other strifes, contended especially to know himself' (III.ii. 226–7). Recognition of his true nature comes as a shock to Angelo which is encapsulated in his expression 'Blood, thou art blood' (II.iv. 15). But not only has the Duke explored his own nature frankly, he possesses a generosity of spirit and receives delight from the joys of others. Again as Escalus puts it in response to a question about the Duke's pleasures: 'Rather rejoicing to see another merry, than merry at anything which professed to make him rejoice. A gentleman of all temperance.' (III.ii. 229–31) Angelo appears so cold-blooded that Lucio suggests that he 'was not made by man and woman, after this downright way of creation'. Indeed, 'Some report a sea-maid spawned him. Some, that he was begot between two stockfishes. But it is certain that when he makes water, his urine is congealed ice.' (III.ii. 100–7) Moreover, Angelo takes an evident delight in seeing others suffer. Before encountering Isabella he dismisses contemptuously the Provost's plea on behalf of Claudio, and leaves the confusion of Pompey's trial expressing the wish to Escalus that he will 'find good cause to whip them all' (II.i. 136). The Duke can even feel compassion for Barnadine; Angelo seems devoid of human warmth or fellow feeling.

What, then, are the prospects for his reformation? The answer can not be obtained from the text. Angelo's disgrace has not diminished his taste for life, for when Claudio appears alive and well his response is one of immediate relief. As the Duke observes,

By this lord Angelo perceives he's safe;
Methinks I see a quickening in his eye.
Well, Angelo, your evil quits you well.
Look that you love your wife: her worth, worth yours.

(V.i. 492–5)

The last line taxes Angelo to be worthy of Mariana, and stresses the need for him to achieve a merit that can counterbalance hers.

Is this a pious hope? Or is there within Angelo the seed of a wholesome spirit that can come to fruition under the warmth of Mariana's love? The structure of romantic comedy calls for a positive response to the latter question, but in this play the question hangs in the air. The audience leaves the theatre pondering the most likely outcome.

Of course, a reader or director of the play has another question to resolve: namely, how does Isabella respond to the Duke's proposal of marriage? Does she accept with alacrity? Does she ponder the question? Or does she recoil at the suggestion? During the Stratford production of 1983 a moment of mutual recognition occurs earlier in the play, as their eyes meet, and the audience has no doubt about the outcome. But this perfectly acceptable device does involve the director's or actor's decision. The reader may feel a considerable sense of uncertainty. Shakespeare provides no clear indication of how Isabella responds. Nevertheless, there is a feeling that this young woman has travelled a long way since the beginning of the play when she sought 'a more strict restraint' (I.iv. 4) than prevailed in the nunnery. Her capacity for empathy has proved to be much greater when contemplating Mariana's situation than her brother's. She may well have come to the conclusion enunciated by the Duke in the opening scene of the play:

> Heaven doth with us as we with torches do,
> Not light them for themselves; for if our virtues
> Did not go forth of us, 'twere all alike
> As if we had them not.

> (I.i. 32–5)

As Elizabeth Marie Pope points out, in her essay on the theological and legal background to the play, Isabella's plea on behalf of Angelo

> is not natural; it is not (as the Duke has carefully pointed out) even reasonable: it is sheer, reckless forgiveness of the kind Christ advocates in the Sermon on the Mount — the great pronouncement which in Luke immediately precedes and forms part of the measure-for-measure passage.[4]

Here it appears that Isabella is responding to Mariana's plea with a depth of spontaneous compassion which she distinctly lacks when castigating Claudio for making his desperate plea to be saved from death by her fornication. Admittedly, the situations are not equal. The one act constitutes the essence of Christian charity and forgiveness, while the other calls for committing a sin in order to save a life. But at the emotional level the contrast in behaviour is so startling as to suggest that the icy current which constituted an essential element in the early Isabella has been warmed. If this is true, then marriage to the Duke would be a fitting conclusion to the play. If, on the other hand, the difference in response between the two situations is due merely to the clarity of Isabella's understanding of the theological issues, what we have is a scrupulous candidate for the nunnery, but a character profoundly lacking a natural human sympathy. This latter interpretation would not prevent Isabella making a first-class judge or ruler; but she would make an uncomfortable wife — in the unlikely event of her accepting such a proposal.

Harriet Hawkins, in her riposte to Arthur C. Kirsch's claim that the problems of *Measure for Measure* can be resolved by means of a clear understanding of vital scriptural texts and the way in which they were interpreted by Shakespeare's audience, maintains that:

> any number of (quite rightly) unanswered questions and unsolved problems seem, whether deliberately or unconsciously, to have been built in to the text of *Measure for Measure* by Shakespeare himself, and these problems and questions are immeasurably more interesting than the solutions to them that have been propounded by modern scholars. For after all, the duty of the artist (as opposed to the scientist) is not to provide us with solutions, but, rather, to make certain that the problems under consideration are accurately posed.[5]

At the heart of her discussion lies the critical exchange between Angelo and Isabella in II.iv. where Isabella describes her willingness to die, rather than surrender her chastity, in highly erotic terms, and Angelo responds with an insistent demand that Isabella succumb to his lust without inhibition. Harriet Hawkins insists that this arousal of the demonic in Angelo (and which may be close to the surface in Isabella) is not removed by the nominal resolution. Rather, she argues, Shakespeare has released upon the audience a veritable Pandora's box of suppressed sexuality which knows no limits. The saintly Isabella is the agent who ignites Angelo's lust; a character who is so much his mirror image — a woman insistent on suppressing her latent sexuality. Ms Hawkins goes so far as to ask what would have happened if Isabella had slept with Angelo? What kind of woman would have emerged from the bed? Of course, that line of investigation is blocked off by Shakespeare, and this is precisely where, for Ms Hawkins, Shakespeare has steered the play away from the intense and deep-seated psychological possibilities that he has raised by the encounter in question. As she expresses the point 'In short, the subsequent action of the play, like many scholarly discussions of it, would seem designed to encourage us to efface from the memory the extraordinary psychological and sexual reverberations of the earlier scenes' and she adds a vital comment: 'Assuming (only assuming) that Shakespeare himself wants us to disregard that dramatic evidence which he himself introduced previously, is it, in the last analysis, possible to do so?'[6]

The answer must be in the negative, and here we come to the nub of the question. No matter how smoothly Shakespeare effects a resolution (and many critics are satisfied that this is a perfectly normal romantic comedy) we are left pondering the questions raised rather than enjoying the satisfaction of the ostensible resolution — which is the essence of the problem play. Moreover, Coleridge's point is germane to the question of the acceptability of the ending. It is not simply a feeling that there has been breach of dramatic decorum by the Duke's generous reprieve of Angelo, but rather, 'cruelty, with lust and damnable baseness, cannot be forgiven, because we cannot conceive of them as being *morally* repented of'.[7]

It would appear, therefore, that a great deal of critical endeavour has been devoted to explaining away the difficulties of this problem play rather than acknowledging them. It is hard to believe that Shakespeare inadvertently created these problems, so they must have been intentional. The dramatist appears to have used the structure of romantic comedy to dramatise difficult psychological, theological and social issues, and even to raise questions about the dramatic mode itself, creating a happy ending about which the audience has doubts. In the real world which Shakespeare has created in *Measure for Measure*, and in the other two problem plays, can there be such a thing as happy ever after?

In all three problem plays Shakespeare is pursuing the connection between the quest for personal realisation and the attainment of socially approved values. Hector wishes to achieve honour and the preservation of his society, but in seeking honour through glory on the battlefield (paying scrupulous attention to the principles of chivalry) he turns his back on the only sure way of protecting Troy: through peace. Personal fulfilment is at odds with rationality (which is clearly revealed at a decisive moment in the debate scene), whether it be in stopping the war or in being totally ruthless on the battlefield. Bertram wants to be a man of honour and distinction, but will spurn the King's earnest entreaty rather than be shackled to one whom he deems a social inferior. He will court honour on the battlefield and have it defined in those limited terms rather than strive for a more widely accepted conception of virtue. If lying is necessary to pass muster in the wider society he will resort to it freely.

Angelo and Isabella are both desperate for the attainment of personal integrity. For Angelo social recognition of his extraordinary detachment or 'gravity' is the crucial objective. In order to achieve his aim he endeavours to comport himself in a way which will ensure respect as a man quite above normal human weakness. When his frailty is exposed to himself, he seeks to retain his status in the community even at the expense of plunging to the lowest level of mendacity. Seeming is an adequate substitute for being. For Isabella there can be no such compromise. She seeks to attain integrity by means of severe self-denial within the nunnery. Sainthood is the goal, and commonplace deprivation will hardly satisfy her. But before she can fully escape the contamination of a befouled world she is called upon to prostitute herself or permit her brother to die. Whereas Angelo can sacrifice the reality of integrity for the appearance, Isabella cannot endure the thought of sacrificing her integrity. For her there is no half-way house between purity and contamination: it is the act that counts not the purpose for which it is undertaken; purity of spirit cannot be achieved without purity of body.

Hector deceives himself by sleight of hand; Angelo is a mature fraud (though he is initially shocked to discover it); Bertram an immature one (who experiences no moral qualms or mental anguish); Isabella can neither deceive nor be self-deceiving in her quest for integrity. Her sexuality constitutes the threat to sainthood. At one level of consciousness she fears her own desire more than she fears brutal violation. The Duke saves her from a fate which to her is worse than death, but only at the cost of engaging in the manoeuvres to which even virtuous people have to resort in the real world. Does this experience cause her to re-define her conception of integrity? Has she become strong enough to achieve integrity outside the protective walls of the nunnnery?

These moral dilemmas which are so integral to the problem plays are of a different order, or are differently structured, from those which are encountered in Shakespeare's tragedies or histories. An awareness of this difference has been glimpsed by David Craig who expresses it as follows:

> It might be said that Shakespeare's tragedies are concerned no less than *Measure for Measure* with such core-values as love and integrity. But the method of the tragedies is to expose humanity to the most terrifying and extraordinary forces conceivable, whereas *Measure for Measure* likens itself to the finest modern fiction by virtue of dealing directly with the kind of experience that comes to us all, exceptional or not, and with the kind of integration we must bring to such personal relations if we are to live them through happily.[8]

There certainly is something more prosaic or down-to-earth about the human choices we encounter in the problem plays. They do not focus on such considerations as regicide, but rather, confront us with such matters as how shabbily we are prepared to behave in order to retain our social standing. Are we more prepared to sacrifice our self-esteem rather than social esteem? And to what extent do vicious or despicable acts infringe our self-love? It would appear that neither Achilles nor Bertram feel tainted by the vilest deeds, while Angelo suffers only momentary anguish at discovering his true nature and his capacity for violence and mendacity. The problem plays don't afford us the consolation of the tragedies, and those who seek productions of *Troilus and Cressida* which accentuate the tragic tones in the close of the play, at the expense of the ironic, lack the moral courage to face up to the bleakness of the reality.

Here, then, is a paradox. The tragedies disconcert us less than the problem plays. The world of tragedy is sufficiently above and beyond us to appear rare and wholly exceptional concatenations of circumstances which owe their power to a terribleness, to being a lesson in the possible. The heroes and victims are men not gods, but whose circumstances are so remarkable that we don't feel that we will ever encounter them — though our inner being is profoundly affected by the experience of watching and listening. In the case of the problem plays we are in very familiar territory: the actions and discourse of these dramas are those of our daily thoughts and dreams. Perhaps it is because we can so easily identify with the concerns and dilemmas of these plays that the dramatist has taken a great deal of trouble to keep us detached and critical, so that we are simultaneously outside and inside the action. The brake is not so necessary in the tragedies, though Shakespeare remains determined to maintain our objectivity whilst at the same time creating emotional intensity. The difference in dramatic technique and in audience response is one of degree rather than of kind.

The prosaic nature of social reality is rendered in the opening scene of *Measure for Measure*. After an exchange of only three words between the Duke and Escalus the former commences the first significant speech of the play with 'Of government'. What follows is not a discourse on good rule or law but a commentary on the 'worth' or value of Escalus and the comprehensive nature of his knowledge:

> The nature of our people,
> Our city's institutions, and the terms
> For common justice, y'are as pregnant in
> As art and practice hath enriched any
> That we remember.

> (I.i. 9 – 13)

Escalus, it seems, has a good working knowledge of the customs and practices in Vienna, the temperament of the people, and the theory and practice of law. Significantly, the word 'pregnant', meaning knowledgeable or full of understanding, commences a verbal patterning suggestive of the process of growth and fruition which is contrasted with death, reaching its climax in Angelo's assertion that pregnancy outside of marriage is equal to committing murder:

> It were as good
> To pardon him that hath from nature stolen
> A man already made, as to remit
> Their saucy sweetness that do coin heaven's image
> In stamps that are forbid.

> (II.iv. 42 – 6)

After what appears to be a polite preamble before handing over power to Escalus, the Duke promptly asks for an opinion on Angelo who, surprisingly, is to deputise for the Duke. Escalus does not express any resentment at being overlooked, but promptly asserts Angelo's 'worth'. The question of value, worth or merit is quickly placed in the foreground and Angelo continues the process, using another common metaphor employed in the play, by asking to have his worth put to the test:

> Now good, my lord,
> Let there be some more test made of my metal,
> Before so noble and so great a figure
> Be stamp'd upon it.
>
> (I.i. 47 – 50)

Ironically, Angelo is about to receive precisely what he requests: a test that will reveal him to be just what the Duke suspects that he is — anything but current gold.

Packed in to this almost businesslike exchange are references not only to value and worth, with the coin imagery serving to call attention to the desirable relationship between extrinsic and intrinsic value, but the contrast between creation and destruction, justice and mercy and wholeness. As the Duke comments to Angelo,

> In our remove, be thou at *full* ourself.
> Mortality and mercy in Vienna
> Live in thy tongue, and heart.
>
> (I.i. 43 – 5)

Angelo is given complete power with the clear implication that compassion and mercy constitute a necessary counterbalance to the rigour of law. Far from being invited to 'clean up' Vienna, Angelo is being cautioned of the need for a balanced outlook. As the scene virtually opens with the word 'government' so it closes with the word 'honour'. Here it is used in the sense of Angelo's title; previously in the scene (line 63) it has been used by the Duke to mean truth or integrity. And so characteristically of the problem plays there is an immediate interweaving of the concepts value or worth and honour, and they are related to personal conduct on the one hand, and socially validated behaviour on the other, in the form of government or law. *Measure for Measure*, it is apparent from the outset, is profoundly concerned with the formation of human values (and the subsequent status attaching to individuals) and the incorporation of those values into the system of law and government. The Duke's comments imply that the law can never be mechanistic, but that the ruler or justice has to employ both his heart and brain.

Another crucial feature of the opening scene is the Duke's assertion that goodness or worth is of little value if it is not employed:

> Heaven doth with us as we with torches do,
> Not light them for themselves; for if our virtues
> Did not go forth of us, 'twere all alike
> As if we had them not.

(I.i. 32 – 5)

Human worth, then, is assessed in terms of human action. By this test Isabella's retreat to the nunnery constitutes an evasion of responsibility. The Duke's expression implies a congruity of spiritual and civil responsibilities. The personal, social, political and spiritual strands are closely interwoven. There is a strong reciprocal relationship between the personal and social: unfettered action by bawds and usurers may turn society into an ungovernable swamp of iniquity; a harsh judgement by a justice may bring misery and death to an essentially good individual. The wholly ordered and 'moral' society requires such discipline that it would be repugnant on the basis of human freedom and the existence of human vitality.

These dilemmas, which lie beneath the surface of abstractions uttered in the opening scene, soon emerge embodied in the entirely realistic characters who move within both the high and low levels of society. And the tension which exists between these social strata is portrayed in a way which intensifies the sense of social realism which characterises the play. There is probably no other play of Shakespeare's where this social dichotomy is so clearly exposed.

Critics of the play who see the Duke's departure as an evasion of responsibility (why does he not clean up Vienna himself?) mistake his actions: he leaves to test Angelo, whose worth he has had cause to doubt through his betrayal of Mariana, and he acquires the opportunity of examining his society from the bottom. He discovers that even a saint could not achieve an untarnished reputation in a world inhabited by characters like Lucio (the very Lucio who is necessary to press the virtuous Isabella into a determined defence of her brother's life), and that it is only by means of stratagems that justice can be achieved. Left to itself the law frequently fails to secure justice, and the more severe and less humble the ruler or justice the greater is likely to be the human suffering involved in the pursuit of justice. Looked at from ground level the social universe is seen as varied and complex; only viewed from the top can it be perceived as susceptible to tight and coherent control that is both just and humane. Barnadine's nine years' imprisonment would constitute severe injustice had he emerged as innocent; his ultimate sentence, in terms of the legal system of Vienna, is overly generous. How is it possible to pin down Pompey and Mistress Overdone when the instrument of law is such a fragile reed as Constable Elbow? Even more significantly, are they merely responding to a social need or are they corrupting society? Might not they constitute an unsavoury but innocuous strand in the social fabric after all?

When Mistress Overdone is informed by Pompey that the houses in the suburbs are to be demolished, she promptly asks what is to become of those in the city. Pompey's reply is ambiguous 'They shall stand for seed: they had gone down too, but that a wise burgher put in for them' (I.ii. 91–2). This may mean that they have been purchased or protected. Either way the implication is that these city houses will become available when the present attack on this activity abates. The suggestion is that prostitution can never be eradicated. The characteristic growth imagery is effective. Pompey is right to be optimistic: 'Come: fear not you: good counsellors lack no clients: though you change your place, you need not change your trade' (I.ii. 98–100).

Fast on the heels of this exchange Claudio appears, being exhibited to the public as a warning to others. Despite Claudio's initial response to the question about the cause of his restraint,

> From too much liberty, my Lucio. Liberty,
> As surfeit, is the father of much fast;
> So every scope by the immoderate use
> Turns to restraint.
>
> (I.ii. 117–20)

he quickly goes on to reveal that he is *effectively* married to Julietta, so that at most his guilt is a mere technicality which contrasts sharply with Pompey's profession:

> Thus stands it with me: upon a true contract
> I got possession of Julietta's bed.

You know the lady; she is fast my wife,
Save that we do the denunciation lack
Of outward order.

(I.ii. 134–8)

It appears that Claudio and Julietta are legally married according
to the common law contract of *sponsalia de praesenti* which was still
valid in England at the time. Shakespeare, then, has made their
breach of legality as slight as possible, even making due allowance
for the legal situation in Vienna. So confident is Claudio that he is
being victimised that he questions Angelo's motives.

Even Isabella, who is unwilling to use the word fornication, is
shocked to discover the penalty for Claudio's crime: 'Doth he
so, / Seek his life?' (I.iv. 71–2) Moreover, she suggests the remedy
for the situation even before discovering the penalty that is being
sought: 'O, let him marry her!' (I.iv. 49) And these lines are being
spoken by the young woman who has just complained of the lack of
severity of the rules of the convent — lines which follow on immediately from the Duke's perceptive critique of Angelo:

> Lord Angelo is precise;
> Stands at guard with Envy; scarce confesses
> That his blood flows; or that his appetite
> Is more to bread than stone. Hence shall we see
> If power change purpose, what our seemers be.

(I.iii. 50–4)

Thus these two characters who so strongly favour restraint,
especially control of natural sexual impulses, are at variance in this
situation. Isabella spontaneously sees no more than a human falli-
bility which is easily remedied; Angelo perceives ingrained vice
which must be extirpated. Isabella seeks to close herself off from
the sullied world; Angelo intends to bend it to his view of orderly
conduct.

Angelo's conception of the law is articulated clearly in the next
scene when he debates Claudio's case with Escalus:

> We must not make a scarecrow of the law,
> Setting it up to fear the birds of prey,
> And let it keep one shape till custom make it
> Their perch, and not their terror.

(II.i. 1–4)

Terror is the vital quality of the law for Angelo. Leaving aside the narrowness of his view on morality, which arises from his repressed sexuality, he appears to be a natural tyrant. He is opposed not only to sexuality but to the forces of life. Whereas Escalus can see the humour in Pompey, Froth and Elbow, Angelo feels total contempt for squirming humanity. When Escalus attempts to secure a more moderate penalty for Claudio he resorts to a metaphor from horticulture:

> Let us be keen, and rather cut a little,
> Than fall, and bruise to death.
>
> (II.i. 5–6)

For Escalus the law should perform the function of the pruning knife, cutting back merely to foster healthy growth.

The suggestion that the law should work with rather than against nature is reinforced by Pompey's claim that 'If your worship will take order for the drabs and the knaves, you need not fear the bawds' (II.i. 231–2). Pompey is right to insist that he is responding to a demand that will persist unless the youth of the city are castrated. Moreover, he points to the equivocal nature of law. Certain actions may invariably be deemed so wrong, such as murder, that they are always illegal, but morality is not a sure guide to legality. When Escalus asks whether being a bawd is a lawful trade, Pompey's riposte is prompt and telling, 'If the law would allow it, sir' (II.i. 224).

Jonathan Dollimore has argued persuasively that at the time Shakespeare was writing *Measure for Measure* the traditional legitimation of law was under severe pressure. Dollimore claims that 'what Machiavelli did for religion, Montaigne did, with equally devastating effect, for law'. In support of this contention, he cites Montaigne's view that

> Lawes are . . . maintained in credit, not because they are essentially just, but because they are lawes. It is the mysticall foundation of their authority; they have none other; which availes them much: they are often made by fooles; more often by men, who in hatred of equality, have want of equity . . . There is nothing so grossely and largely offending, nor so ordinarily wronging as the Lawes.[9]

Florio's translation of the *Essays* was published in 1603 and had been circulating in manuscript for many years before publication, so that *Measure for Measure* articulates in a very subtle way ideas that were in the foreground of intellectual debate. Shakespeare does not take up a position, but rather reveals a complex interrelation between human psychology and institutions. The essence of the problem plays is that the audience is left pondering both the psychology of key characters and the implications of the social situation in which they find themselves. In the case of *Measure for Measure* the main areas of debate have related to the nature of the Duke, Angelo and Isabella both in terms of their motivations and actions, and the apparent contradictions which appear at key moments, such as Claudio's apparent mixture of penitence and defiance.

A good example of the problems being removed from the problem plays is provided by Lawrence's well-known study. He perceives a dichotomy between the realistic characters and the Duke. Whereas many critics have pondered long and hard over the character and actions of the Duke, Lawrence disposes of the difficulties by a simple appeal to the conventions of the Elizabethan theatre:

> The ruler of the degenerate city of Vienna is, I believe, to be regarded as a conventional and romantic figure, whose actions are mainly determined by theatrical exigencies and effectiveness; he is, as it were, a stage Duke, not a real person. In this respect he contrasts strikingly with Isabella and Angelo and Claudio and Lucio, and the low-comedy people . . .
>
> The audience were interested in the Duke's reforms only in so far as these served the plot. They did not care a straw about the triumph of his theories as a reformer or the moral welfare of Vienna. What they did wish was that the play should end, as a comedy should, in a general atmosphere of happiness.[10]

Likewise any doubts we may feel about Angelo's capacity to reform or his suitability as a husband for Mariana become irrelevant in the face of the power of theatrical conventions:

> Our modern feeling may be that Angelo gets off altogether too lightly, but the pardon of the repentant villain and his union to a heroine was a commonplace in Elizabethan drama, and would certainly have been readily accepted by a contemporary audience . . . *Measure for Measure* is not a tract on

equity, any more than it is on government; it is not an
expression of Shakespeare's convictions in regard to the
administration of law, but a story of human passion, sin and
forgiveness.[11]

Lawrence insists that to ponder over-long on the relationship
between the scope for law in human affairs, or the nature of
government, is to be guilty of regarding Shakespeare's play as a
'tract' and to be making assumptions about 'Shakespeare's convictions'. This constitutes a clear case of special pleading: Lawrence
uses emotive terms to give greater plausibility to his unsubstan-
tiated argument.

In expressing dissatisfaction with this response to the perplexing
questions to which the play gives rise, C. K. Stead has suggested
that Lawrence evades the difficulties by 'conventionalising' the
Duke while Wilson Knight achieves the same effect by 'theologis-
ing' him. Stead goes on to enumerate some of the questions which
inevitably arise if resort is not made to 'solutions' provided by
Lawrence and Knight — or Leavis's development of Wilson
Knight's argument in which the Duke 'is a kind of Providence
directing the action from above' — with the moral of the play
consisting in the elevation of mercy over justice because of the
universality of human guilt.

It is unlikely any critic would deny that this very proper
weighing of mercy over justice is one — and one of the most
important — of the many and various ethical propositions
thrown up in the course of the action. Indeed it could hardly
have been otherwise, since the proposition is inherent in the
story Shakespeare had chosen to tell. But that the play is
designed to promote this moral truism is much more difficult
to accept. Once again it is an argument that directs us to look
for ethical rather than artistic consistency, and consequently
leaves us with a host of unanswered questions. Was Angelo,
for example, right or wrong to attempt to stamp out 'the
trade'? If he was wrong, was he wrong only because he was
not himself pure, or would it have been wrong under any
circumstances? Should the prostitutes and panders have been
tolerated and merely subjected to moral harangues of the kind
the Duke, disguised as a friar, delivers upon them? Are those
harangues seriously meant, or are they only an aspect of the
disguise? Was the Duke right in his original intention to

clean up the city? Or was this not his intention at all, but only
a concealment of his real objective, to catch out the 'seemer'
Angelo? If Claudio has 'committed a serious offence' (as
Leavis insists) how should it have been dealt with? And what
of Angelo? He attempts rape and murder, yet he gets off with
rather less suffering than has been imposed on Claudio. Does
the 'new ethic' of which the Duke is supposed to be prophet
imply that theological forgiveness must overrule even the
practical application of the law? Must we see ethical considerations, and not the convention of the comic romance
ending, governing even the pardon and marriage of
Angelo?[12]

Schanzer is probably correct when he claims that 'There is
probably no other play by Shakespeare which has so much perplexed critics as *Measure for Measure*, nor one which has aroused
such violent, eccentric, and mutually opposed responses.'[13] He
attributes a good deal of the perplexity and disagreement to the
complexity of the characters in *Measure for Measure*. Despite
censuring Lawrence, Schanzer insists that 'an understanding of
Elizabethan tenets and feelings on certain matters seems particularly necessary in order to dispel or diminish some of these
perplexities'.[14] No doubt an acquaintance with Elizabethan
customs and institutions does clarify and illuminate certain
features of the play, but what emerges from Schanzer's discussion
is that *Measure for Measure* remains the quintessential problem play,
and he affirms his support for Raleigh's view that 'Of all
Shakespeare's plays, this one comes nearest to the direct treatment
of a moral problem.'[15] Further, Schanzer recognises the significance of disillusionment in the play. He wrongly sees Claudio as
the object of Isabella's disillusionment, but there is substance in
his comment on Angelo that 'What makes his experience unique
among Shakespeare's characters is that the object of this disillusion
is his own person.'[16] Schanzer concludes that the play exhibits two
concerns: the one relating to the public domain, the choice
between justice and mercy, he suggests we feel no doubts about;
the other, the moral choice confronting Isabella, gives rise to a
feeling of uncertainty or ambivalence. Schanzer draws a parallel
between Isabella's moral dilemma and the one confronting Brutus
between assassinating Caesar or sacrificing his country's liberty.
However, apart from this concern with a moral choice the plays
have little in common. There is a good deal of irony in *Julius Caesar*

in that Brutus precipitates the very thing he seeks to avoid (the movement from a republic to a dictatorship); he is essential to the conspiracy, but makes a series of disastrous decisions which brings about the defeat of the conspirators; and even at the moment of his death he seems unaware of the nature of the personal betrayal of which he is guilty. Nevertheless, the play is not characterised by the kind of irony, questioning and open-endedness of *Measure for Measure*. For Schanzer each is a problem play because it reveals

> a concern with a moral problem which is central to it, presented in such a manner that we are unsure of our moral bearings, so that uncertain and divided responses to it in the minds of the audience are possible or even probable.[17]

It is questionable whether *Julius Caesar* can be considered a problem play even in terms of Schanzer's definition (which is much narrower than his implied conception of a problem play in his discussion of *Measure for Measure*). Although we sympathise with Brutus' moral dilemma we know beforehand, as a matter of historical fact, what the outcome of his decision will be. We are fascinated by his reasoning, his capacity for rationalisation, his ability to be both ruthless and squeamish, overbearing and loving, the natural leader and the incompetent decision-maker. In other words we are fascinated by his psychology and his tragedy — and the tragedy of his society. But at the end of the play we see with singular clarity Brutus' path to ruin and recognise the nature of the clash between personal and public values. The consequence of his moral choice and the subsequent moral and political decisions are acted out and a clear line of consequences follows. In *Measure for Measure* both Isabella and Angelo are saved from the consequences of their decisions and we are intrigued by the nature of their *future* decision-making in the light of their experience. Thus the focus is shifted in a way quite unlike anything that happens in Shakespearian tragedy.

The contrast between the feelings engendered by tragedy and those to which the problem plays give rise has been clearly discerned by A. P. Rossiter, perhaps the most penetrating critic on the problem plays, in his discussion of *Measure for Measure*:

> there is no redemption, no hint of immortality in the whole. The only certitudes are existence, uncertainty, disappointment, frustration, old age and death. It mentions values only

as delusions. It determines an attitude of mind in which tragedy is quite impossible; in its sombre light all odds is gone . . . Everything exists: nothing has value.[18]

If the problem plays deny the audience the consolation of tragedy, so too, Rossiter maintains, do they deny the simple satisfaction of comedy. Whereas Lawrence confidently concludes 'I do not think there is any doubt that Isabella turns to him [the Duke] with a heavenly and yielding smile. And I cannot see in the least why she should not',[19] Rossiter asserts that 'The "conventional" comedy ending is a weak plea. There is no need for either Duke or cloistress to marry to end the play — unless', he adds, 'we are being pushed up to an allegorical plane, which is "uncomfortable" with the realism and psychology of Acts I – III.'[20]

The ambiguity which characterises the close of *Measure for Measure* is, for Rossiter, characteristic of ambiguities which run right through a play which is 'full of equivocal speeches, of a kind where there is no resolving the ambiguities, since both meanings "belong" in the play frame'.[21] One of the most telling examples of this feature of the play is Claudio's speech to Lucio in which he seems to be both penitent and resigned yet angry and bitter. An explanation of these apparently antithetical expressions has been provided by C. K. Stead, who argues that Claudio's bitterness is 'directed against "the demi-god, Authority"'[22] which has been responsible for the liberty enjoyed by Claudio and then imposes penalties for the indulgence of such freedoms. This interpretation removes the ambiguity of apparent self-disgust and bitter criticism of authority. However, if this solution is acceptable it merely transfers the problem: in both *All's Well* and *Measure for Measure* Shakespeare created a style which is convoluted and strained so that the language itself contains a tension. Thus even if all the ambiguous speeches could be clarified to the satisfaction of critics and students it would do nothing to remove the sense of ambiguity felt in the theatre which seems to have been deliberately created by Shakespeare. It would appear that the intention of these plays is to promote a feeling of verbal and psychological tension and complexity.

No doubt a director, with the support of convinced actors, can minimise the ambiguities which pervade the play and create a congenial happy ending, but the text is so richly suggestive of uncertainties that only the most determined effort would be capable of persuading the audience that despite its peculiarities this is a piece of romantic comedy and all turns out well in the end. The disturbing features of the play lie so close to the surface that both audience and reader are left pondering the psychology of Isabella, Angelo and the Duke, and the kind of future that they would be likely to forge. Even more significantly there remains the unresolved question of the relationship between people and institutions. Can sexual behaviour be brought within the compass of the law? Can prostitution be suppressed without transforming the mechanism for achieving order into instruments of terror? Which is the greater danger to humanity: having lax laws or severe laws which might be exercised by characters like Angelo? Even the most naive member of the audience would realise that an investigative, manipulative and virtuous ruler on the model of the Duke is unlikely to be encountered in the real world. Lucio is a character of low moral standing yet he commands admiration for his audacity and vitality: the state in which no man, not even a Lucio, dares denigrate the leader has suffered political castration. The real world, this play suggests, is disordered, untidy and perplexing, but manifests life; the creation of a society based on strict moral and political order can be attained only by suffocating the life giving forces. Spontaneity is not compatible with strict order.

Notes

1. Schanzer makes a brief reference to this aspect of the play and draws attention to the critics who have considered the question. Ernest Schanzer, *The Problem Plays of Shakespeare: A Study of 'Julius Caesar', 'Measure for Measure', 'Antony and Cleopatra'* (Routledge and Kegan Paul, London, 1963), pp. 86–7.

2. Keith Thomas, 'The Puritans and Adultery: The Act of 1650 Reconsidered' in Donald Pennington and Keith Thomas (eds), *Puritans and Revolutionaries: Essays in Seventeenth Century History, Presented to Christopher Hill* (Oxford University Press, Oxford, 1978), p. 280.

3. Ibid., p. 281.

4. Elizabeth Marie Pope, 'The Renaissance Background of *Measure for Measure*' in Kenneth Muir and Stanley Wells (eds), *Aspects of Shakespeare's 'Problem Plays'* (Cambridge University Press, Cambridge, 1982), p. 70.

5. Harriet Hawkins, ' "The Devil's Party": Virtues and Vices in *Measure for Measure*' in Muir and Wells (eds), *Aspects of 'Problem Plays'*, p. 87.

6. Ibid., p. 92.

7. T. Ashe (ed.), *The Table Talk and Omniana of Samuel Taylor Coleridge* in C. K. Stead (ed.), *Shakespeare: Measure for Measure* (Casebook Series, Macmillan, London, 1971), p. 46.

8. David Craig, 'Love and Society: *Measure for Measure* And Our Own Time' in Arnold Kettle (ed.), *Shakespeare in a Changing World* (Lawrence and Wishart, London, 1964), p. 196.

9. Jonathan Dollimore, *Radical Tragedy: Religion, Ideology and Power in the Drama of Shakespeare and his Contemporaries* (Harvester Press, Brighton, 1984), p. 15 (from Montaigne, Essays, III 331).

10. W. W. Lawrence, *Shakespeare's Problem Comedies*, 3rd edn (Penguin, Harmondsworth, 1969), pp. 100 – 1.

11. Ibid., p. 111.

12. C. K. Stead (ed.), *Shakespeare: Measure for Measure* (Casebook Series, Macmillan, London, 1971), pp. 18 – 19.

13. Schanzer, *The Problem Plays of Shakespeare*, p. 71.

14. Ibid., p. 73.

15. Ibid., p. 106 from Walter Raleigh, *Shakespeare* (Macmillan, London, 1970), p. 169.

16. Ibid., p. 94.

17. Ibid., p. 6.

18. A. P. Rossiter, *Angel with Horns*, 4th edn (Longman, London, 1970), p. 166.

19. Lawrence, *Shakespeare's Problem Comedies*, p. 103.

20. Rossiter, *Angel with Horns*, p. 162.

21. Ibid., p. 163.

22. C. K. Stead (ed.), *Measure for Measure*, p. 33.

6

Conclusion

In recent years there has been a marked tendency to dismiss the term 'problem plays' as a useful label for encompassing *Troilus and Cressida*, *All's Well* and *Measure for Measure*, or for any other combination of plays. Yet, despite the occasional use of terms such as 'dark comedies' or 'tragi-comedies' no adequate alternative has been found. Some critics, like Northrope Frye, have overcome the dilemma by placing *All's Well* and *Measure for Measure* among Shakespeare's romantic comedies and considering *Troilus and Cressida* as a unique, experimental work. No effort has been made in this study to set forth a thesis which can be used to forge an indissoluble link between these plays. Rather an attempt has been made to explore the conception and evolution of the term 'problem play', as it has been applied to a variety of plays, before engaging in an analysis of major aspects of the individual plays. It was suggested in the introduction that these plays share a number of striking affinities and in the light of these shared characteristics a satisfactory definition could be made which would provide a meaningful framework for consideration of their relatedness.

The subsequent discussion was not undertaken in order to focus on the shared characteristics of the plays, but rather to explore their most salient features paying special attention to the difficulties which have been experienced by literary critics endeavouring to interpret them. In the light of that analysis an attempt will be made to summarise the main conclusions emerging from this study and to suggest that the linkage between these plays is sufficiently strong to merit considering them as a group and that the most useful terminology, both from a descriptive and analytical standpoint, is problem plays.

Before pulling together the threads of the preceding discussion it is worth restating the definition of the problem plays which has been adopted in this study. The term problem play is here used to encompass three plays which defy absorption into the traditional categories of romantic comedies, histories, tragedies and romances, but share striking affinities in terms of themes, atmosphere, tone and style. In particular, they explore fundamental problems relating to personal and social values within a framework which makes the audience acutely aware of the problems without allowing amelioration through the provision of adequate answers or a dramatic mode which facilitates a satisfactory release of emotions.

This definition suggests that the plays present at least two kinds of problems. The first is that of classification. Despite the diversity of the plays within the traditional categories, there is general acceptance of the validity and usefulness of the groupings — romantic comedies, histories, tragedies and romances. The groups of plays share affinities in terms of structure, themes, types of source material and chronology, with the romantic comedies and histories being concentrated mainly during the first half of Shakespeare's dramatic career and the romances right at the end. The problem plays occupy a transitional position. Probably written between 1602 and 1604 (*Troilus and Cressida* in 1602, *All's Well* in 1603 and *Measure for Measure* in 1604) they come after the comedies and histories have been completed (with the exception of *Henry VIII*, written right at the end of Shakespeare's career) and coincide with the onset of the writing of the major tragedies. But not only do these plays sit uncomfortably within any of the generally accepted categories of Shakespeare's plays (in contrast with *Hamlet* and *Timon of Athens* which fall comfortably within the group of tragedies, as do *Julius Caesar* and *Antony and Cleopatra* despite their powerful historical dimension), they also trouble and puzzle theatregoers and critics because of their peculiar open-endedness. Significantly all three plays seem to have been among the least popular of Shakespeare's plays until fairly recently. In 1930 W. W. Lawrence was dismissing them as distinctly second rate. Much more recently as shrewd a commentator as Professor Philip Edwards has described the plays as 'failures':

> Yet these two plays are failures. Each fails in its own particular way, and each has a greatness which perhaps compensates for the failure, yet failure there is in the two of them which is

211

very different from the failure of *Troilus and Cressida*. The latter play purposely fails to answer the expectations of the audience for a pattern which will explain and console. The failure of *All's Well* and *Measure for Measure* is in their insistence on a happy ending in spite of the evidence.[1]

Although the plays still provoke a great deal of critical uncertainty they have become increasingly esteemed in recent years, especially as plays in performance. *Troilus and Cressida* has probably been the least popular of the three, and certainly the most perplexing, but the 1985 production at Stratford represented a culmination in the theatrical appreciation of this play which has been taking place during the past 25 years. The most striking feature of the 1985 production was its modernity. Nothing in the Shakespearian canon appears so astonishingly modern and so full of resonances for contemporary society.

However, it is essential to recognise that the 'space' between *Troilus and Cressida*, *All's Well* and *Measure for Measure* is not equidistant. Although there are significant differences between the quartet of plays referred to as romances (not the least being differences in popularity, with *The Winter's Tale* and *The Tempest* far ahead of *Cymbeline* and *Pericles*) no play of Shakespeare's stands so clearly apart from its generic fellows than does *Troilus and Cressida* from *All's Well* and *Measure for Measure*. The question is whether it has enough in common with the other two plays to make the shared label meaningful. Before attempting a definitive answer it is necessary to underline those features which are common to all three plays apart from their refusal to fall into any other category and their singularly open-ended nature.

Above all else these plays grapple very deliberately with major problems of values which confront all societies. All great literature is concerned with human values but in these plays Shakespeare invites a questioning of fundamental values by characters and audiences. Moreover, and this is critical, each of these societies is experiencing some kind of strain or tension. Troy is confronted by a catalogue of losses incurred through the refusal to return Helen to the Greeks. The crucial debate focuses on two issues. Is Helen a creature of such rarity that her value does counterpoise the past losses and future risks, or is she merely a symbol of the honour of Troy, affording an opportunity for the magnificent Trojan warriors to acquire immortality through fame? To the first question there can be only one answer: no woman is worth the loss of human life which Helen's presence in Troy has wrought, far less can such a woman justify the risk of the desolation of the city. Moreover, although she was captured as an act of retaliation, there can be no doubting the moral impropriety of stealing another man's wife and holding her by force. In the circumstances the Greek offer (unique to Shakespeare) of accepting all past losses without reparation is a generous one. Hector's argument in favour of ending the war is, therefore, up to this point, impeccable. And this is one of the 'stopping points' for the audience. Here is a great civilisation on the brink of destruction having the opportunity of assessing the past and future costs and benefits of pursuing the war. For a modern audience viewing the monstrous carnage of the twentieth century and alert to the prospect of global annihilation this moment in the play is packed with meaning. How do men use their faculties when confronted by a supreme crisis? Hector's logic (supported at various points in the play by such diverse characters as Diomedes and Thersites) demands only one answer. Significantly Troilus denounces this logic. His view is that once a decision is made that decision should be reaffirmed in the face of all subsequent experience. This is human passion and commitment on a grand scale but it is the kind of commitment that abjures reason. Passion triumphs in the debate not by overthrowing logic, but by subverting it. Hector succumbs to the temptation of honour which Troilus reinterprets as fame. Having thoroughly exposed the injustice of the Trojan case, Hector determines to adhere to the set course on the grounds that Helen's 'worth' does not come into the matter; she is merely a symbol. The war is now a matter of principle. Trojan honour is a stake and honour is worth dying for. Such honour can be interpreted in contemporary society as ideology. It is better to die, and even to precipitate universal destruction, than to give ground to antagonistic political and social value systems. But Hector's honour or principle is not merely a matter of self-respect, it offers a means of acquiring immortality through fame. Name or fame is preferred to life and living. Significantly, the decision which determines the fate of Troy is made by the few. The common man has no voice, and the women are over-ruled. The man of principle appears extremely narrow in his calculations. Hector can come to a true evaluation of Helen's worth, but honour and fame are too seductive for him to weigh against past losses and future risks. Ironically he will conduct himself — and Troy is as strong or as fragile as Hector — according to strict principles of fair play even when, as Troilus fully recognises, such principles are outmoded. Hector dies as time's fool: he buys immortality at the cost of Troy through his mistaken act of generosity on the battlefield. The inadequacy of his calculation and misplaced idealism are brought in to sharp focus in his dying words: 'I am unarmed: foregoe this vantage, Greek' (V.viii. 9). Likewise the headstrong lunacy of Troilus so clearly delineated during the debate scene finds expression in his willingness to exchange an arm for a rejected love token ('I come to lose my arm, or win my sleeve' (V.iii. 96)). The question of evaluation, of weighing and assessing which is so central to the debate scene permeates the entire action of the play. The decision and its consequences are continually glanced at and commented on. This display of human folly on a grand scale is demoralising but intriguing.

In *All's Well* there is a patina on the surface of the society, but all is not well below the surface. The play is pervaded by a sense that here is a society in a state of decay rather than of simple transition. The implication of moral decay occurs through statements about what members of the past generation were like (especially the fathers of Bertram and Helena) and through the dignity, humour and humility of its remaining representatives, most especially the King and the Countess. Not that the new generation is seen as uniformly inadequate, but rather that there has been a sharp falling off. The obvious representative of the new generation, Bertram, is a failure in terms of the values extolled by the King and the Countess. Courtesy, respect and fellow feeling for all human beings are stressed by the declining leaders of the society, and were the values most admired by Bertram's father. By contrast Bertram is imbued with a powerful sense of self-importance and social superiority: he lacks insight, modesty, gentleness, compassion, fellow-feeling and most of all honesty. His two claims to honour and a leading place in his society are noble birth and military prowess. Whereas his father had the natural facility for making social inferiors feel his equal, Bertram insists on the primacy of social distance, treats a virtuous young woman of inferior status as a commodity to be used and joked about, and then discarded, finally denouncing her as a prostitute in order to save his own reputation. What can such a man be worth? For the King the worth of any human being is determined by his actions rather than his birth. For the Countess, achievements or actions that are different in kind cannot be traded — military honour cannot make up for shameful social actions. But for Helena her judgement has been made and remains unchanged. She appears to have no doubt about the worth of Bertram. Is this human blindness, or weakness? Or does it represent a power of perception that transcends what *is*, to what *may be*? Whereas in *Troilus and Cressida* we start from the privileged position of knowing that the wrong decisions will be made and that the outcome will be disaster (even though we do not witness it), in *All's Well* we don't know. We are, however, obliged to contemplate the values which are held up to such close scrutiny. And as Hector astonishes the audience by his abrupt reversal, so too does the King in his unequivocal support for democratic values. The implication of his argument is that people who fail to live up to their privileged positions should relinquish them and respect should be allocated in accordance with intrinsic personal qualities, as manifested in actions, rather than in accordance with nominal social status. Taken to its logical conclusion this might imply a high degree of social mobility and the introduction of a mechanism for achieving it. Or is that going too far? Here, then, is an example of values being thoroughly questioned and producing, for Shakespeare's society at least, the possibility of some surprising implications. An alternative view is that the society lived in and valued by the older generation is made up of the ideal aristocratic values with emphasis placed on individual dignity and worth, where power constitutes stewardship not dominance. The justification for this kind of social hierarchy rests on the quality of the values which it embodies.

When contemplating Bertram, the audience is constantly driven back to an examination of his values. If Bertram is capable of change he must change his values. The supreme exemplar of the value system of the society insists on the right of every man to be judged and treated in accordance with his actions rather than in terms of the position which he occupies in the social hierarchy. Indeed, the King implies that special consideration ought to be given by the high born to the low born. Bertram is uninhibited in expressing his disagreement and his treatment of Diana reveals contempt for such values. The single concept of honour to which he adheres is military honour. If, therefore, Bertram is a deceiver right through to the very end of the action, what kind of husband and master will he be? An unreformed Bertram in a position of power is a poor advertisement for his society. It is only when men like Bertram become the norm rather than an aberration that the institutional foundation of such a society becomes questionable. Bertram's abrasiveness and assertion of social superiority is not an aristocratic trait but is much closer to the attitude of the *nouveau riche* exemplified by Natasha in Chekhov's *Three Sisters*. Natasha tramples on an ageing servant and displays total ignorance of, and contempt for, the courtesy and delicacy of the declining aristocracy. The older generation in *All's Well* display a passionate belief in the values which constitute the cement of their society and perceive that they are under threat. Bertram with his fine parentage, upbringing and physical courage should be a guarantee of the future. Instead he represents a threat. What ultimately holds a society together in the long run is not a power structure but a system of shared values. A society that limits characters like Helena to the periphery and has no room for Lavatch, or even Parolles, and allows Diana to be abused, can not preserve its existing shape. Once more, then, as in *Troilus and Cressida*, Shakespeare involves the audience in an examination of the values espoused by individuals but he creates a simultaneous awareness of the social implications. As Ibsen's plays raise questions about social institutions through an examination of personal interaction (as, for example, the collision between Torvald and Nora in *A Doll's House* raises profound questions about the place of women in society) so too do Shakespeare's problem plays provoke a similar questioning. In the kind of hierarchical system operated by the King, Bertram's father and Lafew there is indeed 'place enough for every man alive'; but if the new men who come to the fore are like Bertram the validity of the social system is open to severe critical scrutiny.

It is this connection between personal values and institutions which also occupies the foreground in *Measure for Measure*. If the King in *All's Well* is liberal, warm-hearted, generous and humane, it is the very absence of these values which characterises the new man in Vienna. Angelo is austere, disciplined and devoid of spontaneity, human warmth, or fellow feeling. Once placed in a position of supreme power he determines to create a society in his own image. The first target is instructive: human love and sexuality are the least amenable to state control and are potentially disruptive. Significantly in Orwell's *1984*, and its precursor, Zemyatin's *We*, sexual relations are subject to state control precisely because of their disruptive potential. In creating Angelo, Shakespeare explores the psychology of the character before he falls subject to lust, an aspect totally ignored in all his known sources. The dramatist provokes the question: what makes such a man? Shakespeare seems to imply that repressed sexuality is the chief determinant of Angelo's behaviour. He has exerted unnatural discipline over his own feelings and in doing so has created an image of which he feels proud. But in order to validate it he has to mould society into conformity with his values. Because he expects human beings to be recalcitrant he insists on the full rigour of law: erring humanity cannot be persuaded; it must be driven. This is the stuff of which religious and political fanatics are made. Angelo's equivalents in the source material may be dubious characters, and even tainted with corruption, but none of them possesses Angelo's totalitarian outlook. In Angelo Shakespeare presents a study of the quintessential totalitarian mind. In this sense *Measure for Measure* is Shakespeare's most modern political play. Angelo is more than authoritarian: he is possessed of a vision of a society controlled through rigid discipline, held in awe by the power of the state expressed through the judicial system, and drained of spontaneity.

Critics have tended to focus attention on Angelo's fall and his possible redemption. But it is the quality of his mind before his encounter with Isabella which is most intriguing. The audience is left in no doubt about the kind of society which Angelo would create were he left in control. And at the outset Shakespeare presents the disconcerting fact that Angelo could aspire to that position. He has climbed close to the apex of power through his display of knowledge, competence and conscientiousness. It would seem that Angelo has been subtle enough to conceal his inhumanity even from the Duke with the exception of his treatment of Mariana. But that one act has been enough to alert the Duke and make him want to test Angelo to the full. The implication is that a man who could behave so despicably to Mariana lacks humanity (and the same could be said of Bertram in relation to his treatment of Diana). In one sense the most chilling feature of this play is contemplation of a society controlled by an Angelo without a Duke in the background to put things right. Indeed, an Angelo who did not succumb to lust could be the very worst kind of tyrant as he remains confident of his own moral rectitude. The values of Angelo are both arid and pernicious. Held by unimportant individuals they cause little harm; imposed on society they become monstrous. They attempt to suffocate the life-giving forces, and this is reflected in the imagery of fecundity and growth which characterises sexuality in the play and is epitomised by Lucio's description of Claudio's plight to Isabella (I.iv. 40 – 4).

What defence is there against the creation of the arid society visualised by Angelo? Ironically the virtuous Isabella would offer no defence were she not impelled to fight for her brother's life. First, she shares Angelo's abhorrence of fornication; and secondly, she is endeavouring to avoid participating in her society by escaping to the nunnery. It would seem, therefore, that the disruption of the realisation of the totalitarian vision is to be sought in the low life of burgeoning sexuality and vitality. Lucio stands for spontaneity as the supreme value and recognises sexual vitality as the central feature of human nature. For him, and the less articulate Pompey Bum, Angelo's ambitious reforms are impractical because of human nature. Paradoxically the very values which animate the world of Pompey and Mistress Overdone provide a surface justification for the kind of regime visualised by Angelo. However, it emerges clearly from the action that the kind of reforms necessary to minimise prostitution are not legal constraints but wider social opportunities.

Isabella presents a powerful case against the tyranny so warmly desired by Angelo, and the values which she extols during the debate scene reveal the necessity of tempering rigour with humanity and compassion. But Isabella cannot defeat Angelo. In the absence of the Duke, Angelo would triumph over Claudio and his kind but not over the low-life characters. Whereas Whetstone provides a picture of the lower echelons to indicate how corruption spreads from top to bottom, Shakespeare depicts this stratum as representing a bastion of freedom. Unbridled sexuality debases human relationships but at least resists tyranny through spontaneity. Likewise, brothels turn sex into a commodity and market diseases, but exemplify the determination and energy of lesser mortals to gain a livelihood.

This view of values in Vienna does not provide an ideal moral formula for seeking a middle way between the extremes of Angelo and Pompey. Rather it implies something more paradoxical and disconcerting. The power of sexuality is reinforced by Angelo's fall, but sexual suppression does not give way to healthy desire; rather it produces the passion of cruelty. If there is something worse than sex turned to commodity, it is Angelo's attempted judicial rape. Because Angelo is capable of using the law for his own ends, doubt is cast on the institutionalisation of such individual power. The question which inevitably arises is, can any man be trusted with such power? In real life there is not going to be a benign Duke at hand to intervene at crucial moments. So it is that not only are Angelo's values held up to close critical scrutiny, but so too are the formation of social values and the nature of the institutions which embody them. Whatever the ultimate source of values, be they Christian theology or humanist ethics, they are articulated through institutions. The values may be ideal, but, they can still be distorted by the institutional framework. Consequently it seems impossible in *Measure for Measure* to escape from the examination of values, human nature and social institutions.

In each of the three problem plays Shakespeare explores the values which animate individuals and societies by means of a central confrontation. 'Intellectual' and 'analytical' are characteristic of the epithets applied to the problem plays and that aspect is to the fore in the debate scenes. However, they are not just cerebral: they contain a powerful cross-current of emotion. But the collision is not between will or passion and reason; nor is cold reason always superior to hot passion. Isabella's intellect is not engaged until ignited by passion. She finds her strongest arguments only after she has forgotten her own narrow morality in a desperate attempt to free her brother from the powerful grip of the law. It is Lucio who instigates the intense encounter between the two cold intellects. Initially it is only he who seems to grasp that what is at stake is a warm human life. Denigrating the Duke may be seen as good fun, and abandoning his own child may be thought of as a necessary manoeuvre in the hurly-burly of life, but Lucio is incapable of standing by while a friend is executed for what he sees as a trivial offence.

In *Troilus and Cressida* the situation is different. Hector attempts to take the heat out of the debate by claiming that Helen is 'not worth what she doth cost the keeping' (II.ii. 52). Troilus' riposte is immediate: 'What's aught but as 'tis valued?' (II.ii. 53) No sooner has Hector attempted to quantify the costs and benefits or values than Troilus asserts that there is no means of making such an assessment. Hector's reply is crucial. When he claims that 'But value dwells not in particular will' (II.ii. 54) Hector is insisting on the necessity of a social valuation. It is the society that bears the cost of the action and so it is the society that must make the calculation of worth. Troilus accepts this argument but goes on to claim that once an evaluation has been made it must be accepted as binding; there is no justification for a re-evaluation. The Trojans supported Paris' expedition and applauded its success. It is not possible, therefore, to relinquish Helen without suffering indignity. It is at that very moment that Cassandra intervenes to prophesy the entire destruction of Troy if Helen is not returned.

Thus the ultimate possible cost of keeping Helen is made clear, and the Trojans have already endured years of bloodshed and suffering without being able to drive away the Greeks. In claiming that no decision should ever be reversed Troilus is denying the wisdom of reconsideration in the light of experience. Before overturning these arguments Hector exposes the nature of the basis upon which they are constructed:

> The reasons you allege do more conduce
> To the hot passion of distemper'd blood
> Than to make up a free determination
> 'Twixt right and wrong: for pleasure and revenge
> Have ears more deaf than adders to the voice
> Of any true decision.

> (II.ii. 169–74)

What both Troilus and Paris are engaging in is not honest exploration of the situation in which they find themselves, but the utilisation of any arguments that can be found to support the continuation of the war and their quest for honour. The worth of Helen is never in doubt: Diomedes provides a devastating assessment of her in terms of the blood that has already been spilled; Thersites describes the Trojan war succinctly: 'All the argument is a whore and a cuckold: a good quarrel to draw emulous factions and bleed to death upon' (II.iii. 76–8). Eventually, when Hector has turned his back on the impeccable logic with which he has denounced the war, Troilus admits that Helen is a pretext, not the cause of the continuation of the war:

> Why, there you touch'd the life of our design:
> Were it not glory that we more affected
> Than the performance of our heaving spleens,
> I would not wish a drop of Trojan blood
> Spent more in her defence. But, worthy Hector,
> She is a theme of honour and renown,
> A spur to valiant and magnanimous deeds,
> Whose present courage may beat down our foes,
> And fame in time to come canonize us;

> (II.ii. 195–203)

The values that animate Trojan society emerge in the debate. The perpetuation of the war is for fame and immortality; the risks involved are pushed on one side. And the very man who insisted that 'value dwells not in particular will' is prepared to lend his decisive voice to an action which may bring glory to the few but disaster for the many. Those critics who see Ulysses' speech on order as Shakespeare's assertion of the necessity of social hierarchy with decision-making determined at the top must be oblivious to the implications of the debate scene. Hector makes a moral and legal case for returning Helen which is impregnable before declaring himself in favour of the perpetuation of the war. Like so much in this play the debate is a sham. The audience has the facts and implications laid before it and observes the central characters turn their backs on reason in favour of glory. The implications for our world are so stark and so obvious that is is not surprising that *Troilus and Cressida* has exerted a greater fascination over audiences during the past 25 years than at any other time. Not only are the values questioned, but also the way in which decisions are arrived at. The silent soldiers so derided by Pandarus bear eloquent testimony to the nature of Trojan society. Their silence is more telling than the complaints made by the messengers, in Homer. Likewise the silence of Antenor — 'one o'th'soundest judgements in Troy' (I.ii. 193–4) — speaks for itself.

As in *Troilus and Cressida* the debate in *All's Well* is a public affair. The former possesses all the trappings of a genuine debate but is really a hollow exercise. In the latter the debate is genuine and breaks out in what is intended to be a festive occasion. Helena has wrought a miracle: the whole court should be celebrating and eagerly awaiting the choice of the lovely miracle worker. By rejecting Helena on the principle of social inferiority and in a manner which shows slight regard for the King's personal well-being or authority, Bertram mars the celebration and challenges the reciprocal principle of privilege and duty. Both the King and Helena are slighted and humiliated by Bertram's response. What is astonishing is the King's patience and temperate behaviour and the principle which he enunciates with such conviction and vigour. Bertram surrenders not because he is convinced by the power of the King's 'democratic' argument, but because he knows that he cannot enjoy the fruits of patronage without acceding to royal authority. Even then he accepts only the form of the arrangement that is required of him rather than the substance. What is surprising is that despite the supposed gap between the generations no one, except Parolles, supports Bertram. What is being portrayed is an ideal aristocratic society with a genuine mutual respect between individuals and social levels with a willingness to accept social evaluation. But what are the social implications if Bertram represents a strong strain rather than an aberration?

Part of this probing of the values which underpin societies and motivate individuals is associated with one of Shakespeare's favourite perceptions: the contrast between appearance and reality. But if this dichotomy is explored in many of Shakespeare's plays it possesses a particularly sharp cutting edge in the problem plays. *Troilus and Cressida* portrays the most famous heroes in history and they belong to the world of medieval chivalry. Yet, underneath the surface gloss of the heroic and chivalric there is the practical, sagacious and ruthless. For all his compelling generalisations about time and human nature Ulysses is a manipulator; Agamemnon, the famous leader of the Greeks is devoid of perception or charisma; Ajax, is, for the most part, a muscular blockhead; Menelaus is a taciturn fool; the mighty Diomedes is a hardheaded, insightful opportunist; the famed warrior Achilles is a ruthless coward who in the midst of conviviality brags of how he will kill Hector but willingly resorts to murder when he discovers that he has met a better man. The face that launched a thousand ships belongs to a woman who is pathetic rather than enchanting, while her lover Paris is a self-indulgent non-entity. The mighty Hector is the most attractive character in the play but also the greatest fool: he adheres to a code of chivalry to which few others subscribe; by turning his back on reason in the debate scene and by his misplaced generosity in sparing Achilles' life he precipitates his own death and the destruction of Troy. Troilus possesses passion and energy in abundance but is contemptuous of reason; he becomes disillusioned but he never learns from experience. Cressida remains an enigma: is she a lovely woman who aspires to fidelity but finds she lacks the capacity for genuine love? Or is she one of nature's whores? Perhaps she is neither of these things but a woman who as a victim of war learns quickly to look out for herself. Whatever she is, she is not a woman deeply in love and capable of enduring all weathers as she insists before her departure from Troy and Troilus. As Hector discovers that the man whom he has pursued for his sumptuous armour (a momentary breach of his principles which contributes to his death) is diseased, so too does the audience discover that the Trojan war does not consist of a glorious battle between noble warriors. Even if Thersites' view of this world is considered an exaggeration (and many critics denounce his views as a grotesque parody of what happens in the play), he continually guides the audience through to an examination of the diseased interior that lies beneath the surface of generalship, strategy, martial prowess and love. Those who have so passionately denounced Thersites seem to fear the ugliness of the truth which he exposes. It is not a congenial thought that the Trojan war was ultimately a matter of a 'whore and a cuckold' (II.iii. 74 – 5); or that the love affair of the eponymous hero and heroine falls into the same category.

Although Lucio and Parolles cannot be cited as literary brothers to Thersites, they are at least second cousins, and serve to expose the contrast between the fair surface of things and the underlying reality, and to provide a point of detachment for the audience. All three railers have uncontrollable tongues: but whereas Thersites can be accused of not more than exaggeration, Lucio and Parolles are given to slander and fantasy. All three provide a major centre for comedy in the plays and function in such a way as to point up significant contrasts. Lucio's comments on Angelo emphasise that he is unnatural: he is a bigger aberration and a greater danger to society than the worst perpetrator of sexual licence; he also demonstrates in his denigration of the Duke that even when a man is as good as he seems he cannot escape calumny. But Lucio, who is undoubtedly a rascal, is necessary for transforming Isabella from novice to advocate. Likewise, his insubordination is an essential element in a world where there is a greater tendency for people to be subservient under harsh laws than to protest about them. Parolles is most effective in highlighting the contrast between appearance and reality through his own person than by means of commentary. He is the embodiment of clothes and words; decoration without substance. But when he is exposed he is not outraged; he accepts a new and humbler role with such alacrity that his vices are seen to be as shallow as his virtues. If he is not what he seems, neither is Bertram, whose own unmasking produces pain rather than amusement and provokes serious doubts about the appropriateness of the role that he is to occupy. 'Seemers' like Parolles are easily exposed. Bertram and Angelo are formidable because their honour is validated by birth and public office respectively. Moreover, they are more intelligent, subtle, and self-deceiving than Parolles. Consequently they are much more dangerous. They also present a serious challenge of psychological interpretation: are they capable of reform even when guided by such loyal and loving women as Helena and Mariana? If their honour remains open to question, that of Achilles does not, at least to the playgoer.

Shakespeare strips Homer's hero of his finer qualities and exposes him as an impostor. However, the dramatist reveals how difficult it is to know what really happens when dealing with historical events. Having had his adversary murdered in a corner of the battlefield Achilles has his men relay the story that he has killed Hector. Hence his reputation as the greatest warrior is perpetuated. In this way Achilles preserves honour in the form of public reputation but discards it in his soul. The accounts of Achilles' abuse of the bodies of Hector and Troilus probably influenced Shakespeare in his interpretation of his 'true' character. What man of genuine honour would do such a thing? Even so Shakespeare's presentation goes much deeper in that the whole code of honour in such circumstances is held in question. Can there be anything honourable in a war fought for personal glory that inflicts privation, mutilation and death on thousands who are not consulted about their participation? In *Troilus and Cressida* the questioning of the concept of honour and the social implications surrounding it appears more starkly than in *All's Well* and *Measure for Measure*.

Honour is also linked to sex in all three plays. Love is a major concern in many of Shakespeare's plays but none of them possesses the acute juxtaposition of love and lechery which is displayed in the problem plays. Angelo succumbs to lecherous impulses on a brutal scale while Bertram treats the seduction of Diana as a joke before denouncing her as a prostitute. Nowhere else in Shakespeare do 'heroes' treat women with such contempt. Diomedes' evaluation of women is equally harsh. He finds Cressida beautiful but treats her as a whore. Astonishingly the woman who so recently pledged her love to Troilus accepts Diomedes valuation and satisfies his demands for instant gratification. Here there is no Helena or Mariana to display female fidelity: Helen has moved in the opposite direction from Cressida but with equal facility. There is a suggestion (beautifully developed in the RSC's 1985 production at Stratford) that Helen recognises the excesses and self-indulgence of her affair with the unthinking Paris, but she lacks the vitality to do anything about it. Once more Thersites' assessment appears very accurate: 'lechery, lechery, still wars and lechery! Nothing else holds fashion' (V.ii. 193–4). In *All's Well* and *Measure for Measure* the actions of Bertram and Angelo reveal their contempt for women; they are saved by the bed-trick — though this 'elegant' solution involves some disparagement in itself, as Helena's reflection seems to imply (IV.iv. 21–5). In *Troilus and Cressida* women are used and abused. Both Helen and Cressida are viewed as whores but this is a man's world in which they are counters and victims. Greeks and Trojans bleed in order to restore Menelaus' honour — even though he is viewed with contempt by those who are fighting in his cause.

The feeling which is paramount in *Troilus and Cressida*, in both audience and characters, is disillusionment. Troilus is disillusioned with love and war; Hector's illusions are shattered seconds before his death; and virtually all the protagonists are disillusioned with Helen and the war; Cressida and Helen are disillusioned with themselves; the audience is disillusioned by the inability of human beings to act rationally and humanely. Shakespeare's most fascinating play is also his most disillusioning. The feeling of disillusionment which is to be detected in the other two problem plays is nothing like as pervasive as in *Troilus and Cressida*, but it is potent. There is a sense of disillusionment deeply embedded in the atmosphere of *All's Well* and articulated during the first half of the play by the King. This feeling becomes overt after Bertram's treatment of Helena and Diana and his behaviour during his 'trial'. Unless the 'happy ending' is uncritically accepted the audience experiences a feeling of disillusionment. Belief in Angelo's capacity for reform doesn't remove the disillusionment that occurs in *Measure for Measure*. Mariana, like Helena, knows precisely what Angelo intended. What kind of individual is most likely to occupy positions of power, a man like the Duke or characters like Angelo? Evidently every citizen is vulnerable to harsh laws or inhumane justice. And what hope is there of eliminating prostitution and the transformation of women into commodities? This task is beyond even the Duke who possesses remarkable insight, energy and compassion. Evidently the task of creating a free and just society is extremely difficult and one of the most destructive forces is lechery which comes so naturally to such diverse characters as Lucio and Bertram.

Whatever else these plays do, they do not present an optimistic view of life. There is a consciousness of the striving after ideals, of a desire by individuals to believe in and possess integrity. Both Hector and Troilus have this vision despite their weaknesses; Helena and Mariana are women of remarkable integrity but the objects of their love fail hopelessly to live up to their vision — in the end they may prove to be just as deceived as Hector is. Nevertheless, throughout these plays there is passion for goodness which involves a deep respect for fellow human beings. And the problem of the human condition is to preserve that aspiration and to embody the highest ideals in institutions which nurture the good in man rather than attempting to bludgeon him into a predetermined pattern of existence. One of the most vital forces in human beings is spontaneity and that is to be prized even when found in such dubious characters as Lucio. The biggest threats reside in the cold-eyed vision of an Angelo, or the egotism of a Bertram or Paris. These three plays challenge the human intellect to face up to the weaknesses and vices in men and to attempt to construct societies which foster the finest qualities and discourage the worst; stimulate idealism while recognising the existence and potency of cynicism.

A number of comments have already been made on the nature of language in these plays but at least one aspect calls for further comment. Of the three plays only *Troilus and Cressida* is rich in imagery. Disease, food (cooking, eating and regurgitating), animal and body imagery abounds. And there are numerous references to trade and commerce. Whereas the imagery in *Troilus and Cressida* is vigorous, persistent and clustered, in *All's Well* it is spread thinly, always remaining subordinate to the verbal reticence which characterises the play. The planetary references carrying an association with fortune are significant; so too is the growth imagery which though not frequent is highly effective. References to age and time are numerous but infiltrate the text in a way which conveys a sense of an ageing society experiencing a stillness and slowing of time.

The linguistic feature which most closely links this play with *Troilus and Cressida*, and appears to have been virtually ignored by critics, is quantification or measurement. The Countess instructing Reynaldo to write to Bertram says:

> Let every word *weigh heavy* of her worth
> That he does *weigh too light*; my *greatest* grief,
> Though *little* he do feel it, set down sharply.

> (III.iv. 31–3)

The King makes his famous comment on blood pointing out

> Strange is it that our bloods,
> Of *colour*, *weight*, and *heat*, pour'd all together,
> Would quite confound distinction, yet stands off
> In differences so *mighty*

> (II.iii. 118–21)

And in going on to guarantee Helen's dowry to Bertram promises

> A *counterpoise*, if not to thy estate,
> A balance *more replete*

(II.iii. 175–6)

In dismissing Lafew's lavish introduction of Helena the King muses, 'Thus he his special *nothing* ever prologues'. (II.i. 91) Accepting Bertram at court, the King asserts, 'My son's no *dearer*' (I.ii. 76). Diana responds to Bertram's protestation with the caution ''Tis not the *many* oaths that makes the truth' (IV.ii. 21). Parolles insists 'I love not *many* words' (III.vi. 80). Bertram in accepting his charge from the Duke of Florence claims that it is '*too heavy* for my strength', but promises to bear it 'To th' *extreme edge* of hazard' (III.iii. 4–6). The Countess tells the distressed Helena

> If thou *engrossest* all the griefs are thine
> Thou robb'st me of a *moiety*. He was my son,
> But I do wash his name out of my blood
> And thou art *all* my child.

(III.ii. 65–8)

Helena in referring to the receipt of the remedy from her father tells the King

> Which, as the *dearest* issue of his practice,
> . . .
> He bade me store up as a *triple* eye,
> Safer than mine own two; *more dear* I have so,

(II.i. 105–8)

And there are more complex and extended examples, such as those which occur in the King's description of Bertram's father where quantification is interwoven with references to time and the imagery of growth (I.ii. 24–67).

If references to measurement, weighing and quantification occur widely in the play without being as ubiquitous as in *Troilus and Cressida*, the awareness of the kinship network is almost as powerful. There are constant references to relationships through blood, marriage and friendship. The influence of dead fathers is strongly felt in the play. It is not just the number of such references that is so significant but their quality in terms of the feeling which

227

they generate, whether they consist of extensive descriptions or fleeting touches such as the Countess's reference to the affection of her husband for Lavatch. This is one of the features which gives *All's Well* an astonishing sense of depth: the texture of a generation, of a society, is tangible.

In contrast *Measure for Measure* conveys no sense of the *presence* of an older generation. In the light of the obvious youth of Claudio and Isabella the marked absence of their parents accentuates the feeling of their vulnerability and Angelo's power. The fatherly and protective qualities are manifested in the Duke. There is no sense of family in *Measure for Measure*. The embryonic family of Claudio, Julietta and their unborn child hovers on the brink of destruction: Isabella is bound for the nunnery; Lucio disowns his child and despises the mother; Mistress Overdone would be hard pressed to remember the names of her nine husbands. Even so, the most potent and almost sole imagery in the play relates to growth and fecundity, the finest example being Lucio's description of the embrace of Claudio and Julietta:

> As those that feed grow full, as blossoming time
> That from the seedness the bare fallow brings
> To teeming foison, even so her plenteous womb
> Expresseth his full tilth and husbandry.
>
> (I.iv. 41–4)

Apart from this speech the growth imagery is confined to single lines or odd words. That the infrequency of imagery in *Measure for Measure* has provoked little comment is partly to be explained by the vigour of the language. There is none of the verbal reticence which informs *All's Well*. References to value, worth and profit are pervasive; comments on the contrast between appearance and reality occur with considerable frequency; the word 'honour' is used constantly. Thus at the level of the verbal structure the problem plays share significant affinities.

In his survey of the critical writing on the problem plays John Wilders comments, 'Of all Shakespeare's plays, these three have probably provoked the most extreme critical controversy. They have sometimes baffled the critics . . . and they have been given extremely divergent and conflicting interpretations'.[2] Thus not only has the meaning and relevance of the term problem plays been the subject of intense controversy, but each of the plays has evoked bewilderment and widely differing interpretations. As

John Russell Brown suggests, 'no one can read or see these plays without being involved with, and in some measure perplexed by, deep and serious issues'.[3] Increasingly these plays have been seen as possessing a particular appeal to the modern consciousness. The most modern and most peculiar of the three plays is *Troilus and Cressida* which was effectively dismissed until the last few decades. As recently as 1933 John Dover Wilson encapsulated much of the previous feeling about the play when he wrote disparagingly of the 'disillusionment and cynicism', in which the 'air is cheerless and often unwholesome, the wit mirthless, the bad characters contemptible or detestable, the good ones unattractive'.[4] Kenneth Muir, one of the most recent editors of the play, rightly states that 'The play has been more widely appreciated during the past thirty years than in the previous three and a half centuries.' But in an introduction which makes several sound observations and a number that are questionable or require serious qualifications, he adds, 'Few would regard it as one of the supreme plays, but only a great dramatic poet could have written it.'[5] This conclusion may be valid at present but the argument advanced here is that *Troilus and Cressida* is one of Shakespeare's greatest plays and his finest achievement — and will soon be widely recognised as such. The most brilliant of Shakespeare's plays shares with *All's Well* and *Measure for Measure* a desire to engage the intellect in an examination of the formation and transmission of values and their embodiment in institutions. But Shakespeare was not advancing a thesis about the inadequacy of his own society or adumbrating the principles which should underpin some ideal society. Rather he sought to explore the complexity of social reality whilst keeping in the foreground the greatest enigma of all: the human mind. These dramas so aptly called 'problem plays', present difficult problems of interpretation because they seek to explore the needs, passions, desires, vices and weaknesses inherent in human life within the context of attempting to change or preserve the existing social universe. Human societies, like families, constitute a kinship network in which the strains and stresses arising out of individual needs and aspirations have to be resolved by rules and institutions which are flexible enough to accommodate the stresses. Hence society can never be static because of the reciprocal interplay between human beings and institutions. Of all the undoubted affinities which these plays share they are united most strongly by focusing on this problem. And the dramatist implies that like life the drama itself must be open-ended, inviting constant exploration and reinterpretation. If this conclusion is implicit in much of Shakespeare's dramatic work it appears singularly explicit in the problem plays.

Finally, the problem plays leave the audience with an acute sense of the gap which may exist between human aspirations and social realities. Helena and Mariana have the capacity to love wholly, but the objects of their love are deeply flawed. Isabella seeks purity within the confines of the nunnery, but is left with the dilemma of seeking fulfilment in a defiled world or retreating to the inaction of the cloistered life. In *Troilus and Cressida* the division between aspiration and achievement is sharply felt and persistently articulated. Agamemnon asserts that failure is merely the means by which the gods seek to discover 'persistive constancy in men', testing and 'winnowing the light away' so that what remains 'Lies rich in virtue and unmingled' (I.iii. 21–30). Troilus expresses a longing to Cressida

> That my integrity and truth to you
> Might be affronted with the match and weight
> Of such a winnow'd purity in love —
>
> (III.ii. 163–5)

He loves her with a purity that is 'strain'd' (Iv.iv. 23) and swears he is convinced there is 'no maculation' in her heart (IV.iv. 63). When Troilus discovers that Cressida does not possess such spotless love he feels a sense of dissolution which is universal: 'The bonds of heaven are slipp'd, dissolv'd, and loos'd' (V.ii. 154). Thus division, infection and dissolution triumph over the passion for wholeness and integrity. As Cressida recognises a division within herself as she surrenders her love of Troilus (V.ii. 106–7), so Hector dies recognising Achilles' violation of the code of honour. Whether the play ends with the words of the defiant Troilus or the diseased and sniggering Pandarus the final note is not that of tragedy. As with *All's Well* and *Measure for Measure* we are left contemplating the past events and attempting to visualise the future, both in the world of the stage and in the wider world of human action. These plays provide no simple consolations or easy solutions. The problem plays articulate the problems but don't attempt to solve them.

Conclusion

Notes

1. Philip Edwards, *Shakespeare and the Confines of Art*, 2nd edn (Methuen, London, 1972), p. 110.
2. John Wilders, 'The Problem Comedies: *Troilus and Cressida*, *All's Well*, and *Measure for Measure*' in Stanley Wells (ed.), *Shakespeare Select Bibliographical Guides* (Oxford University Press, London, 1973), p. 94.
3. John Russell Brown, *Shakespeare and his Comedies*, 5th edn (Methuen, London, 1970), p. 184.
4. John Dover Wilson, *The Essential Shakespeare*, 4th edn (Cambridge University Press, Cambridge, 1935), p. 116.
5. Kenneth Muir (ed.), 'Shakespeare: *Troilus and Cressida*' (The Oxford Shakespeare, Oxford University Press, Oxford, 1982), p. 38.

Bibliography

Bayley, J. *Shakespeare and Tragedy* (Routledge and Kegan Paul, London, 1981)

Boas, F. S. *Shakspere and his Predecessors* (John Murray, London, 1896)

Boccaccio, *The Decameron*, translated by G. H. McWilliam (Penguin, Harmondsworth, 1986)

Bradbrook, M. C. *Shakespeare and Elizabethan Poetry*, 3rd edn (Chatto and Windus, London, 1965)

Bradshaw, G. *Shakespeare's Scepticism: Nature and Value in Shakespeare's Plays* (Harvester, Brighton, 1986)

Brower, R. A. *Hero and Saint: Shakespeare and the Graeco-Roman Tradition* (Oxford University Press, Oxford, 1971)

Brown, J. R. *Shakespeare and his Comedies*, 5th edn (Methuen, London, 1970)

Bullough, G. (ed.) *Narrative and Dramatic Sources of Shakespeare*, vols. II and VI (Routledge and Kegan Paul, London, 1966)

Campbell, O. J. *Comicall Satyre and Shakespeare's 'Troilus and Cressida'*, 4th edn (Huntington Library Publication, California, 1970)

Charlton, H. B. *The Dark Comedies* (Haskell House Reprints, 1986)
—— *Shakespearean Comedy*, 5th edn (Methuen, London, 1969)

Chaucer, G. *Troilus and Criseyde*, translated into Modern English by N. Coghill, 8th edn (Penguin, Harmondsworth, 1982)

Dollimore, J. *Radical Tragedy: Religion, Ideology and Power in the Drama of Shakespeare and his Contemporaries* (Harvester Press, Brighton, 1984)
—— and Sinfield, *Political Shakespeare: New Essays in Cultural Materialism* (Manchester University Press, 1985)

Donaldson, E. T. *The Swan at the Well: Shakespeare Reading Chaucer* (Yale University Press, New Haven and London, 1985)

Dowden, E. *Shakspere: A Critical Study of his Mind and Art*, 3rd edn (Routledge and Kegan Paul, London, 1875)

Eagleton, T. *Shakespeare and Society: Critical Studies in Shakespearean Drama*, 2nd edn (Chatto and Windus, London, 1970)

Edwards, P. *Shakespeare and the Confines of Art*, 2nd edn (Methuen, London, 1970)
—— *Shakespeare: A Writer's Progress* (Oxford University Press, Oxford, 1986)

Ellis-Fermor, Una edited by K. Muir, *Shakespeare's Drama* (Methuen, London, 1980)

Evans, B. *Shakespeare's Comedies*, 4th edn (Oxford University Press, Oxford, 1969)

Frye, N. *Fools of Time: Studies in Shakespearean Tragedy*, 2nd edn (University of Toronto Press, Toronto and Buffalo, 1973)
—— *The Myth of Deliverance: Reflections on Shakespeare's Problem Comedies* (Harvester Press, Brighton, 1983)

Geckle, G. L. (ed.) *Twentieth Century Interpretations of 'Measure for Measure': A Collection of Critical Essays* (Prentice-Hall, New Jersey, 1970)

Hawkins, H. *Likeness and Truth in Elizabethan and Restoration Drama* (Oxford University Press, Oxford, 1972)

Hunter, G. K. (ed.) *The New Arden Shakespeare: 'All's Well that Ends Well'* (Methuen, London, 1967)

Kettle, A. (ed.) *Shakespeare in a Changing World* (Lawrence and Wishart, London, 1964)

Knight, G. W. *The Wheel of Fire: Interpretations of Shakespearian Tragedy*, 4th edn (Methuen, London, 1972)

Knight, S. *Geoffrey Chaucer* (Basil Blackwell, Oxford, 1986)

Knights, L. C. *Drama and Society in the Age of Jonson* (Chatto and Windus, London, 1937); (Peregrine Books, Penguin, Harmondsworth, 1962)

—— L. C. *Some Shakespearean Themes*, 4th edn (Chatto and Windus, London, 1966)

Lascelles, M. *Shakespeare's 'Measure for Measure'* (Athlone Press, London, 1953)

Lawrence, W. W. *Shakespeare's Problem Comedies*, 3rd edn (Penguin, Harmondsworth, 1969)

Leavis, F. R. *The Common Pursuit*, 5th edn (Penguin, Middlesex, 1969)

Lever, J. W. (ed.) *The New Arden Shakespeare: Measure for Measure*, 2nd edn (Methuen, London, 1966)

Lewis, C. S. *The Allegory of Love: A Study in Medieval Tradition*, 5th edn (Oxford University Press, Oxford, 1985)

Martin, P. (ed.) *Troilus and Cressida* (Casebook Series, Macmillan, London, 1976)

Maxwell, J. C. *Measure for Measure: The Play and the Themes*, British Academy Lecture (Oxford University Press, Oxford, 1974)

Muir, K. (ed.) *Shakespeare: The Comedies. A Collection of Critical Essays* (Prentice-Hall, New Jersey, 1965)

—— *The Sources of Shakespeare's Plays*, 2nd edn (Methuen, London, 1977)

—— and Wells (ed) *Aspects of Shakespeare's 'Problem Plays'* (Cambridge University Press, Cambridge, 1982)

—— (ed.) *The Oxford Shakespeare: Troilus and Cressida* (Oxford University Press, Oxford, 1985)

Palmer, D. J. (ed.) *Shakespeare's Later Comedies* (Penguin, Middlesex, 1971)

Palmer, K. (ed.) *The New Arden Shakespeare: Troilus and Cressida* (Methuen, London, 1982)

Parker and Hartman (eds) *Shakespeare and the Question of Theory* (Methuen, London and New York, 1985)

Pennington and Thomas (eds) *Puritans and Revolutionaries: Essays in Seventeenth Century History, presented to Christopher Hill* (Oxford University Press, Oxford, 1978)

Pettet, E. C. *Shakespeare and the Romance Tradition*, 2nd edn (Methuen, London, 1970)

Robinson, F. N. (ed.) *The Complete Works of Geoffrey Chaucer*, 2nd edn (Oxford University Press, London, 1957)

Rossiter, A. P. *Angel with Horns*, 4th edn (Longman, London, 1970)

Schanzer, E. *The Problem Plays of Shakespeare: 'Julius Caesar', 'Measure for Measure', 'Antony and Cleopatra'* (Routledge and Kegan Paul, London, 1963)

Shaw, G. B. *Plays Pleasant and Unpleasant*, 2 vols., revised edn (Constable, London, 1906)

Spencer, T. *Shakespeare and the Nature of Man*, 4th edn (Macmillan, London, 1971)

Spurgeon, C. *Shakespeare's Imagery and What It Tells Us*, 7th edn (Cambridge University Press, Cambridge, 1971)

Stead, C. K. *Shakespeare: Measure for Measure* (Casebook Series, Macmillan, London, 1971)

Thomson, A. *Shakespeare's Chaucer: A Study in Literary Origins* (Liverpool University Press, Liverpool, 1978)

Tillyard, E. M. W. *Shakespeare's Problem Plays*, 3rd edn (Penguin, Harmondsworth, 1970)

Turner, F. *Shakespeare and the Nature of Time: Moral and Philosophical Themes in Some Plays and Poems of William Shakespeare* (Oxford University Press, Oxford, 1971)

Ure, P. *Shakespeare: The Problem Plays*, 3rd edn (Longman, London, 1970)

Wagenknecht, E. (ed.) *Chaucer: Modern Essays in Criticism*, 2nd edn (Oxford University Press, New York, 1971)

Walker, A. *Cambridge Shakespeare: Troilus and Cressida*, 4th edn (Cambridge University Press, Cambridge, 1972)

Wells, R. H. *Shakespeare, Politics and the State* (Macmillan, Basingstoke, 1986)

Wells, S. (ed.) *Shakespeare: Select Bibliographical Guides* (Oxford University Press, London, 1973)

Wilson, J. D. *The Essential Shakespeare*, 4th edn (Cambridge University Press, Cambridge, 1935)

Index